FOCUS ON

Advanced

English

C.A.E.

Longman

SUE O'CONNELL

With additional Grammar and Listening material by

Mark Foley
and Russell Whitehead

Map of Focus on Advanced English CAE

Key: SB - Study Box; LC - Language Check; ET Exam Tip; GT Gapped Text; MM - Multiple Matching; MuC -Multiple Choice.
Numbers in brackets refer to a part of the relevant paper in the exam.

Unit/Topic	Grammar	Reading	Writing	English in Use	Listening	Speaking
The Certificate in Advanced English: overview *page 4*						
Language Focus 1: Grammatical Terms *page 8*; **Learning Focus 1: Reading Strategies** *page 9*						
1 Use Your Head *page 10*	Conditionals Phrasal Verbs SB: *despite /in spite of*; *although/but*	Your mind – do you make the most of it?	Informal Letter (2)	1 Word Formation (4) 2 Error Correction (3)	Learning a Language (3)	Your Expectations (1)
2 Severe Weather *page 23*	Review of the Passive 1 SB: Contrast links	1 Today is cancelled! 2 Where snow means go	Formal Letter (2)	1 Spelling (3) 2 Lexical Cloze (1)	1 Climate Change (1) 2 Weather and Mood (2)	
Language Focus 2: Vocabulary Skills 1: What's in a word? *page 36*; **Learning Focus 2: Planning for Writing** *page 37*						
3 Time Eaters *page 39*	The Future 1 Modal Verbs 1 SB: *no matter*	Time-eaters and what you can do about them (MM)	Personal Notes and Messages (1)	1 Structural Cloze (2) 2 Discourse Cloze (6)	1 Ways of Wasting Time (4) 2 Adventure Sports (2)	1 Visual Prompts (2) 2 Problem Solving (3, 4)
4 Stress *page 51*	Expressing Cause and Effect -*ing* Forms and Infinitives SB: Expressing cause and effect	1 Stress Test (MuC) 2 Stress Busters (MM)	Leaflet (2)	1 Lexical Cloze (1) 2 Register Cloze (5)	1 Causes of Stress (1) 2 A Company Fitness Centre (1)	
Language Focus 3: Coherence/Cohesion *page 65*; **Learning Focus 3 Editing Skills 1: Revising your Draft** *page 66*						
5 Globe Trotting *page 67*	Past/past perfect simple/continuous SB: Three-word phrasal verbs SB: Common reference links	1 When the locals are friendly (MM) 2 Holiday claims too hot to handle (GT)	Letter of Complaint (1)	1 Register Cloze (5) 2 Structural Cloze (2)	1 Sun Facts (2) 2 Customer Complaints (3)	1 What kind of traveller are you? 2 Visual Prompts (2)
6 Language Matters *page 81*	Relative Clauses Comparison SB: *like* v *as*, *alike* SB: Punctuation	1 The Day a Language Died (GT) 2 US and them (MuC)	Review (2)	1 Spelling and Punctuation (3) 2 Lexical Cloze (1)	1 Which Language? (4) 2 Critics' Choice (3)	1 Proverbs 2 Visual Prompts (2)
Language Focus 4: Vocabulary Skills 2: Making the right choices *page 94*; **Learning Focus 4: Editing Skills 2: Polishing** *page 95*						
7 The Ages of Man *page 97*	Present perfect simple/continuous Reported Speech SB: *used to* + inf; *be/get used to* + -*ing* LC: Word formation	Where old folks learn new kicks (MM)	1 Articles: An Introduction (2) 2 Information Report (2)	1 Discourse Cloze (6) 2 Word Formation (4)	1 Attitudes to Age (4) 2 Young Achievers (1)	Problem Solving (3)

The Certificate in Advanced English: overview

The examination consists of five papers and each of the papers has equal weighting (i.e. 20%).

Paper 1 Reading (1 hour 15 minutes)

There are four texts and up to 50 questions, which test a range of reading skills. Texts may include newspaper and magazine articles, extracts from non-fiction books and brochures or leaflets. Questions include various types of multiple choice, gap filling and multiple matching.

Paper 2 Writing (2 hours)

There are two parts, with one task of approximately 250 words in each. In Part 1, the task is compulsory and candidates have to read and respond to written information by producing one, or sometimes two pieces of writing, e.g. a letter and a note. In Part 2, candidates have to write one piece from a choice of four topics. One topic is usually work-related.

Paper 3 English in Use (1 hour 30 minutes)

There are six parts and 80 questions, which test candidates' knowledge of features of the language system such as grammar, register, spelling, punctuation, cohesion and coherence (the way language is used to link different parts of a text or different ideas together).

Paper 4 Listening (45 minutes)

There are four parts consisting of four texts and approximately 30-40 questions, which test a wide range of listening skills. The questions include various kinds of multiple matching, completion and multiple choice items. In Part 2, the recording is heard once only. In the other three parts, the recording is heard twice.

Paper 5 Speaking (15 minutes)

Candidates are examined in pairs by one interlocutor and one assessor. There are four parts, designed to test general social language, transactional language, and negotiation and collaboration skills. Pictures and other visual prompts are used in Parts 2 and 3 to cue various tasks.

Marking

There is more detailed information on the questions and marking criteria below.

Advice on how to tackle specific questions is given in this book under the headings STRATEGY, EXAM TIP and EXAM SKILLS.

Paper 1 Reading

There are three main kinds of questions.

Multiple matching (Texts 1 and 4)

You are given a list of questions or 'prompts' (e.g. 1–12) and a list of possible answers (e.g. A–L) to choose from. You have to match the correct answers to the questions according to the information in the text. You may have to match more than one answer to a question and you may have to use an answer more than once.

These questions are usually fairly straightforward because the answers are stated in the text – but as the text may be long and the time is short, it's a test of how quickly you can find the answers. For this reason, it's important to scan effectively for the information you need and not to spend time on other parts of the text.

See pages 178 and 186.

Gapped text (Text 2)

The text has a number of gaps in it where paragraphs have been removed and placed below the text. You have to choose one for each gap. There is one paragraph which you won't need.

To answer these questions, you need to be very clear about the development of the writer's argument or, if it's a narrative, about the sequence of events. So read the text carefully and think about what kind of information might be missing in each gap. When you are choosing an answer, look for grammatical and logical clues to help you.

See pages 172 and 198.

Multiple choice (Text 3)

You are given an unfinished statement or a question and you have to select the best answer from four choices. Multiple choice questions test your understanding of the text and the questions so make sure you study the exact words in the question before making a choice. The questions follow the order of the text.

See page 204.

Marking

For Paper 1, answers have to be filled in on a special mark sheet, which is checked by computer. You can write your answers on the exam paper first if you like, but be sure to leave time to transfer them to the mark sheet.

Paper 2 Writing

Part 1

There is no choice in this section. You will be asked to produce one or sometimes two pieces of writing (250 words in all) in response to various kinds of written information.

You will have to use the information some way – by selecting and summarising from it, for example, or by responding to it – so the question tests effective **reading** as well as **writing**.

See pages 176 and 190.

Part 2

In this section, you will be asked to write one piece of about 250 words from a choice of four tasks.

Each task is described in detail so that you know **why** you are writing, **who** you are writing to, and **what** kind of information to include. Make sure you follow these instructions exactly.

See pages 182 and 194.

Marking

Your work in each section will be marked on the same two scales.

Accuracy and Range of Language looks at how:
• accurate your grammar, spelling and punctuation are
• precisely you use vocabulary
• broad your range of grammar and vocabulary is.

Handling the Task looks at whether:
• you do everything the question asks for
• you use an appropriate style and register
• your work would achieve the required objective.

There are equal marks for each scale, so make sure you consider both aspects of the task carefully.

Paper 3 English in Use

There are six parts in this paper.

Part 1 Lexical cloze
This focuses mainly on vocabulary: you choose the best answer in each case from four options to fill in 15 gaps in a short text. See pages 195 and 221.

Part 2 Structural cloze
This focuses mainly on grammar and here there are no multiple choice answers to help you. You have to fill in 15 gaps in a short text with one word. See pages 184 and 208.

Part 3 Error correction
You have to read a short text with 16 numbered lines. Some lines contain an error which you must identify and correct. There are two task types. In one, you have to find an extra word that shouldn't be there. These words are always structural words, e.g. articles, pronouns, etc. In the other, you have to identify mistakes in spelling and punctuation. See pages 209 and 231.

Part 4 Word formation
This consists of two short texts with a total of 15 gaps. You have to fill in the gaps with the correct form of the prompt words given. See page 183.

Part 5 Register cloze
You have to transfer information from a text in one register (e.g. formal) to a text in another register (e.g. informal) by writing one or two words in gaps in the second text. See pages 135 and 231.

Part 6 Discourse cloze
You have to choose the best phrase or sentence from a given list to complete six gaps in a text. There are three items which you will not need. One item is always given as an example. See pages 122 and 196.

Marking
Each section carries approximately equal marks. Before the exam it's a good idea to experiment to find out which questions take you longer to answer. You may find, for example, that you can do a lexical cloze exercise or an error correction task quite quickly, while a discourse cloze takes longer. When you take the exam, make sure you plan your time well so that you can give the necessary amount of time to each section.

Paper 4 Listening

The four parts in this paper focus on different kinds of spoken English such as monologues and dialogues, formal and informal conversations, public announcements and private messages. The voices you hear will be in standard English in terms of grammar and vocabulary; some may reflect a slight accent. Don't worry about this; you should have no problems in understanding any accents you hear in the exam.

Questions
The questions provide different reasons for listening – listening for specific facts, for gist, to understand the speaker's attitude, etc. – and together they require a variety of listening skills to be used.

Parts 1 and 2
In Part 1 you will hear a monologue which lasts about 2 minutes. In Part 2 you will hear a monologue, or possibly two speakers. The text could be a short talk, a radio announcement or a recorded message, for example. The questions will test your understanding of **specific information** in the recording and you will usually have to fill in up to four missing words or figures in a set of notes, perhaps in table or chart form.

Note: The recording is played twice in Part 1 but **only once** in Part 2. However, in Part 2, you will normally hear some of the key information more than once.

Part 3
A longer recording (about 4 minutes) of a discussion or conversation, played twice. The questions test your understanding of the recording as a whole, including the gist of what is said, specific information that is given, and also the speakers' attitudes. You will usually have to complete notes or sentences with single words or short phrases, or answer four-option multiple choice questions.

Part 4
Five short extracts (up to 30 seconds each), played twice. You may be asked to identify the situation or topic, to say whether each speaker is making an enquiry, complaining, explaining and so on, or to identify specific information from the extracts. You will either have to do two multiple matching tasks, or answer up to 10 three-option multiple choice questions.

Paper 5 Speaking

The interview is in pairs and there are two examiners. One examiner (the interlocutor) works with you, explaining the tasks, while the other (the assessor) generally sits apart, assessing your English. The interview is in four parts, which each test different speaking skills. The examiners may arrange the chairs in different ways at different phases of the interview.

Part 1

In this part there will be a relaxed conversation round a table where you and your partner meet the two examiners and answer general questions about yourselves. During this part, your general social English and your ability to interact with other people in English will be assessed. Be prepared to:

- introduce yourself and say where you come from.
- introduce your partner (if you know them) and say something about them. See page 176.
- talk about your family in a general way. See page 176.
- talk about how long you have been studying English, and why. See page 15.
- talk about your job or course of study and your future plans. See page 15.
- talk about your interests and hobbies. See page 176.

You may also have to ask your partner questions in the same areas.

Part 2

In this part you and your partner sit facing each other and you will take it in turns to speak for a minute or so about a visual prompt – a photograph, cartoon, or set of pictures. When you have finished, your partner responds briefly – by saying what's similar or different about their own visual, for example.

This part tests your ability to give information clearly. See pages 42 and 190.

Part 3

In this part, you and your partner will have a problem-solving task to discuss for about two minutes. You might have to put points in order of importance, give advice, or come to a decision.

This part tests your ability to negotiate and collaborate with your partner. It does not test your ability to find the correct solution. If you can't agree on a solution, it will be perfectly acceptable it you 'agree to disagree'. See pages 46 and 202.

Part 4

In this last part you will be asked to report and explain the decisions you reached in the Part 3 task, as well as answer further questions which extend the discussion. In this part, your ability to report, explain, summarise and to develop a discussion naturally is tested.

Marking

Your speaking skills in Paper 5 as a whole will be marked on four scales.

- **Grammar and vocabulary:** Do you use a wide range of structures and vocabulary and make only a few minor mistakes?
- **Discourse management:** Do you express ideas and opinions clearly and coherently, and without long hesitations?
- **Pronunciation:** Are you easy to understand? Do you use English pronunciation features naturally?
- **Interactive communication:** Do you contribute fully and effectively to the discussion with your partner and with the examiners?

There are equal marks for each scale.

Language Focus 1 *Grammatical Terms*

1 What kind of word is it?

Here are some basic grammatical terms used in dictionaries and grammar reference books. Choose a term to fit each definition 1–8 and then match each definition with examples (a–h) from the box below.

preposition	adverb
noun	article
pronoun	conjunction
adjective	verb

1 ...... a word which refers to a person, a thing or an abstract idea such as a feeling or a quality. e.g. ...

2 ...... a word which is used to replace a noun that has already been mentioned or that will be mentioned later. e.g. ...

3 ...... a word which gives more information about a noun or pronoun. e.g. ...

4 ...... a word which is concerned with what people and things do, and what happens to them. e.g. ...

5 ...... a word which adds information about a verb, or about an adjective or adverb. e.g. ...

6 ...... a word or group of words often placed before a noun or pronoun to indicate place, direction, source, method, etc. e.g. ...

7 ...... a word or group of words that join together words, groups of words or clauses. e.g. ...

8 ...... a word with no meaning on its own which is used in front of a noun or noun phrase. e.g. ...

a	*I, you, him, it*	b	*and, although, if*
c	*run, make, behave*	d	*a, an, the*
e	*Tim, clock, strength*	f	*long, heavy, difficult*
g	*in, from, by*	h	*easily, fast, extremely*

2 Other terms

a Match each term 1–5 to an explanation a–e.

1 *Base Form*   4 *Participle*
2 *Auxiliary Verb*   5 *-ing Noun*
3 *Modal*

a An auxiliary verb which is used with a main verb to show a particular attitude such as possibility, obligation or prediction.

b A form of the verb that can be used in compound tenses of the verb or as an adjective. There are two types: the past, usually ending in *-ed*; and the present, ending in *-ing*.

c A noun formed from a verb and ending in *-ing*. Also called a gerund.

d The form of the verb which has no letters added to it. Also called the infinitive.

e A verb which is used with a main verb to form tenses, negatives, questions, etc.

b Find and underline examples for each of the terms (1–5) in the following letter.

PACKAGING GONE MAD

SIR: Take a bottle of typewriter correcting fluid. It is quite small and very strong. In all my years of letter-writing, I've never seen one broken. A smart hammer blow on a hard surface might do the trick, but I don't keep a hammer beside the typewriter.

It's exactly the sort of small object that would be found miraculously unharmed in the ruins of a heavy bombardment.

Now, stick it to a piece of stout cardboard, swaddle it in shrink-wrapped plastic and put it on a supermarket shelf. There you have it: the ultimate in wasteful packaging. Are marketing consultants really so stupid and irresponsible that they can't think of a better way of drawing the shopper's eye to their products?

They cut down trees for this. And that's not all. We pay for this pointless rubbish in the price of the product, too.

Geoff Dawson,
Carstensz Street,
Griffith (ACT).
July 24

---

3 Dictionary abbreviations

What do the following common abbreviations in dictionaries refer to?

adj	......	*n*	....	*prep*	......
adv	....	*obj*	....	*pron*	....
C	....	*pass.*	....	*sing.*	....
conj	....	*phr v*	....	U	....
infml	....	*pl.*	....	*v*	....

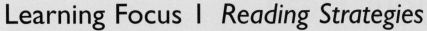

Learning Focus 1 *Reading Strategies*

1 Think about how you would read the following pieces of written language, then discuss the questions below with another student.

1   a   A list of results for an exam you've taken. (3 pages)
    b   A letter from a friend who's studying in Australia. (3 pages)
2   a   Detailed instructions for reaching a friend's house. (half a page)
    b   A review of a film you were thinking of going to see. (half a page)
3   a   A newspaper in your own language. (16 pages)
    b   A newspaper in English. (16 pages)

1   Would you read all six pieces in the same way? If not, why not?
2   Would each pair take the same amount of time to read? Why/Why not?
3   Would you be likely to read any of the pieces above a second time and in a different way? If so, which ones and why?
4   What kinds of things affect the way we read?

2 Read the descriptions below of three basic strategies for reading:

Skimming

If you skim a newspaper or other piece of writing, you read through quickly to understand the main points without bothering about the details. e.g. *Just skimming through the papers, I noticed an article on the Olympics which I thought I might read later.*
The best way to get an idea of the main points of a text is usually by:

- reading the headline/title
- reading the first and last paragraphs
- looking for the *topic sentences* in each paragraph

Scanning

When you scan something, you look at it or through it to find some particular information. e.g. *The lifeguards scanned the sea for shark fins. I only scanned his letter for news of my sister.*
Depending on the information you are interested in, you can save time by looking for particular features:

- names of people, products, places, etc., capital letters, words in a special type (e.g. bold or italics)
- dates, ages, prices, quantities, etc., numbers, abbreviations such as AD, C, £, $, kg

Reading for detail

When you read part or all of a text for detail, you study it carefully in order to understand it fully and not to miss any information.

3 Which of the examples in exercise 1:
1   would you only skim?
2   would you only scan?
3   would you skim first and read for more detail later?
4   would you scan first and read for more detail later?
5   would you read for detail immediately?

Work with a partner and think of other examples of reading where you would a) skim, b) scan and c) read for detail.

EXAM SKILLS ▶ Paper 1

In the CAE Reading Paper you have only 1 hour 15 minutes to read four texts and answer up to 50 questions. This is quite a challenging task, but it is intended to reflect real life, where information needs to be processed rapidly for a particular purpose. To do well in this paper, you will need to read both efficiently and effectively. That means using the right skills at the right time and for the particular type of task.

Which skill should you use when you:

- read the instructions and the questions?
- read the text for the first time?
- need particular facts or figures from the text?
- are choosing the right answer to a multiple choice question?

I ▶ Use Your Head

'Tell me and I'll forget. Show me and I may not remember. Involve me and I'll understand.'
Native American saying

Lead-in

1 **Work with one or two other students and discuss the following questions.**
1   Think of something you have learnt to do successfully (e.g. a sport, driving a car, playing the piano, using a computer). Why do you think you were successful? How did you succeed?
2   Think of something you had less success in learning (maybe at school). Why do you think you were less successful? What went wrong?

2 **Discuss whether you think the following statements are true or false.**
1   Most people have better memories than they think.
2   Drinking black coffee can help people to remember information.
3   We learn better at certain times of the day than at others.
4   When you're studying, it's best not to take many breaks.
5   Our memories are bound to get worse as we get older.
6   We learn best when we are relaxed.
7   It's possible to learn while you sleep.
8   When studying a book, it's best to remember information in the author's own words.

You will find information on all these points in the following text.

Text

1   The text deals with several different aspects of memory and learning. The main topics are listed below in the order they appear in the text.

SKIMMING

Skim through the text fairly quickly and write the numbers of the paragraphs which deal with each topic.

Topic	Paragraph(s)
Memory	......
Learning rhythms	......
Effects of ageing on intelligence	......
Learning: psychological factors	......
Learning strategies	......

SCANNING

2   In which paragraphs does the writer give the following advice? Use your answers to Exercise 1 to guide you to the relevant part of the text.

	Paragraph
A Make your own notes.	......
B Find out what your best time for learning is.	......
C If you want to remember something, try to reproduce the conditions you were in when you were learning it.	......
D Keep mentally active.	......

Lifeplan psychology adviser John Nicholson explains how to reveal the hidden potential of your mind, and how to improve your mental efficiency

YOUR MIND

Do You Make The Most Of It?

'Other people can provide you with information, but only you can learn it.'

1 PSYCHOLOGICAL research shows we consistently underestimate our mental powers. If you think this does not apply to you, then here is a simple test to show you are wrong.

2 Write down the names of all the American states you can remember. Put the list away and then set yourself the same task a week later. Provided you have not cheated by consulting an atlas, you will notice something rather surprising. The two lists will contain roughly the same number of states, but they will not be identical. Some names will have slipped away, but others will have replaced them. This suggests that somewhere in your mind you may well have a record of virtually every state. So it is not really your memory letting you down; just your ability to retrieve information from it.

3 We would remember a lot more if we had more confidence in our memories and knew how to use them properly. One useful tip is that things are more likely to be remembered if you are in exactly the same state and place as you were when you learned them.

4 So if you are a student who always revises on black coffee, perhaps it would be sensible to prime yourself with a cup before going into the exam. If possible, you should also try to learn information in the room where it is going to be tested.

5 *When* you learn is also important. Lots of people swear they can absorb new information more efficiently at some times of day than at others. Research shows this is not just imagination. There is a biological rhythm for learning, though it affects different people in different ways. For most of us, the best plan is to take in new information in the morning and then try to consolidate it into memory during the afternoon.

6 But this does not apply to everyone, so it is essential to establish your own rhythm.

You can do this by learning a set number of lines of poetry at different times of the day and seeing when most lines stick. When you have done this, try to organise your life so that the time set aside for learning coincides with the time when your memory is at its best.

7 Avoid learning marathons – they do not make the best use of your mind. Take plenty of breaks, because they offer a double bonus: the time off gives your mind a chance to do some preliminary consolidation and it also gives a memory boost to the learning which occurs on either side of it.

8 Popular fears about the effects of ageing on intelligence are based on a misconception. Research shows that although we do slow down mentally as we approach the end of life, becoming stupid or losing your grip in the world is not an inevitable consequence of the ageing process. On some measures – vocabulary, for example – we actually improve in the second half of life. In old age, intellectual functioning is closely related to physical health. But there also seems to be a lot of truth in the old adage: If you do not want to lose it, use it.

9 Learning goes well when people feel challenged and badly when they feel threatened. Whenever a learning task becomes threatening, both adults and children feel anxious. Anxiety interferes with the process of learning because it is distracting. In order to learn effectively you have to be attending closely to the task. An anxious person is likely to be worrying about what will happen if he fails, to the detriment of his attempts to succeed. If his mind is full of thoughts such as "I'm sure I'm going to fail this test", or "What are my parents going to say?", he will not do as well as he should.

10 Learning is an active process. Despite claims to the contrary, you cannot learn when you are asleep. "Sleep learning" (accomplished by having a tape recorder under the pillow, playing soothing but improving messages while you are recharging your tissues) is unfortunately a myth. Any learning that seems to have occurred in this situation will actually have been done after you woke up but were still drowsy.

11 Other people can provide you with information, but only you can learn it. It also has to be "chewed over" before it can be integrated into your body of knowledge. That is why just reading a book is no way to acquire information unless you happen to possess a photographic memory. Parroting the author's words is not much better. You have to make your own notes because this obliges you to apply an extra stage of processing to the information before committing it to memory. Effective revision always involves reworking material, making notes on notes, and perhaps re-ordering information in the light of newly-observed connections.

12 As a general rule, the greater your brain's investment in a body of information, the better its chances of reproducing it accurately and effectively when you need it.

11

READING FOR DETAIL

3 Work in pairs. Read through the questions below and see if you can answer them without looking back at the text. If you need to check, scan through the text till you find the information you need, then read more carefully.

1 If you try the memory test suggested, how much time should pass between the first and second test?

2 What two conditions should be the same if we want to help our memories to recall something that has been learnt?

3 How can learning poetry help us understand how we learn best?

4 What are the advantages of taking breaks during study?

5 What aspect of intelligence gets better as we get older?

6 Why can't we learn effectively if we are anxious?

7 Why doesn't 'sleep learning' work? If you try it, when will learning actually take place?

8 You can only learn by just reading if you have a special quality. What is it?

Focus on Vocabulary *Dictionary Skills*

DICTIONARY SKILLS

1 a Look at the two meanings of *cheat* described in this extract from the *Longman Dictionary of English Language and Culture* and then answer the questions.

> **cheat** *v* **1** [I (**at**)] to behave in a dishonest or deceitful way in order to win an advantage, especially in a game: *He always cheats at cards.* | *Any student found cheating will be disqualified from the exam.* **2** [T (**of, out of**)] to take from someone deceitfully: *They cheated the old woman (out) of her money by making her sign a document she didn't understand.*

1 What part of speech is the word *cheat*? How do you know?

2 Can *cheat* in the first meaning take an object – can you cheat a game? How do you know?

3 Can *cheat* in the second meaning take an object – can you cheat a person? How do you know?

4 What other useful information is given about the way *cheat* is used?

b What is the meaning of *cheat* in this example from the text on page 11? 'Provided you have not cheated by ...' (para. 2)

2 Now find other words or phrases in the text to match these dictionary definitions:

Word	Grammatical information	Definition	
1	*v* [T] (**from**)	to find and bring back (usually formal or technical)	(para. 2)
2	*v* [T] (**with**)	to prepare (e.g. a machine) for working	(para. 4)
3	*v* [I/T]	to (cause to) become stronger and firmer	(para. 5)
4	*v* [I] (**with**)	to happen at the same time	(para. 6)
5	*n usually sing.*	something pleasant in addition to what is expected (*infml*)	(para. 7)
6	*n usually sing.*	an increase or improvement	(para. 7)
7	*phrase*	have less understanding, control or skill in a subject or activity	(para. 8)
8	*n*	an old, wise saying, a proverb	(para. 8)
9	*phr v* [T]	to think about (a question, problem, etc.) (*infml*)	(para. 11)
10	*v* [T]	to repeat someone else's words without thinking or understanding	(para. 11)

3 Answer these questions using words or phrases from the list in Exercise 2.
Example:
> Why are you looking so cheerful? (*You've been on holiday and that's improved your spirits a lot.*)
> *Going on holiday has given my spirits a real boost.*

1 Why are you so fed up? (*One of your exams takes place on your birthday.*)
2 Why are you going back to the office again? (*You left your briefcase there.*)
3 Why don't you think Tim's history essay deserves an 'A'? (*He copied most of it word for word from A J P Taylor's book on the subject.*)
4 Why are you working overtime? (*They're offering an extra payment to people who exceed their sales targets.*)
5 Why are you worried about your boss? (*He doesn't seem to be able to concentrate for more than two minutes and he keeps forgetting things.*)

EXPRESSIONS WITH 'BRAIN'

4 Work with a partner. Choose the definition which you think is correct for each of the expressions below.

1 bird-brained (*adj*) a stupid, silly
  b imaginative

2 scatterbrained (*adj*) a well-informed about a lot of subjects
  b careless, forgetful

3 brainchild (*n*) a someone who behaves in an immature way
  b someone's idea or invention

4 brainwash (*v T*) a to make someone change their beliefs by very strong persuasion
  b to relax and clear one's mind of problems, worries, etc.

5 brainwave (*n*) a a sudden inability to think clearly
  b a sudden clever idea

6 brainy (*adj*) a intelligent (of a person) e.g. *She's beautiful **and** brainy. It's not fair!*
  b intellectually demanding (of a topic or treatment) e.g. *Economics is a very brainy course to take.*

7 pick someone's brains (*phrase*) a to question someone who knows a lot about a subject.
  b to steal someone else's ideas.

5 Once you've checked your answers to Exercise 4, complete these sentences.
1 Don't let all those TV adverts ...... you into buying that new toy.
2 This is the best job offer he's going to get but he's too ...... to realise it.
3 You don't have to be ...... to succeed, you just need common sense.
4 You're the computer expert, Jane. Could I ...... a minute?
5 She would be a marvellous organiser if she wasn't so ....
6 I couldn't think how to raise the money we needed and then Jim had a ...... : a car boot sale!
7 The advertising campaign was the ...... of one of the junior managers.

Focus on Grammar 1 *Conditionals*

1 Match the following examples to these three types of conditional sentence. Write 0, 1 or 2 in the space provided.

Type 0 Conditions which are always true
Type 1 Conditions which are very probable in the future
Type 2 Conditions which are impossible or improbable in the present or future

...... 1 Provided you have not cheated, you will notice something very unusual. (Text)
...... 2 We would remember more if we had more confidence in our memories. (Text)
...... 3 If you do not want to lose it, use it. (Text)
...... 4 ... just reading a book is no way to acquire information unless you happen to have a photographic memory. (Text)
...... 5 You can borrow my car as long as you bring it back on the dot of six.
...... 6 If you're hoping to get there for the start, leave now!
...... 7 If you tried a bit harder, you might actually succeed.
...... 8 He never fails to check the answering machine in case anyone's left a message.

2 **Great conditional myths**

Some of the 'rules' you may remember about conditionals are not the whole picture. Cross out the word *always* in each rule and answer the questions.

> In conditional sentences, the conditional clause always starts with *if*.

1 Find four other conditional links in the examples above.

....

Can you think of any more?

(There is a list of conditional link words in the Grammar File, page 138.)

> In Type 1 conditionals, the verb in the main clause is always *will* and ...

2 Find two other verb forms in the examples.

....

(Modal verbs are dealt with in Units 3 and 9 and also in the Grammar File, pages 142–144.)

> ... the verb in the conditional clause is always the simple present.

3 Find two other verb forms in the examples.

....

Notice that these tenses are both ways of referring to present time.

> In Type 2 conditionals, the verb in the main clause is always *would*.

4 Find one different verb in the examples.

....

3 Match the two halves of the following conditional sentences.

1 If you need to make a phone call,
2 If you tidied your desk,
3 If you didn't complain so much,
4 Unless you've made other plans,
5 If there was an emergency,
6 As long as you still love me,
7 If I knew what the answer was,
8 Provided you've done your best,
9 If I told you a secret,
10 In case there's an urgent message,

a people would be more sympathetic.
b I'll leave a number I can be contacted on.
c everyone will be satisfied.
d why would I be asking you?
e you might actually be able to find things.
f would you keep it to yourself?
g please keep it short.
h I'd like you to have dinner with me.
i I wouldn't have a clue what to do.
j nothing else matters.

4 Complete these conditional sentences.

1 If they ...... (still/make) that awful racket at midnight, I ...... (not/hesitate) to call the police.
2 I ...... (be) quite willing to go as long as someone ...... (lend) me the money for the fare.
3 If you haven't got a dictionary, ... !
4 Don't forget to bring the map, in case ....
5 No one would mind you coming in after midnight, provided that ....
6 I find it hard to concentrate on studying if ....
7 I can't learn a new word unless ....
8 If I weren't studying English now, ...

Focus on Speaking *Your Expectations*

▶ Paper 5, Part I

1 Reasons for learning English

Why are you studying English at advanced level? Tick the reasons that apply to you, or add your own.

1 to get a better job
2 out of interest
3 to live in an English-speaking country
4 ....

Compare your reasons with a partner.

2 Factors in learning

How important do you expect the following factors to be in your English course? Rank them in order of importance (1 = most important).

your teacher   ......
your coursebook   ......
yourself   ......

Discuss your answers and your reasons with your partner.

3 How can your teacher help you most?

Here are some possible ways your teacher can help you to learn (and you can add more if you like). Tick the six which you consider most important.

1 by revising all major areas of grammar thoroughly
2 by concentrating on areas of advanced grammar
3 by working on your use of functional language (e.g. complaining/apologising)
4 by explaining all new vocabulary clearly
5 by giving regular tests
6 by correcting every mistake you make
7 by giving practice in pronunciation
8 by setting regular homework
9 by working through past examination papers
10 by giving plenty of practice in speaking
11 by giving practice in different types of writing tasks
12 by getting students to work in pairs or groups
13 by helping you to develop good learning methods
14 ....

Compare your choices with another student.

4 How can you help yourself?

a Here are 17 language learning habits. Tick the things which you already do.

1 translate from my own language before I speak or write
2 keep a vocabulary notebook and revise new vocabulary regularly
3 record new vocabulary in a short phrase or sentence
4 write new vocabulary with just a translation in my language
5 use only a bilingual dictionary

6 use only a monolingual dictionary

7 use a grammar reference book

8 speak only English in class

9 read English newspapers or magazines outside class

10 listen to spoken English outside class

11 translate every unknown word as I read

12 guess unknown words as I read

13 only speak in class when I'm sure I won't make a mistake

14 ask questions in class

15 revise each lesson before the next

16 set myself learning targets (e.g. five new phrasal verbs each week)

17 find out which areas of language I am weak in and give myself extra practice in them

b Some of the above habits may, in fact, be unhelpful in the long run. Which are they? (You will probably be able to find about five.) Compare your answers with your partner's and discuss why certain habits might be helpful or unhelpful.

c Underline or highlight the good language learning habits which you will definitely try to adopt. Refer back to this page from time to time to see which good learning habits you have developed.

Focus on Listening *Learning a Language*

 Paper 4, Part 3

You will hear a Japanese woman being interviewed about her experience of learning English. You will hear the recording twice. In this task, you have to choose the correct answer, A, B, C or D.

STRATEGY

- Before you listen the first time, read through the stems or questions, but not the multiple choice options.

- Before the second hearing, read the options A–D. As you listen, choose which answer best fits the question.

1 Ayako started studying English in England because
   A she was keen to improve her language skills.
   B she had nothing else to do with her time.
   C her husband encouraged her to do so.
   D her employer sent her on a course.

2 At first, she found that the classes she attended
   A were quite easy and rather boring.
   B focused on grammar exercises.
   C were a good way to meet people.
   D were well taught and organised.

3 She says that football interviews on TV were difficult for her because
   A they spoke very quickly.
   B she didn't understand the subject.
   C they contained different accents.
   D she wasn't interested in football.

4   What method for building up vocabulary does she recommend?
    A   reading part of a dictionary every day
    B   keeping a written list of new expressions
    C   repeating new words until they are memorised
    D   focusing on expressions from newspapers

5   How does she measure her success?
    A   Her accent is better.
    B   Her writing skills have improved.
    C   She has a wider vocabulary.
    D   Her teacher gives her feedback.

6   What difficulty does she say Japanese causes her in relation to English?
    A   The writing system is very different and hard to translate.
    B   There are many English words that are confusingly similar.
    C   Japanese people speak more slowly than the English.
    D   Japanese contains American words with different meanings.

7   She says that the best advice for people arriving in England is to
    A   have friends from your own country who understand you.
    B   follow your interests in reading newspapers and watching TV.
    C   go shopping in supermarkets so you don't need to speak.
    D   try to make friends with English people who can teach you.

STUDY BOX ▶ *despite/in spite of; although/but*

Despite and *in spite of* are prepositions and are followed by nouns (including *-ing* nouns) or noun phrases. They cannot introduce finite clauses (clauses containing a verb with a tense).

> *Despite/In spite of* claims to the contrary, you cannot learn when you are asleep. (Text)

> ... that made [listening to football interviews] more difficult, *despite/in spite of* my interest. (Listening)

Although and *but* are conjunctions which introduce clauses. Compare the following examples.

> *Although* we do slow down mentally as we approach the end of life, becoming stupid is not an inevitable consequence of the ageing process. (Text)

> Other people can provide you with information, *but* only you can learn it. (Text)

Tick the correct sentences below. Correct any which have mistakes in them.

1   I'll definitely come and see you although I can't promise when that will be.

2   In spite of take the fast train, we still arrived 20 minutes late!

3   Although I'm sure the bill was absolutely correct, but I'd still like to check it.

4   They still got burgled in spite of all their elaborate security precautions.

Focus on Writing *Informal Letter*

TASK

> Some English friends, Peter and Sue Hall, have written to you for advice. Their 20-year-old son, Tom, wants to get a job teaching English in your country. This is part of the letter you have received from them.

Tom's doing a teacher training course at the moment, as you know, but he thinks he ought to learn something of the language before he comes, which seems like a good idea. He's bought a 'Teach Yourself' book on the language, but we were wondering if you had any other suggestions which would help him. It's quite a while since he studied a language at school, so he'd also be really grateful for some general tips on learning a language.

> Write a **letter** to Tom giving advice and any helpful suggestions that you can. Write about 250 words excluding the address.

UNDERSTANDING THE TASK

1 Read the question carefully and highlight the key points. Ask yourself:

- What's the purpose of your letter?
- What two things do you need to give advice on?

CONTENT

2 Work with another student – one who speaks your language if possible.

a What would be the advantages of Tom being able to speak a bit of your language when he arrives?

b Think about the language: is there anything an English speaker would find particularly unusual or difficult (pronunciation/grammar/writing system, etc.)?

c Make a list of all the things Tom could do to learn your language, from having private lessons or buying a cassette course to tuning into radio broadcasts. Think about the pros and cons in terms of cost, time and effectiveness. Decide which method seems most realistic. Is there anything you could do to help – e.g. send magazines or simple books?

d Write down any general tips on learning a language that you think would be helpful. Use your own experience as far as possible.

ORGANISATION

3 Working individually, make a plan for your letter. Decide on the main sections you want to have and think about the best way to organise them. Jot down the main points for each section. Think of a suitable introduction and conclusion.

LAYOUT

4 Before you begin, check the Writing File, page 157, for an example of the layout of an informal letter and for useful language.

Focus on Grammar 2 *Phrasal Verbs*

1 Underline the phrasal verbs in these two extracts from the text on page 11. What do they mean?

> So it is not really your memory letting you down, just your ability to retrieve information ...
> Information has to be 'chewed over' before it can be integrated into your body of knowledge.

A phrasal verb consists of a verb + a particle (either an adverb or a preposition). In order to use a particular phrasal verb correctly you have to know not only its **meaning** but also its **grammar.** For example:

Is it **transitive** or **intransitive** (does it take an object or not)? If it's transitive, is it **separable** or **inseparable**? Can the object go before the particle (e.g. Put *your shoes* on) or must it come after the particle (e.g. They got on *the bus*)?

2 How much do you know? Not all the phrasal verbs in these sentences are used correctly. See if you can spot which ones are incorrect.

1 He didn't speak much English but he managed to get his meaning across. (A)
2 He didn't speak much English but he managed to get across his meaning. (A)
3 The police ordered him to hand over his gun. (A)
4 When the police saw his gun, they ordered him to hand over it. (A)
5 Hold on and I'll put through the manager to you. (B)
6 Hold on and I'll put him through to you. (B)
7 I looked through all the questions and I couldn't answer any! (C)
8 I looked all the questions through and I couldn't answer any! (C)

Check your answers by reading the rules below. The letters A, B and C in brackets refer to the patterns described.

Separable

A In the most common type of phrasal verb, the object can come either before the particle or after it, e.g.

> I *chewed over* the problem for a few days. *or*
> I *chewed* the problem *over* for a few days.

But if the object is a pronoun (*him, her*, etc.), it always comes **before** the particle, e.g.

> I *chewed it over* for a few days.

B In a second type of phrasal verb the object must come **before** the particle, e.g.

> If I miss the meeting, I'll feel I've *let* everybody *down*. (Not ~~let down everybody~~)
> e.g. *let down, put through, move around, send away, ask out*

Inseparable

C In a small third group, the object must come after the particle, e.g.

> Could you see to this customer while I answer the phone?
> e.g. *look through, see to, stick to, make for, summon up*

3 Complete these sentences using phrasal verbs from the list below. Write no more than three words for each.

> *jot down   break off   let in   wind up   let down
> put off   fit in   make up*

1 There's one more bag to go in the boot. Can you ...... ?
2 They were engaged for a while but they've ....
3 None of those stories he told you were true. He ....
4 Give me your phone number and I'll just ....
5 That'll be the police at the door. You'd better ....
6 The clock's stopped. I must have forgotten to ....
7 I'm relying on you. Don't ....
8 I wouldn't want to go myself, but don't let me ....

4 Use phrasal verbs from the list to rewrite these sentences less formally.

> *ask out   send away   send out   take in
> pick out   move around*

1 It's a demanding course because there's a lot of new information to assimilate in a short time.
   The course is hard work because you ....

2 I was required to identify the man from a selection of photographs.
   They asked ....

3 She dismisses any salesmen without exception.
   She always ....

4 You should obviously try and arrange a date with her.
   Why don't you ....

5 The furniture needs rearranging for the party.
   We'll have to ....

6 Details of the pay offer will be circulated to all employees.
   The company ....

English in Use I *Developing Skills: Word Formation*

1   In this task, you have to form words to fill the gaps in a text. The words you need could be nouns, verbs, adjectives or adverbs. To form them you may need to make any of the following changes:

- add a **suffix**, e.g. retire → retirement (*n*);
- add a **prefix**, e.g. intelligent → unintelligent (*adj*);
- make a spelling **change**, e.g. long → length (*n*);
- combine two words to make a **compound**, e.g. stair → staircase (*n*) head → bigheaded (*adj*)

a   Make **nouns** from these words by adding one of the following suffixes:
-tion, -ity, -ment, -ness, -ship, -ance
stupid   kind   concentrate   appear   member   judge

b   Make **adjectives**, using one of the following suffixes: *-able, -ful, -y, -ly, ive, -al, -ial*
harm   education   salt   friend   proverb   profit   co-operate

c   Make these verbs and adjectives negative by adding one of the following **prefixes:** *un-, dis-, mis-, in-, ir-, im-*
probable   credible   pack   lead   like   responsible

d   Make nouns by changing the spelling as necessary:
prove   thieve   strong   high

2   Read the text below. Use the words in the box to form **one** word that fits in the same numbered space in the text. The exercise begins with an example (**0**).

RISE AND SHINE!

Starting the day with a good breakfast and making the right (**0**) ....*decision*.... about what to eat can have an important effect on your (**1**) .... during the day, according to a professor of psychology. Studies carried out by Andrew Smith of Bristol University showed that eating breakfast leads to a ten per cent (**2**) .... in mental function. Students who ate breakfast had faster (**3**) .... , were more (**4**) .... in lectures, and reasoned more (**5**) .... than their colleagues who ate nothing. Professor Smith also found that people who had breakfast on a (**6**) .... basis experienced more positive moods than those who did so more (**7**) .... And the best (**8**) .... of food? Well, forget the (**9**) .... cooked English breakfast of fried eggs and bacon – apparently a bowl of cereal has the most (**10**) .... effects of all.

(**0**)	**DECIDE**
(**1**)	PERFORM
(**2**)	IMPROVE
(**3**)	RESPOND
(**4**)	ATTEND
(**5**)	LOGIC
(**6**)	DAY
(**7**)	REGULAR
(**8**)	CHOOSE
(**9**)	TRADITION
(**10**)	BENEFIT

English in Use 2 *Developing Skills: Error Correction*

▶ Paper 3, Part 3

1 In this task you have to find a number of extra and unnecessary words in a text.

STRATEGY

a You should:

- read the text once quickly to get the general picture.
- read it again very carefully. It's easy to miss an unnecessary word when you're thinking mainly about the meaning.

TYPICAL ERRORS

b Here are some words to look out for while doing this type of task.

Articles (*a/an, the*)
Look at the second example in the text on page 22, *the researchers*, a typical mistake with a definite article. This is the first mention of *researchers* and we don't know who they are yet, so we use the general plural without *the*. Later in the text, when they are mentioned again, the definite article can be used. There are three more mistakes with articles in this text.

Auxiliary verbs (e.g. *be, do, have*) + **modal auxiliaries** (*can, may, will, would,* etc.)
Think carefully about each auxiliary verb and make sure that it is grammatically correct and also fits the meaning. (two mistakes in this text)

Relative pronouns (e.g. *who, which, that*)
Sometimes a relative pronoun looks correct at first but when you read the whole sentence, you realise that it makes no sense. (one mistake in this text)

Prepositions (e.g. *on, in, for*)
Look carefully at each preposition. (one mistake in this text)

2 Underline the unnecessary word in each of the following sentences and say which part of speech it is.

1 It was the first comet to can be seen in the night sky for over 50 years.

2 The importance of revision which is stressed by teachers, who test you regularly on what you know.

3 You must take a care when you go upstairs because some of the steps are rather uneven.

4 They spent a long time discussing about the results of the recent election.

5 He went on to repeat what he had been said several times before.

HH LEARNING CENTRE
HARROW COLLEGE

3 In **most** lines of the following text, there is **one** unnecessary word. It is either grammatically incorrect or does not fit in with the sense of the text. Underline every unnecessary word and then write it in the space on the right. If a line is correct put a tick (✓). There are two examples (0) at the beginning, and 11 more unnecessary words to find.

A sonata for two can aid your IQ

BY NIGEL HAWKES, SCIENCE EDITOR

Listening to Mozart can significantly increase your intelligence,	0 ✓
according to <u>the</u> researchers in America. Unfortunately, the	0 _the_
effect is temporary and only lasts about 15 minutes long.	1 ......
Dr Frances Rauscher and two colleagues from the University of	2 ......
California were reported the findings in the journal Nature. They asked	3 ......
36 college students to undergo standard of psychological tests	4 ......
after listening to a tape of Mozart's sonata for the two pianos in D major.	5 ......
They found that the students did better after listening to this music	6 ......
than they did so after hearing a ten-minute tape of instructions	7 ......
designed to make them to relax, or ten minutes of silence. Although	8 ......
the researchers could offer no explanation for the finding, but they	9 ......
said that there had long been a belief that people who are interested	10 ......
in music are tend to perform better at intellectually demanding tasks.	11 ......
They believe that the beneficial effect which depends on the complexity	12 ......
of the music played and they intend to try the other compositions	13 ......
and musical styles to prove the point. They also plan further tests	14 ......
to see if a listening for longer periods produces even greater effects.	15 ......

2 ▶ Severe Weather

'When two Englishmen meet, their first talk is of the weather.'
Samuel Johnson (1709–1784)

Lead-in

1 From the list of 16 words below, cross out the 6 words which are **not** connected with weather conditions.

typhoid	*draught*	*hail*	*gale*
sleet	*tornado*	*typhoon*	*slump*
harpoon	*flooding*	*cholera*	*blizzard*
hurricane	*hazard*	*fog*	*drought*

2 Which sets of adjectives a–h go with the nouns 1–8?
1	rain	a	temperate/mild/tropical
2	sea	b	severe/violent/electrical
3	wind	c	dry/humid/intense/scorching
4	climate	d	light/heavy/driving/torrential
5	heat	e	thick/dense/freezing
6	fog	f	bright/dazzling/warm
7	sunshine	g	calm/choppy/rough
8	storm	h	gentle/light/strong/icy/biting

▶ Paper 5, Part 2

3 a Describe these photographs using some of the weather words above.

   b Discuss the impact these severe weather conditions may have had on the people in the photos and the local community.

Text 1

SKIMMING

1 The newspaper article opposite comes from the *London Evening Standard*. Read through the main article quickly to find out what the chief effects of the severe weather were. When you've finished reading, work with a partner and see how much you can recall.

SCANNING

2 Now scan the article to find answers to these questions as quickly as possible. Look for names and numbers.
1 BR is mentioned in the headline. What does it stand for?
2 How many rail travellers were unable to travel?
3 Four counties outside London were affected by the weather. Which ones?
4 How many buses were running north of the river Thames?
5 Which two Underground lines had near normal service?
6 Which railway station was completely closed?

READING FOR DETAIL

3 Read the short reports in the 'In brief' section to find answers to the following questions.
1 Where did rescuers have to be rescued?
2 Where were winter sports events cancelled, and why?
3 Where did winter conditions give someone's game away?
4 Where was the temperature especially newsworthy?
5 Where was there a warm welcome for the elderly?
6 Where was warm water a life-saver, and why?
7 Where was hot water potentially dangerous, and why?
8 Who or what might have benefited from some frozen water?
9 Who found two legs better than four wheels?

GUESSING UNKNOWN VOCABULARY

4 Find words or phrases in the two reports which mean the same as:

Main article

First paragraph   1 people who travel to and from work regularly (*n*)
Left-hand column   2 urgent request (*n*)
     3 alarming (*adj*)
     4 piles of snow blown up by the wind
     5 a very slow speed (*n*)
Right-hand column   6 surrender/giving up a fight (*n*)
     7 unable to get away (*adj*)
     8 have no false beliefs (*phrase*)

In brief   9 in a desperate situation (*adj*)
     10 keep away/deter (*phrasal verb*)
     11 hiding place (*n*)

STYLE

5 a Look at these extracts from the text. Notice the words in italics. What are these words usually associated with? Why have the writers used them?

The weather has *beaten* us.
The chilling admission of *defeat* ...
... the greatest *threat* so far to commerce and industry

b The writers deliberately use a number of other words and expressions for dramatic effect. Add some more examples to these lists:

Nouns: nightmare, chaos, ...
Adjectives: *chilling* admission, *blinding* blizzards, ...

c How appropriate is this language to the topic? How serious do you think the writers are?

Forget it, says BR, the weather has beaten us

And don't try by car, it's a nightmare

TODAY IS CANCELLED!

by Colin Adamson and Patrick McGowan

BLINDING BLIZZARDS brought London to a virtual standstill today and British Rail told 700,000 commuters: 'Forget it. There's no way we can get you to work.'

As Arctic conditions spread eastwards from snowbound Essex and Kent into Sussex and Surrey, rail chiefs extended their 'stay at home' plea to the whole of the Southern and Eastern regions.

The chilling admission of defeat was the greatest threat so far to commerce and industry in the capital. Weather men warned there could be worse to come.

The nightmare was no better on the roads. Millions of commuters forced to take to their cars faced the worst conditions since the big freeze began.

Heavy overnight snowfalls, driven into huge drifts by fierce winds, brought chaos to every major route into London and reduced traffic to a crawl.

Even in the heart of London, where snow rarely settles, the heavy falls gave roads the appearance of isolated country lanes.

South of the Thames, only one bus in ten was running on some routes. Others had no more than a one-in-five service.

North of the river, only half the usual number of buses were running. They were caught up in huge traffic jams in many areas.

The Jubilee and Victoria Underground lines were the only ones with anything like a normal service. All the others ran into trouble as soon as lines came up onto the surface.

The rail capitulation reached its lowest point at 6 am with the total closure of Waterloo Station, caused by major drifts.

As thousands of freezing commuters were left stranded on empty platforms and trapped in dozens of London-bound trains, British Rail said: 'That's it. We can no longer guarantee any sort of service. The weather has beaten us.'

Only a tiny number of trains were still attempting to move across the Eastern and Southern Regions.

An Eastern Region spokesman said: 'If people have any sense at all they will stay indoors and forget trying to make it to work.

Those who do make the effort should be under no illusions that they will get there. Even if by some miracle they do, it will be a rotten journey. The service everywhere is awful.'

IN BRIEF

MOTORISTS stranded in snow and traffic yesterday were overtaken by a man on a pair of skis on the A12 in Essex.

HOVE's swimming pool complex, which is kept at a steamy 80 degrees F, is to open its doors free to pensioners today so they can keep warm.

A FIRE crew was called in to help dig out five ambulances snowed in at Chelmsford Ambulance Station in Essex overnight.

A POLICEMAN who went to pull a stricken schoolboy from a frozen lake in Dagenham had to be rescued himself ... when he fell in.

In LINCOLNSHIRE, an outdoor skating championship at Baston Fen, near Spalding, was cancelled because there was too much snow on the ice.

At LONDON ZOO, lion keepers kept the animals indoors to prevent them escaping when the moats surrounding their enclosures froze. Elephants were given warm baths to stave off hypothermia.

In BLYTH, Northumberland, the snow trapped burglars who had raided a supermarket. Their footprints led police to their hideout.

In SWITZERLAND, the village of La Brevine recorded a record low temperature for the country of -41.8°C. The village lies on an exposed plain known as the Siberia of Switzerland, more than 3,000 ft above sea level near the French border.

Parts of NORWAY were colder than the North Pole yesterday. The Norwegian ice skating championships at Hamar were cancelled because officials considered temperatures of – 30°C too dangerous to the contestants. Doctors there warned people against taking hot drinks immediately after coming in from the extreme cold, to avoid cracking tooth enamel.

Text 2

1 This article describes how the Swiss deal with problems of severe weather. Read it and underline the differences between the British and the Swiss response to severe winter conditions. Why do you think there is this difference?

HOW SWISS SKATE OVER THE PROBLEMS OF A BIG FREEZE-UP

Where snow means go

from John Marshall in Berne

AS SNOW and ice bring chaos to Britain, life in Switzerland – experiencing a record minus 41.8°C – runs as smoothly as an expert skier.

'The latest any train has been this week was 20 minutes,' said a railway spokesman.

At the slightest hint of snow, engines fitted with ploughs and blowers are out clearing the tracks.

• Trains: longest delay only 20 minutes

Where there is a train hold-up due to freezing points or failure of the electrical contract points, teams of repair men on stand-by quickly move into action.

In fact the use of trains goes up by 10 per cent as drivers switch from road to rail.

The unemployed are kept busy clearing minor roads and sweeping the snow off open-air railway platforms.

To obtain unemployment benefit, a claimant must show

• Roads: jobless sweep up the snow

that he or she has applied for at least 10 jobs in the past month.

Work done for the state, such as clearing snow, counts as a job application.

Most roads and all motorways are cleared of snow by 7 a.m. and regularly during snowfalls throughout the day.

Custom posts warn foreign drivers they should drive with snow tyres or carry chains.

Chains are obligatory in almost all of the ski resorts.

• Pavements: residents must keep them clear

Anyone trying to drive without them will be stopped by the police.

Keeping the pavement outside a house or business clear is the legal responsibility of the owner.

Hospitals report a slight increase in the number of accidents involving aged people falling on icy pathways, but say it is only slight.

Farmers in the mountain regions are well stocked up. Food for cattle is flown in, as many towns have communal helicopters.

Reproduced by permission of the Evening Standard Company Ltd

2 a Describe the differences between Britain and Switzerland by combining the sentences in the two columns below, using contrast links from the Study Box on page 27.

Britain	Switzerland
1 Snow and ice bring chaos.	Life continues to run smoothly.
2 Motorists get stranded when it snows.	Most cars have snow tyres or chains.
3 Slippery pavements are a hazard.	Householders have to clear the pavement outside their house.
4 Many farms are completely cut off.	Food for cattle is flown in by helicopter.

Examples:
While snow and ice bring chaos to Britain, life continues to run smoothly in Switzerland.
Snow and ice bring chaos in Britain. In Switzerland, *by contrast*, life continues to run smoothly.

b Use the information in the two articles to make more, similar sentences contrasting the following in London and Switzerland:
  • rail travel • roads • use of cars

..., *while* ...	
..., *whereas* ...	Tim is idealistic *while/whereas* Jane is more practical.
..., *but* ...	
..., *yet* ...	He caused the problem, *but/yet* she's the one who solved it.
Although ...,	*Although* Pete eats a lot, he never puts on weight!
... *by contrast* ...	Summer in Scotland is mild and wet. Summer in Italy, *by contrast*, is hot and dry.

DISCUSSION POINTS
▶ Paper 5, Part 1

3 As a group, discuss the effects that climate has on lifestyle. Think of things like housing, clothes, food, entertainment, holiday destinations. Compare your country with Britain, or another country you know. What differences or similarities can you think of between them that might be related to climate?

4 In Britain, the weather is a favourite topic of conversation, often used as an ice-breaker. What are typical topics of conversation in your country? What topics can you talk about when you don't know someone very well?

Focus on Writing *Formal Letter*

▶ Paper 2, Part 2

TASK

You are attending a course in London. Last week, because the trains were delayed by bad weather, you were late for college every day. On the worst day, the train was 1 hour 20 minutes late and you missed two classes.

This is an extract from an information leaflet you have picked up at the station.

> **We hope you have a pleasant journey with Capital Rail, but if you have any comments or complaints about our services, please write to the Customer Care Manager at the address below.**
>
> ## What we promise to do when things go wrong:
>
> • If you are delayed for more than one hour you may claim rail vouchers to the value of 50% of the journey made.

Write a **letter** to the Customer Care Manager at Capital Rail complaining about the poor service you have experienced and asking for compensation. Use your own words as far as possible. Write about 250 words. You do not need to include addresses.

Do exercises 1–5 in pairs.

UNDERSTANDING THE TASK

1 Read the instructions on page 27 carefully and highlight the key points. Ask yourself:

- What is the purpose of your letter
- What do you want it to achieve?

CONTENT

2 Consider whether your letter should include the following points. Cross out the points which you don't think are relevant.

- Where you come from
- Why you are in England
- Why you are writing
- How weather problems are dealt with in Switzerland/your country
- Which of your journeys were delayed
- How long the delays were
- How railway staff behaved
- How comfortable the trains were
- What happened as a result of the travel delays
- How you suggest improving the rail service in Britain
- What compensation you require

Compare your answers with other pairs.

ORGANISATION

3 Look at the remaining points and divide them into about four paragraphs.

Compare your paragraph plan with other students and make notes about the kind of things you could say in each paragraph.

Make sure your letter is clear and that you have included all the relevant points.

STYLE/REGISTER

4 Thinking about what you want the letter to achieve, consider these questions.

1 Should the letter be formal, semi-formal or fairly informal?
2 What tone is appropriate, e.g. angry, humorous, sarcastic, cool and factual?

LAYOUT

5 Discuss these questions.
1 Where exactly do you write the beginning (*Dear Sir or Madam*) on the page?
2 Where do you begin the first sentence?
3 When do you use the ending *Yours faithfully* and when *Yours sincerely*?
4 Where do you write the ending? Is it followed by a full stop, a comma or nothing?
5 How do you sign your name in a formal letter?

Check your answers by referring to the model letter on page 159 of the Writing File.

Before you begin, look at the **Useful Language** on page 160 of the Writing File.

Focus on Listening I *Climate Change*

▶ Paper 4, Part I

1   What do you know about 'global warming'? What do you think could be the connection between global warming and the severe weather conditions described in this unit?

2   You will hear part of a radio science programme in which an expert on climate and environmental issues talks about the link between climate change and global warming. You have to complete the notes below with up to three words. You will hear the recording twice.

STRATEGY

- Before you listen, read through the notes, which summarise the information in the recording. Think about what kind of information could fill the gaps – it could be a name, a number, a date or a key phrase.

- As you listen the first time, fill in the missing information in **no more than three words**. Remember that these are **notes**, rather than complete sentences. Write only key words.

- Check your answers when you listen a second time.

Climate changes

British Isles: large part of [＿＿＿ 1] now classified as semi-arid.

Northern and central Europe: increased incidence of [＿＿＿ 2]

Southeast Asia: violent cyclones ruining [＿＿＿ and ＿＿＿ 3] more frequently

North America: [＿＿＿ 4] in spring

Global warming

Rise in temperature of 0.5 degrees C over [＿＿＿ 5]

Most recent Ice Age caused by fall of [＿＿＿ 6]

Moisture in atmosphere has increased by [＿＿＿ 7]

Additional moisture affects [＿＿＿ 8]

Global warming thought to result from [＿＿＿ 9]

Focus on Grammar *Review of the Passive I*

1   **a**   Underline the passive forms in these examples.

1   Buses were caught up in huge traffic jams in many areas. (Text 1)
2   Food for cattle is flown in, as many towns have communal helicopters. (Text 2)
3   Anyone trying to drive without snow chains will be stopped by the police. (Text 2)
4   Most roads and all motorways are cleared of snow by 7 a.m. (Text 2)
5   A policeman who went to rescue a schoolboy had to be rescued himself. (Text 1)
6   Global warming may be caused by the build-up of greenhouse gases. (Listening 1)

b   Complete the table below to show how the passive is formed.

Verb: .... + ...

(Check your answer on page 145 of the Grammar File where you can find more detailed information on the passive.)

c   Which tenses (or other forms) are used in each of the examples?

2   **a**   Complete this note on the use of the passive using three words:

> We use a passive form when we are more interested in what .... than in the **agent** (the person or thing that .... it).

b   A very common use is when the agent is not known or is not important. All but one of the sentences in Exercise 1 are examples of that use. Which one is the exception?
(There is a fuller list of uses of the passive in the Grammar File on page 146.)

3   Because the passive is more impersonal, it is normally used in more **formal** contexts. Convert these spoken statements into a more formal written form, using the passive.
Example:
> While the meeting was going on, some rotten person stole my overcoat from the cloakroom!
> *During* the meeting, my overcoat *was stolen* from the cloakroom.

1   Some idiot obviously didn't set the burglar alarm properly.
It appears that ....
2   To my knowledge, nobody said anything at all critical about you.
Nothing ....
3   Remember that you can't use dictionaries or grammars in the exam.
No ....
4   I know it's a great shame but we've cancelled the summer party.
Unfortunately ....
5   Normally we send out the goods as soon as we receive an order.
Goods ....
6   There just haven't been enough people showing an interest in the event.
Not enough interest ....
7   I think it'll be quite some time before they can repair all the storm damage.
The storm damage ....

4   *get* + **past participle**

Get is sometimes used as an alternative to *be* + past participle to form the passive. It is less formal and tends to suggest accidental or chance events, rather than planned or intentional ones, for example:

> We *got stuck* in a traffic jam in the town centre.
> Maybe your letter *got lost* in the post.
> The college ~~got opened~~ was opened by the Queen.

Complete the following sentences, using verbs from the list below in *get* + past participle constructions.

> *beat up   chase   sweep   fine   pay   catch steal*

1   Just my luck! I ...... in the rain and arrived for the interview dripping wet!
2   If you leave that briefcase on the seat, you're asking for it ....
3   We ...... $100 on the spot for speeding.
4   I wonder how much he's ...... for appearing in that TV advertisement.
5   The cat's been a nervous wreck since it ...... by next door's dog.
6   He thought if he tried to stop the fight he might ...... himself.
7   It was blowing such a gale that my hat ...... into the sea.

Focus on Listening 2 *Weather and Mood*

► Paper 4, Part 2

You will hear a doctor talking about how the weather affects us. As you listen, fill in the missing information for questions 1–8. You will need to write between one and three words for each answer.

In the examination, the recording will be played **once** only. However, the important information is repeated using different words, so you have a better chance of catching it. For practice, see if you can answer all the questions during the first hearing, but listen again if you need to check your answers.

Weather	Effect	Advice
Low pressure [_____ 1] Warm winds	Slow reflexes	[_____ 2]
Low pressure [_____ 3]	[_____ 4]	Don't do too much exercise
Low pressure and above-normal humidity [_____ 5]	[_____ 6]	Don't do complicated work
High temperatures and humidity [_____ 7]	Irritability, edginess Increased proneness to [_____ 8]	[_____ 9]

Focus on Vocabulary *Weather Idioms*

1 The phrase *a chilling admission of defeat* in the article 'Today is cancelled' is a metaphor. The literal meaning of *chill* is 'make colder' but here the word suggests that it was an admission which made people feel worried or alarmed. Words to do with weather are often used metaphorically.

Put the words on the right into the gaps in A and B to make some common phrases. Then say what you think they mean.

A
1   a ...... relationship
2   a ...... look
3   a ...... smile
4   a ...... manner
5   a ...... remark

sunny
biting
breezy
stormy
frosty

31

B
1 a storm of ......
2 to shower (someone) with ......
3 a hail of ......
4 gales of ......
5 to be in floods of ......

tears
gifts
laughter
protest
bullets

2 Complete the sentences below with one of these weather idioms.

blow hot and cold   *the foggiest (idea)*   *a storm in a teacup*
under the weather   *like (greased) lightning*   *on cloud nine*
(be) snowed under

1 'You're not ill, are you?' 'Not really, I'm just feeling a bit ...... at the moment.'
2 'Why don't you join us for lunch?' 'I'd like to, but I'm completely ...... with work.'
3 'What was all the arguing about?' 'Don't worry, it was only ....'
4 'How do you work this photocopying machine?' 'Sorry, I haven't ....'
5 'Didn't anyone help you wash up?' 'No, when the meal was over, they were all off ....'
6 'Is Henry in favour of the idea?' 'I don't really know, he keeps ....'
7 'What's Jane looking so happy about?' 'Oh, she's been ...... ever since she got engaged.'

English in Use 1 *Developing Skills: Spelling*

▶ Paper 3, Part 3

In Part 3 of Paper 3, you sometimes have to find and correct spelling mistakes. Some typical spelling mistakes you should look out for are shown in Exercise 1.

1 **a** The three verbs in italics below illustrate one kind of spelling change that can occur when you add *-ing* or *-ed* to the stem of a verb. What is the spelling change?

Today is *Cancelled!*
... only one bus in ten was *running*
The snow *trapped* burglars

There are also a few other possible changes. Try the exercise below to see how accurate you are in this area of spelling.

b Not all the verbs below are spelt correctly. Underline and correct those which are wrongly spelt. (Ignore the numbers in brackets for the moment.)

beating (2.1.1)	raiding (2.1.1)	panicked (2.2.5)
blinded (2.1.1)	clearing (2.1.1)	admitted (2.1.1)
aging (2.2.1*)	controling (2.1.3)	signalled (2.1.3)
benefiting (2.1.2)	refering (2.1.2)	happenning (2.1.2)
occurring (2.1.2)	fitted (2.1.1)	fulfiled (2.1.3)
travelled (2.1.3)	swimming (2.1.1)	forgeting (2.1.2)
enterring (2.1.2)	dying (2.2.4)	sweeping (2.1.1)
developping (2.1.2)	enjoied (2.2.3)	kidnapped (2.1.2*)

Compare your answers with another student. There are spelling rules which may be helpful if you have problems with this area of spelling. The reference numbers in brackets refer to these rules and exceptions (*), which you can find in the Grammar File on pages 148–149.

2   There is a spelling mistake in 13 of the numbered lines in the following text. Underline every word which is wrongly spelt and write the correct spelling in the space at the end of the line. If there is no spelling mistake, put a tick (✓) in the space. There are two examples at the beginning.

Weather Hazards

High Winds

In strong winds, never walk on narrow mountain ledges or
peaks: you could easily get blown off by a guest. If it suddenly
becomes windy, tuck your clothes into your trowsers; a
flaping coat or jacket can catch the wind and throw you
of balance. If the wind is very strong, lie flat on the ground.

Floods

Try to avoid camping close to a river. There is a posibility
of heavy rain occurring up-river and flood water could come
rushing down when you are asleep or away from the tent.
If their is a flood warning, take food, drinking water and
spare cloths, and make for high ground. If you are swept
away by flood water, try to grab hold of a floatting object
such as a log or a peace of wood. If it is big enough,
clime on top and use it as a ratt. Paddle to safety using
your hands.

Avalanches

Avalanches are extremly dangerous and can happen very
suddenly; they are especially likely to occur during a thaw
and after a new fall of snow. Listen to the whether
forcasts for your area and if there are any warnings of
avalanches, don't go out walking or skiing.

0	✓
0	_gust_
1	......
2	......
3	......
4	......
5	......
6	......
7	......
8	......
9	......
10	......
11	......
12	......
13	......
14	......
15	......
16	......

33

English in Use 2 *Developing Skills: Lexical Cloze*

▶ Paper 3, Part I

STRATEGY

In this task you have to choose the correct word A, B, C or D to fill each space.

a It's important to have a general understanding of the text before you start the task. Read the text quickly and answer these questions.
1 What are some of the bad effects the wind can have?
2 What good effects are mentioned?

b Now begin reading the text again very carefully. When you come to a gap, think about the general meaning you would expect, then look at the possible answers. The correct answer must have the correct meaning and must combine correctly with other words in the sentence.

The first answer has been done for you as an example.

WIND

The untameable weather machine

On 15 October 1987, the southern counties of Britain were (0) .... by the strongest winds they had experienced in 200 years. Gusts of over 130 kilometres per hour slammed across the region and £1.5-billion-worth of damage was (1) .... in just a few hours.

Extreme weather events like this are dramatic (2) .... of the power of the wind. It's one part of the weather we generally don't (3) .... a second thought to in Britain but it (4) .... a vital role in people's lives across the world. Without the formation and circulation of winds there would quite (5) .... be no climate.

Some parts of the world seem to (6) .... more than others from the effects of 'ill winds', and links between particular winds and psychological problems (7) .... back centuries. The Föhn, the hot dry wind that slides off the slopes of the Alps, is (8) .... of boosting temperatures quite suddenly by 10°C or more. It affects as many as one in three people in its (9) .... , making them feel anxious, irritable and generally ill. In California, many people (10) .... the arrival of the Santa Ana, which rushes down from the high Mojave desert. Lyall Watson, in his book *Heaven's Breath*, (11) .... that when the Santa Ana blows, murder rates soar.

The wind may get into the headlines when it comes in the form of tornadoes and hurricanes, but for the (12) .... part it goes about its job of shifting huge masses of air around the planet. Plants take (13) .... of this free ride to send their pollen grains far and wide. Trees (14) .... on it to remove old leaves and make way for new growth. Spiders have been caught (15) .... a lift at altitudes of almost 4.5 kilometres.

	A		**B**		**C**		**D**	
0	A	knocked	B	blown	C	struck	D	punched
1	A	made	B	caused	C	destroyed	D	completed
2	A	reminders	B	recollections	C	mementos	D	memorials
3	A	pay	B	give	C	have	D	spend
4	A	plays	B	does	C	makes	D	works
5	A	easily	B	rightly	C	surely	D	simply
6	A	experience	B	share	C	suffer	D	bear
7	A	last	B	originate	C	pass	D	date
8	A	possible	B	capable	C	powerful	D	able
9	A	line	B	road	C	path	D	bypass
10	A	despair	B	respect	C	dread	D	warn
11	A	claims	B	pretends	C	expects	D	predicts
12	A	most	B	maximum	C	majority	D	general
13	A	benefit	B	chance	C	occasion	D	advantage
14	A	need	B	trust	C	hope	D	rely
15	A	travelling	B	hitching	C	borrowing	D	making

▶ **Question 2**

Only one of these words can refer to something in the present or future. Make sure you know how the others are used.

▶ **Question 6**

Find the dependent preposition. Only one of the verbs combines with it.

▶ **Question 8**

The adjective you choose must combine with *of*.

▶ **Question 13**

Which of these nouns can be used in the phrase *take ... of*?

Language Focus 2 *Vocabulary Skills 1: What's in a word?*

What does *light* mean? How many meanings can you think of? What else is there to know about a word? Use a good dictionary to check your answers to the questions below.

> **light**² *adj* **1** pale and not dark: *a light blue dress* → see colour picture on page 126 → opposite DARK¹ **2** not weighing much or weighing less than usual: *Your bag's lighter than mine.* → opposite HEAVY **3** not having much force or power: *a light wind* | *a light tap on the door* **4** thin and not very warm: *a light sweater* **5** a room that is light has plenty of light from the sun in it: *a light and airy studio* **6** food or drink that is light does not make you feel too full: *a light white wine* **7** not serious: *a light comedy on TV* **8** **it is light** used to say that there is enough light to see by: *It was still light when we got home.* **9** small in amount or less than usual: *Traffic is much lighter on Sundays.* **10 light sleep** sleep from which you wake up easily **11 make light of sth** to joke about something or treat it as if it were not important
>
> ...³ **lit** /lɪt/ or **lighted** lit... light-

> ...might help prevent crime.
>
> **light·ly** /ˈlaɪtli/ *adv* **1** without force; GENTLY: *He touched her li... shoulder.* **2** in small light amoun... *sugar lightly over the cake.* **3** not ... to think very carefully and seri... *make this decision lightly.* **4** escap... **off lightly** to not be harmed or punis... as you could have been
>
> **light·ning**¹ /ˈlaɪtnɪŋ/ *n* [U] a bright trical light in the sky during a sto... *trees were struck* (=hit) *by lightning.*
>
> **lightning**² *adj* extremely fast or sud... *ning attack*
>
> **light·weight** /ˈlaɪt-weɪt/ *adj* we... little: *a lightweight jacket*
>
> **lik·a·ble** /ˈlaɪkəbəl/ LIKEABLE
>
> **like**¹ /laɪk/ *prep* **1** similar...

1 Meaning

a What **group of words** does this one fit into? For example, we can say '*light* blue'. What other adjectives can we use in front of colours?

b Does the word suggest a particularly **positive** or **negative** attitude, or is it neutral in meaning (connotation)? How is *lightweight* used in these examples?

> a *lightweight* suit; a *lightweight* intellectual

c Does the word occur in any **metaphors** or **idioms**? *Light-* can be combined with three of the following participles to make compound adjectives. Which are they and what do the adjectives mean?

> fingered   faced   headed
> bodied   handed   hearted

2 Grammar

a What **part of speech** is it?

> Some bicycles had no rear *lights*.
> The fire took a long time to *light*.
> You're standing in my *light*!
> She was only wearing a *light* jacket.

b What are the **parts of the verb**?

> *to light,* .... , ...

c Is the verb **transitive** or **intransitive**? Is the phrasal verb **separable** or **inseparable**?

- Can we say both 'He lit.' and 'He lit a cigarette.'?
- Can we say both 'Fireworks *lit up* the sky.' and 'Fireworks *lit* the sky *up*.'?

3 Use

a How **formal/informal** is the word or expression? (register/style)

> Have you got a *light*?
> In the *light* of recent experience, ...
> As soon as I got into bed I went out like a *light*.

b What other words can it **combine with** (collocation)? Which words below can we use the adjective *light* with?

> colour   headache   work   sound   meal
> cigarette   sleeper   wind   coffee   price

c Is there a word which means the same (synonym)? And one which means the opposite (antonym)? Think of synonyms and antonyms for *light* in the examples in b .

4 Word formation

a What **other words** can be made from *light* (derivations)?

- What verb means 'to make something *lighter*'?
- What is the difference between *lighting*, *lightning* and *lightening*?
- What prefix can you add to the participle *lit* to make an adjective to describe a street with no lights, for example.

b How do you **spell** it?
Which of the following should be written a) as one word, b) with a hyphen, or c) as two words?

> light/bulb   light/house   light/hearted

c How do you **pronounce** it? Which of these words have the same vowel sound as *light* /laɪt/?

> trial   height   straight   bite   buy
> weight   fly   sieve   quiet

EXAM SKILLS ▶ Paper 1

If you come across a word you don't know in a CAE reading text, first make sure you **need** to understand it in order to answer the questions. If not, don't waste time on it. If it is important, try to guess the meaning by:

- looking carefully at the **context**
- thinking about the **grammar** of the word (e.g. what part of speech is it?)
- looking for clues in the **parts of the word** (e.g. prefixes and suffixes)

Learning Focus 2 *Planning for Writing*

1 Reasons for writing

a If you wanted to do the following things (1–6) would it be better to telephone or to write? Discuss your answers and the possible reasons for them.

1 make a complaint about a holiday you've been on
2 thank someone for a present they've sent you
3 arrange a date to play tennis with someone
4 report to your boss on a conference you've attended
5 make a booking at a hotel
6 let people know about a new sports club you're setting up

b Decide which of the following are advantages of writing.

a more personal
b more immediate
c easier to be precise
d more convenient
e provides immediate feedback
f more concise
g more formal
h provides a record
i allows time for thoughts to be organised
j layout can clarify information
k stress/intonation can clarify information

2 Purpose and target reader

a There are several different factors which determine the kind of writing we choose to do. Think of some further examples to add to the following tables.

Subject and Purpose	
General	Specific
e.g. to inform	e.g. to say you can't attend a meeting
to persuade	to encourage people to buy something
to complain	....
to apologise	....
....	....

Audience and Relationship
e.g. close family/friends
acquaintances
colleagues
potential employers
....
....

Special Circumstances
e.g. you want to catch people's attention
you want to make a very good impression
you want to clarify a number of details
you haven't got much time
this could be important legally
....

b With these factors in mind, we need to decide about the following points:

Format	*Style*	*Layout*
e.g. note	e.g. chatty/casual	e.g. formal letter layout
memo	informal	informal letter layout
postcard ➔	neutral ➔	heading(s)?
leaflet	formal	numbered points?
letter	humorous	eye-catching features?

3 Layout, style, language

a Look at 1–7 below and match each one to a writing task a–g.

a Formal letter
b Informal letter
c Personal note/message
d Leaflet
e Article
f Report
g Review

1 plenty of food in the fridge but you'll probably need to buy more coffee. See you on Wednesday.
Julia

2 **HOW TO FIND US**
Blazes Museum is situated just off the A358 at Bishops Lydeard, very close to the West Somerset Steam

3 With reference to your letter of 5th November, I should like to confirm my interest in taking up a

4 **Accommodation**
While the majority of conference delegates expressed satisfaction with the standard of the hotel, there were a small number of complaints about noise late at night coming from

5 When she sang the opening words to 'Here We Are' the applause was heart-felt. The show followed the familiar

7 the weekend? It would be lovely to see you both and we would have a chance to catch up on all the news. Let me

6 Professor David Marshall will be remembered as much for his colourful character as for his pioneering work

b Discuss the following questions about each of the extracts in a.

1 What features of **language** or **style** helped you decide what type of writing it was?
2 What is the **purpose** of the piece of writing?
3 Who is the intended **audience**?
4 How would the complete piece of writing be **laid out**?

4 Work with another student. Look again at the items in Exercise 1 which you thought would be better expressed in writing. For each one, identify the audience and your relationship with them, and any special circumstances. Then select an appropriate format, style and layout.

5 Planning
Which of the following approaches to writing a formal letter, report or exam composition seems most sensible, and why?

'I write out the whole thing first in rough and then copy it out neatly or type it afterwards. That way I can correct most of my mistakes.'

'I'm too impatient to do a rough version first. I think it's better to be spontaneous, so I tend to start writing the final version immediately.'

'I like to collect my ideas and make sure I haven't forgotten anything important, so I make notes about what I want to say before I write out the final version.'

6 Making notes
Making notes before you start is a very good idea and essential in an exam.

How to make notes:
- Make a list of all the points you want to include – so nothing is left out.
- Decide on the best order for the points – so the organisation is logical.
- Make a note of any useful expressions and vocabulary – so you make the most of your knowledge.

7 Choose one of the writing tasks you discussed in Exercise 4. Make a plan of the main points you think should be included. Decide how many paragraphs you need. Then compare your plan with another student's.
Remember: you can refer to the Writing File for notes on any special layout and language for particular types of writing.

3 ▶ Time Eaters

'Lost time is never found again.'
Benjamin Franklin

Lead-in

Discuss these questions with a partner.

a Are any of these statements true for you?
1 When I have free time, I like to do something useful with it.
2 I work hard, so when I have a chance to relax I like to switch off completely.
3 Although I only mean to watch one programme, I often end up spending the whole evening in front of the box.
4 I do things on the spur of the moment without planning in advance.

b Which of these activities would you consider a) useful b) a waste of time?
- writing a diary
- reading a magazine
- window shopping
- gossiping on the phone
- walking the dog
- cooking
- gardening
- doing jigsaw puzzles
- sorting the photo album

c What are the 'time eaters' in your life? How much time do you spend on them? Do you ever try to cut down on this?

Focus on Listening 1 *Ways of Wasting Time*

Paper 4, Part 4

You will hear five people talking about ways of wasting time. You will hear the recording twice. There are two tasks, so it's a good idea to do the first task during the first listening, and the second during the second listening.

TASK ONE lists the different ways of wasting time which the speakers mention. Match the extracts as you hear them with the topics listed A–G. Write the correct letter in each box. Two topics will not be used.

A cutting the grass
B not being able to make up one's mind
C making typing mistakes
D doing puzzles
E putting things in order
F working slowly and inefficiently
G reading books

	1
	2
	3
	4
	5

TASK TWO lists points mentioned in the five extracts. Put them in order by writing the correct letter, A–G, in each box. Two points are not needed.

Which extract is about somebody who:
A wastes most time thinking about small things?
B is criticised by other people for wasting time?
C is afraid of what other people will think?
D says they'd like to have a secretary?
E is poorer than they used to be?
F has lost their old habit?
G tries to limit the time they waste every day?

	6
	7
	8
	9
	10

Text

PREDICTION

1 Thinking about the topic of a text in advance will help you to read more effectively. Read the title of the article opposite. Write down the sub-headings A–C on a piece of paper, then discuss with a partner the different ways these things can be a problem when you're working.

SKIMMING

2 a Skim-read the whole article quickly and check your ideas.

b **Which sentence best summarises the advice given by the writer?**
1 Disconnect the telephone.
2 Experiment with relaxation techniques.
3 Study the principles of Business Management.
4 Identify the problems and make changes to overcome them.

c **Was the article written mainly for:**
1 students planning their studies?
2 people in business?
3 parents of children taking exams?
4 people working at home?

MULTIPLE MATCHING
▶ Paper 1, Part 1

3 The writer makes a number of suggestions about ways we can work more efficiently. Match each suggestion below to one of the four sections of the article A–D.

STRATEGY

• Try to guess which section each suggestion comes from. Check that section first. If you were wrong, try another section.

• Scan the section to find the part which seems to deal with the point.

• Read that part carefully to check that it really matches the suggestion. Look for words or phrases which say the same thing in a different way. Don't waste time reading the whole text in detail.

Ask someone to answer the phone on your behalf.   **1** ......
Make a list of interruptions you have during the day.   **2** ......
Work on a group of similar tasks together.   **3** ......
Put a sign on your office door.   **4** ......
Make sure you have everything you need before you start work.   **5** ......
Be aware of the danger of all sorts of interruptions.   **6** ......
Give yourself some private time each day.   **7** ......

**VOCABULARY:
PARALLEL EXPRESSIONS**

4 Suggestions 1–3 in question 3 above are expressed in different words in these extracts from the text. Look at the words in italics.

a Decide what part of speech each one is, and what the general meaning is, then match the words in italics with the meanings listed on page 42.
1 **Suggestion 1**   Have someone else *screen* your calls (line 98)
2   make an arrangement with a *peer* to take messages (line 102)
3 **Suggestion 2**   keep an interruptions *log* ... (line 115)
4   analyze the listing to *isolate* the cause (line 120)
5 **Suggestion 3**   the Principle of *Consolidation* (lines 11–12)
6   ... group *like* activities and ... (line 13)
7   *execute* them all in one time frame (line 14)
8   When you *intersperse* activities ... (lines 17–18)

40

TIME-EATERS AND WHAT YOU CAN DO ABOUT THEM

A INTERRUPTING YOURSELF

In business or in homework, your time gets wasted because you think of something that had slipped your mind, so you drop everything and are
5 off to complete it before you forget it again. What's the solution? There are several things you can do to reduce the amount of time stolen from you by yourself.

10 Firstly, remember two principles governing time. The Principle of Consolidation states that you get more done if you group like activities and execute them all in one time
15 frame. The reason behind this logic is that the preparation time period occurs once for all the tasks. When you intersperse activities, you are winding up and winding down,
20 reducing your concentration and not functioning at peak mental effectiveness. And so it takes longer to complete each task.

The other law that affects your time
25 is one you've heard for years. 'A stitch in time saves nine'. In other words, if you spend some time in preparation before actually beginning to work on a job, you will be able to work right
30 through and complete it. The total time for the getting ready and the doing will be less than the time you would spend if you just started right in performing the task. If you clear
35 your work area, before beginning an activity, you won't be distracted by some paperwork your eyes fall on as you're on your priority task. So if you want a drink while you work or need
40 to get some supplies or reference material, do so before you actually being working. Once you do start, use conscious self-discipline to stick to it until it's finished. Don't have your
45 time stolen by interrupting yourself. The second major time-eater occurs when others visit your work area:

B DROP-IN VISITORS

You know the person. Every organization has one or two or three,
50 or maybe you're it. You have just sat down to your desk to tackle your daily tasks and knock, knock 'How's it going?' or they arrive with a fast business question then stay to visit
55 long after.

The solution can be two-pronged – you can discourage the visitors altogether or reduce the length of their stay when they do drop in. To
60 discourage visitors, adopt a closed door policy for at least 1 hour a day. A Quiet Hour. Pick an hour during the day when you feel at your best, or sharpest. It might be from 10.00 a.m. to 11.00
65 a.m. or it may be in the afternoon.

The procedure is straightforward, just tell your fellow employees, and those with whom you deal outside the company that you are not available for
70 that specific hour unless it is an emergency.

Then, close your door. Maybe you want to make a sign like they have in hotels to hang over the door knob –
75 DO NOT DISTURB UNTIL 11 A.M. – If you don't have a door, pin a notice on the divider or stand it on the corner of your desk – GONE FISHING UNTIL 4 P.M.
80 This quiet hour will take a few days or even a week to begin to pay off for you. Once people who work with you get the idea, they will plan to see you before your quiet hour begins or be
85 content to wait until it is over. You will be more and more enthusiastic as well when you realize the amount of work that you will accomplish during this hour.

C TELEPHONE INTERRUPTIONS

90 No matter what we are doing or what project we are working on, we usually allow the almighty telephone to butt in. Telephone company literature even exhorts us to answer before the third
95 ring. This practice drastically reduces our concentration. How do we control this intruder? Have someone else screen your calls during your quiet hour. If you do not have a secretary or
100 assistant, ask the switchboard operator to take messages for you or make an arrangement with a peer to take messages for you during your quiet hour if you take their messages during
105 their quiet hour. A polite 'I'm sorry, (s)he is busy right now. May I have him/her return your call after 11?' Screening the calls properly should not annoy anyone. If it is an
110 emergency, by your definition of an emergency, of course the call should be allowed to interrupt you.

D WHAT YOU CAN DO

If you suspect that interruptions are a major time-eater, you should keep an
115 'interruptions log' from time to time. On a separate piece of paper, jot down the time and date, the type of interruption and who it is that is interrupting. After a week or so,
120 analyze the listing to isolate the cause of the interruption that is wasting the greatest percentage of the total time. It may be your insecure boss, the lack of an assistant, or an untrained staff
125 member. Or it could be you.

Perhaps you think you are the only person who can answer questions, handle telephone calls, etc. The big step is to isolate the cause, the next
130 step is to deal with it.

I urge you to recognize the importance of the interruptions to your time management programme and the power of interruptions to eat
135 away at your time. By minimizing the effect of interruptions, you could save up to 2 hours a day. Just think of all those things you will be able to find time for in an extra 2 hours a day.

41

b   Match the words in italics on page 40 with the meanings listed below.

a   include or scatter things here and there amongst other things (*v*)

b   someone who is the same as you in position, profession, etc. (*n*)

c   perform or do (e.g. a piece of work) (*v*)

d   combining things to become more effective (*n*)

e   similar (*adj*)

f   check things and select only those which are acceptable (*v*)

g   a written record of events with dates and times (*n*)

h   identify something in order to deal with it (*v*)

STUDY BOX ▶ *no matter*

Look at these examples. The first is from the text on page 41.

> *No matter what* we are doing or *what project* we are working on, we usually allow the almighty telephone to butt in.

> I'll certainly meet you, *no matter when* you arrive.

The phrase *no matter* is followed by *what/who/where/when/which/how* and *whose* + a clause. It means that something is true in all circumstances.

The present tense can be used with future meaning after *no matter* as in the second example.

Complete these sentences.

1   I've set my heart on buying that house, no matter how …… .

2   You won't make me change my mind, no matter what …… .

3   No matter where …… , he's constantly being asked for his autograph.

4   Don't believe any of the rumours, no matter who …… .

5   It's a 24-hour service so you can speak to someone, no matter when …… .

6   We must all take responsibility for the mistake, no matter whose …… .

Focus on Speaking 1 *Visual Prompts*

▶ Paper 5, Part 2

1   a   Work in pairs. In this activity, Student A and Student B will look at two different photographs. You each have one minute to describe your photos (without showing them to each other).

Student A should turn to the photograph on page 235.
Student B should turn to the photograph on page 238.

b   When you have both finished, you should discuss what is similar and what is different about your photographs.

Useful Language

Both pictures show ...

There are some similarities between the two study areas. For instance ...

The main difference between the two study areas is that ...

There are a number of differences between the two study areas, *including* ...

The desk in my photo is ... , *while/whereas* the desk in the other photo is ...

The study area in your photo seems more ... but *on the other hand* it ...

2   Now look at each other's photographs together. What does each photograph indicate about the person who works there? Which of these words would you use to describe them/their style of organisation?

very/extremely well-organised/neat and tidy

highly/extremely efficient

absolutely meticulous

rather disorganised/untidy/scatterbrained

somewhat erratic

DISCUSSION POINTS

3   Discuss these points in pairs.

1   How do you prefer to study? Alone or with other people around?

2   Where do you usually do your private studying? At home in a special room?

3   What time of day do you find you study best? How late into the evening can you study effectively? Have you ever studied all night?

4   Do you like to listen to music while you're studying? If so, what kind?

5   Who or what is the most common cause of interruptions to your work?

Focus on Vocabulary 1 *Idiomatic Expressions*

1   **Match verbs and particles from the following lists to make phrasal verbs from the text on page 41. Use these to complete the sentences below.**

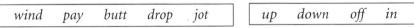

| wind | pay | butt | drop | jot | | up | down | off | in |

1   Must you keep ...... ? Can't you at least let me finish a sentence?

2   Why don't you ...... when you're next in the area? We'd love to see you.

3   They found that all that fitness training had really ...... when they finally set sail in the round-the-world yacht race.

4   It takes him at least a week to ...... before he can enjoy the holiday.

5   If you've got a slip of paper I'll just ...... that telephone number.

"For God's sake, Gerald, wind down gradually!"

2   **Complete the sentences with a suitable verb from the list.**

speak   bear   slip   take   cross   set

1   He said he'd send written confirmation but it must have ...... his mind.

2   I must admit that it ...... my mind to call the police. I wish I had done now.

3   Why not come to the pub with us? It might ...... your mind off your worries.

4   I always ring to say I've arrived safely, just to ...... my mother's mind at rest.

5   Thanks for the warning. I'll ...... it in mind.

6   You can be sure Jack will ...... his mind. Let's hope he doesn't offend too many people!

Focus on Grammar I *The Future I*

I *going* to versus *will* (Future simple)

a Sentences 1–6 are examples of the main uses of *going to* and *will*, which are described below. Write the number of the sentence which best illustrates each use in the space provided.

1 I doubt if he'll have enough money to pay the fine.
2 You've put too much in that shopping bag – the handle's going to break.
3 Your father will be absolutely furious!
4 I'm going to have a steak with salad for dinner.
5 She'll be 21 next birthday.
6 That's the doorbell. I'll see who it is.

The *going to* future is mainly used:

● to talk about **personal intentions** and **plans** e.g. ......

● to make **predictions** which are based on evidence we can see now e.g. ......

The *will* future is used:

● to express a **future fact** e.g. ......

● to make a **prediction** based on our knowledge or intuition rather than on present evidence e.g. ......

● to give an **opinion** about the future (often after verbs like *think*, *suppose*, *expect* and *doubt if* or with *probably*) e.g. ......

● to announce a **decision** at the time of making it e.g. ......

b Some of the following sentences contain inappropriate future forms. Make the necessary corrections and then compare your answers with another student.

1 Aren't you going to take a lunch break today?
2 That smell of paint is making me feel awful – I think I'll be sick.
3 Will you do anything interesting this weekend?
4 He'll be fifty by the time his son starts school.
5 Why not ask Mike? He's probably going to help you.
6 Stop worrying, you'll sail through the exam, no problem!
7 Don't tell me how the book ends. It's going to spoil it for me.

2 Tenses in time clauses with future reference

a Look at the verb forms in italics in these sentences from the text on page 41. Find the verbs in the future simple tense. These are in the main clauses. The other verbs are in subordinate clauses. What tense is used?

You *will be* more and more enthusiastic **when** you *realise* the amount of work that you will accomplish during this time.
Once people who work with you *get* the idea, they *will plan* to see you **before** your quiet hour *begins*.

b Now complete this explanation.

In subordinate clauses with future meaning, the .... tense is normally used after conjunctions of time such as .... , ... and .... The present simple is also used after question words such as *what*, *who* and *where*.

c Now look at another example and complete the sentence which follows.

We'll cut the cake **when** all the guests have arrived.

The .... tense is used to make it clear that an action will be complete before the action in the main clause.

3 Make sentences by joining a clause 1–6 with a clause a–f using a suitable conjunction. Each complete sentence refers to a piece of equipment. What are the six items?

1 It won't work
2 You'll find it easier than writing by hand
3 A red light will come on
4 You'll be able to leave a message
5 You'll have to take the lens cap off
6 I'll put it back in the cupboard

until	before	after	while	when	as soon as	once

a it's recording a programme.
b you put a battery in.
c it has cooled down.
d you get used to the keys.
e you hear the tone.
f you take any pictures.

4 Complete the following sentences with suitable subordinate clauses.

1 You'd better clear up this mess before ....
2 He won't pass his driving test until ....
3 Once .... I'll be a lot happier.
4 The 'No Smoking' sign will be switched off ....
5 I promise I'll let you know as soon as ....
6 She'll be exhausted ....
7 .... you'll be amazed!

Focus on Writing *Personal Notes and Messages*

TASK

You are working as an assistant in the offices of an English company. You are finishing some work after your colleagues have left when the phone rings for you. As a result of the call, you need to take the following day off work.

Write two **notes** explaining the situation, one to your boss, and one to a colleague and friend, with whom you had a lunch date. Write 60–80 words in each note.

CONTENT

1 A task like this will be more realistic and more successful if you decide on some concrete details before you start. If you can use true facts, it's very easy, but if you can't, invent some interesting and believable ones!

a On your own, decide on answers to the questions below.

Your work: What kind of work do you do for the company?
How long have you been with the company?
How will you be able to make up for the time you will miss?

The phone call: Who was it from? What was the message?
Why is it important? Why was there such short notice?

Your boss: Male/female? How well do you get on with him/her?
How are they likely to react to your being away?

Your colleague: Male/female? How long have you known them?
Have you had lunch together before?

The lunch: Where were you going to go?
Will there be any problem about cancelling?
When could you have lunch instead?

b Work in pairs. Ask your partner about their telephone call, their boss and their friend. Ask for more information if necessary.

STYLE/REGISTER

2 a Work in pairs to discuss these questions.
1 What is the difference between a letter and a note?
2 What difference might there be between a note to your boss and a note to a colleague? Think about the style of language, the register (the level of formality) and the tone (how friendly/polite/apologetic).

b Which phrases from the following list might be more appropriate in the note to your boss (A) or the note to your colleague (B), and which would be appropriate in either note (C)?

Note: The level of formality will depend on your relationship with each person, so your answers may be slightly different from your partner's.

a just to let you know   ......   f I'll gladly make up the time   ......
b I received a telephone call ......   g I'm really sorry   ......
c out of the blue   ......   h in the circumstances   ......
d rang me   ......   i I apologise for any inconvenience ......
e such short notice   ......   j some other time?   ......

ORGANISATION/LAYOUT

3 Before you begin, look at the information about notes and messages and the **Useful Language** in the Writing File on pages 161–162.

Focus on Speaking 2 *Problem Solving*

▶ Paper 5, Parts 3 & 4

1 In pairs, discuss which of the inventions in the pictures:

- is the most useful
- saves the most time
- wastes the most time
- is largely a waste of money
- you would choose if you could only have one of them

> **Useful Language**
> The (main/biggest) *advantage* of a ...
> The (best/worst) *thing* about a ...   is (that) ...
> The (main/only) *problem/trouble/drawback* with a ...
> The *reason* I'd choose a ...

2 Tell the class about the main points of your discussion.

> **Useful Language**
> *We both agreed/thought/felt* that the X was the most useful because ...
> *We disagreed/We couldn't reach an agreement* about ... because ...
> *We couldn't decide between* X and Y because we thought they were equally useful.
> My partner said that ... *but/while/whereas* I thought/felt that ...
> In my opinion, X was ... *but/while/whereas* my partner disagreed.

Focus on Vocabulary 2 *Expressions with 'time'*

Choose verbs from the list to complete the sentences below.

while away   keep   make up   make up for   save   spare   take   kill

1 I wonder if you could ...... the time to answer a few questions?
2 Although the flight was delayed, strong tailwinds enabled us to ...... time and we arrived on schedule.
3 You can ...... your time, the taxi isn't coming for half an hour yet.
4 This watch belonged to my grandfather but it still ...... perfect time!
5 A telephone bank account would ...... you an awful lot of time.
6 We played cards to ...... the time until you got here.
7 I'd rather ...... time at the airport than risk missing my flight.
8 You'll have to work over the weekend if you want to ...... lost time.

Focus on Listening 2 *Adventure Sports*

Paper 4, Part 2

1 a Look at the leisure activities in the pictures.
Can you say what they are?

b Discuss these questions in pairs.
Which activities:

- have you done?
- would you like to do?
- would you never dream of doing? Why not?

2 You will hear the conclusion of a TV programme about adventure sports, which are becoming an increasingly popular way of spending our leisure time. As you listen, complete the notes for questions 1–9 using a number or a few words. You will hear the recording once only.

STRATEGY

- Before you listen, read through the notes below to see what kind of information is needed.

ADVENTURE SPORTS

LAND

Compton Off-road Racing Centre

Course includes all necessary [___1___]

4 x 4 Galore Centre allows use of [___2___]

Sessions last for either [___3___] hours.

AIR

Sky High Centre – phone 01884 753922

Course consists of [___4___]

Price includes [___5___]

Essential to book [___6___] in advance.

WATER

Contact John Hunter – South Seas Club

Most important aspect of yachting is [___7___]

Number of crew: [___8___]

Cost of hiring equipment: [___9___]

Focus on Grammar 2 *Modal Verbs 1*

Modal verbs are used to indicate our attitude to what we say. They can express ability, willingness, obligation, possibility, certainty and so on. For general information about modal verbs, and detailed information about the verbs below, see the Grammar File pages 142–144.

1 Ability: *can, could, be able to*

a Look at the verb forms in italics in the sentences below. Which ones refer to:

- the present?   • the future?
- general ability in the past?
- a specific ability in the past?

1 Perhaps you think you are the only person who *can* handle questions? (Text)

2 You *couldn't* use a scythe on grass that was less than three inches. (Listening 1)

3 Although my passport was stolen, I *was able to* get a replacement from the consulate.

4 When I finish the course, *I'll be able to* service my own car.

5 The doctor *can* see you at three o'clock.

6 I looked for you at the party, but I *couldn't* find you!

b Complete the following sentences using suitable verb forms expressing ability.

1 My engine stalled, but with the help of a passer-by, I ...... push the car to the side of the road.

2 I'm sorry I'm late. I ...... find a parking space.

3 If you'll be sitting at the back of the theatre, ... hear clearly?

4 She was such a clever child that she ...... read by the time she was four.

5 These days I've got so much energy that I ...... run for miles and miles.

6 He used to ...... run a marathon but he's got less stamina now.

7 Sorry I'm late. I ...... get here any earlier, the traffic was just too heavy.

8 He was so good at science at school, he ...... a doctor, but he went into politics instead.

2 Likelihood and certainty: *could, can't, must, may, might*

Can and *could* are not only used to express ability. Along with *must, may* and *might* they can also be used to indicate degrees of possibility and certainty, to express assumptions or deductions.

a Make sentences by matching the sentence halves.

1 He must have taken the train to work
2 He might have got caught in a traffic jam
3 She must be at home
4 He can't have left the country
5 She could've gone away for the weekend
6 There may be another way out
7 She can't be a grandmother
8 He could well save a lot of money

a – she keeps a little cottage by the seaside.
b – all the lights are on in the house.
c – the car's still in the drive.
d – she doesn't look a day over 30!
e – their rates are very low.
f – they usually provide at least three exits.
g – there was an accident on the motorway.
h – he hasn't got a passport.

b Write the numbers of the sentences (1–8) in the space provided to answer these questions.

1 Which sentences refer to:

- the future? ......   • the present ? ......   • the past? ......

2 Which sentences express:

- possibility? ......   • impossibility? ......
- certainty (an unavoidable deduction)? ......

Check your answers by referring to the Grammar File on pages 142–143.

3 Complete the following sentences using suitable modal verb forms expressing possibility and deduction.

1 I thought he would come and visit us, but he ....
2 Don't touch it! It ....
3 If you imagine I'd lend you any more money, you ....
4 I don't know who telephoned, but it ....
5 I gave her such good directions that she ....
6 The exam was so easy, nobody ....
7 I think you've added up the bill wrongly. The meal ....
8 Just look at her brand new car! She ....

English in Use I *Developing Skills: Structural Cloze*

In this task you have to fill in **one** word in each space. The missing words are usually structural words such as pronouns, prepositions and particles, conjunctions and link words.

STRATEGY

a   It's important to have a general understanding of the text before you start the task. Read the text quickly and answer these questions:
1   Who would find the information in the text useful? Why?
2   Where does the information come from?
3   What kind of person would behave in the ways described?

b   Now begin reading the text again, sentence by sentence, very carefully. Think about the **kind** of word which is needed in each space. Is it an article, a preposition, a noun or a verb, for example?

Remember, the correct answer must be **grammatically correct** and must **make sense in context**. The exercise begins with an example (**0**).

▶ **Question 1**

Several prepositions can combine with *a meeting*: e.g. *in, at, for, to.* Which is correct here?

▶ **Question 2**

This refers back to the first sentence: more examples.

▶ **Question 4**

You need to decide on the correct verb form (infinitive or gerund).

▶ **Question 12**

manage to or *try to* would be grammatically correct but they would not make sense here. To fit the context, you need a verb with negative meaning.

How to win friends and influence colleagues

The worst sins that office workers can commit in the eyes of colleagues are interrupting people (**0**) *on* the telephone, talking loudly in front of someone's desk and arriving late (**1**) .... a meeting. It is almost (**2**) .... bad to eat at your desk, (**3**) .... personal calls or leave coffee cups (**4**) .... around, according to *Bodytalk*, a guide published by the Industrial Society, (**5**) .... lists the 30 traits most likely to annoy colleagues.

High (**6**) .... the list are signing on at someone else's computer terminal (**7**) .... signing off afterwards, messing up the photocopier (**8**) .... jamming the paper or leaving (**9**) .... set to produce multiple copies. Reading newspapers, doodling, chewing gum, keeping cuddly toys or ornaments on your desk, and putting up postcards or supposedly witty slogans (**10**) .... invite disapproval. Also unpopular are (**11**) .... who never fetch a colleague a drink from the machine, or who (**12**) .... to hold the lift door open when others are approaching. (**13**) .... conduct, according to the guide's author, Judi James, not only gives you an unprofessional image (**14**) .... is downright anti-social and could result (**15**) .... dismissal.

English in Use 2 *Developing Skills: Discourse Cloze*

This task tests your understanding of text structure. A number of phrases have been removed from a text and you have to choose the correct phrase from the list below to fill each gap.

STRATEGY

a First read through the text and answer these questions.

1 Look at the way the words 'procrastinator' and 'procrastination' are used in the text. What do you think they mean?

2 Are you ever a procrastinator? If so, when?

3 What is the danger with procrastination?

b Look at the first question, which has been answered as an example. Cross through the answer in the list below. For each gap, try to think what to expect before you look at the list of phrases. Cross through each answer you choose (in pencil) so that the choice gets easier each time.

▶ **Question 1**

This must refer to people who *don't* procrastinate. There are two answers to consider – think carefully which tense is appropriate.

▶ **Question 3**

There's a clue at the end of the sentence in '*the* deadline'. What does the use of the definite article suggest?

▶ **Question 5**

What does 'those' refer to? Is it people or things?

Don't delay: it's enough to make you sick

If you are one of those people who delay doing the Christmas shopping and sending off cards (**0**) .... , you may well be spending Christmas ill in bed. According to new research, procrastinators put themselves under so much stress by delaying action that they succumb to illnesses much more easily than those (**1**) .... .

The link between procrastination and illness emerged during a study of students (**2**) .... . Professor Dianne Tice of Case Western Reserve University, Ohio, set a class of students a project (**3**) .... , and measured their psychological state as the deadline approached.

Early results suggested that the procrastinators had the right idea; they seemed to be enjoying life immensely, having fun playing video games, going to see films, and generally doing anything

(**4**) .... . The conscientious ones, in contrast, had knuckled down and were showing mild signs of stress and ill-health.

But as the research continued, it became clear that virtue did indeed have its own rewards. With the deadline looming and lack of progress staring them in the face, stress levels soared, and the procrastinators started to crack. Their happy-go-lucky attitude had collapsed into higher rates of headaches, stomach pains, colds and other health problems than those (**5**) .... .

Yet despite the obvious effects (**6**) .... , Professor Tice doubts that procrastinators will ever change their ways. 'What makes procrastination so habitual is that for many people it works most of the time, and they feel good early on,' she said.

A with a deadline to work to

B which delay has on their health

C who had worked steadily from the start

D apart from working on their projects

E who persistently fail to finish work on time

F who simply get on with things

G until the last possible moment

4 ▶ Stress

*'**Stress:** Collective term for the insults a body must endure when thrust into a less-than-congenial environment; e.g. overwork, unemployment, a shopping mall in December or a vacation with one's in-laws.'*
Rick Bayan, *The Cynic's Dictionary*

Lead-in

1 Work with another student to discuss the following questions.

1 Which of the following activities causes the most stress? When and why?
2 Number the activities 1–6 according to their level of stress (1 = most stressful).

2 Discuss these questions.

1 What level of stress do you have in your life – high, medium or low?
2 What situations typically cause you stress?
3 What are the ways you deal with stress?

Text 1

PREDICTION

1 a Before you read, say whether you think these statements are true or false.

1 We should try to get rid of any stress in our lives.
2 Stress can have damaging physical and mental effects on us.
3 Stress can be caused by a poor diet.

b Read the first section of the text (lines 1–30) on the next page and check your answers.

A certain degree of stress is unavoidable in life. But the pressures of modern, urbanised societies can push stress to
5 dangerously high levels. While we can't completely eliminate stress, we can learn to modify our behaviour in ways that lessen its harmful effects on our
10 minds and bodies. Experts have identified a number of indicators that affect our vulnerability[1] to stress. Some of them have to do with physical factors, some are
15 related to mental and emotional behaviours, and some have to do with nutrition.

The following questionnaire was developed by psychologist
20 researchers at the Boston University Medical Centre, to evaluate vulnerability to stress, and to highlight those areas in which improvement can be
25 made.

To answer the questionnaire, rate each item according to how often it is true of you. Answer all the items, even if they seem not
30 to apply.

[1] *vulnerability* – our ability to be affected or harmed by something

GUESSING UNKNOWN VOCABULARY

2 **Discuss in pairs what you think the following words might mean.**
- Look at the way they are used in **context**.
- Ask yourself what **part of speech** they are.
- Look for clues to meaning in the **parts** of the word, e.g. *evaluate – value*

1 urbanised (line 3)   4 evaluate (line 22)
2 modify (line 7)   5 highlight (line 23)
3 indicators (line 11)

DISCUSSION POINTS

3 **a** Work with a partner to discuss the points in the Stress Test below. Fill in the scores **for your partner.**

b Read the first paragraph on the next page in order to check each other's results.

Stress Test

1	I eat at least one hot, balanced meal a day.	(......)
2	I get 7–8 hours of sleep at least four nights a week.	(......)
3	I regularly give and receive affection.	(......)
4	I have at least one relative within 50 miles on whom I can rely.	(......)
5	I exercise to the point of perspiration at least twice a week.	(......)
6	I smoke less than half a pack of cigarettes a day.	(......)
7	I take fewer than five alcoholic drinks a week.	(......)
8	I am at the appropriate weight for my height.	(......)
9	I have an income to meet my basic expenses.	(......)
10	I get strength from my religious beliefs.	(......)
11	I regularly attend club or social activities.	(......)
12	I have a network of friends and acquaintances.	(......)
13	I have one or more friends to confide in.	(......)
14	I am in good health.	(......)
15	I am able to speak openly about my feelings when I am angry or worried.	(......)
16	I have regular conversations with the people I live with about domestic problems.	(......)
17	I do something for fun at least once a week.	(......)
18	I am able to organise my time effectively.	(......)
19	I drink fewer than three cups of caffeine-rich drinks (coffee, tea, soft drinks) a day.	(......)
20	I take some quiet time for myself during the day.	(......)

(1) Almost always   (2) Frequently   (3) Occasionally   (4) Almost never   (5) Never

Add up the figures of your answers and subtract 20. If you have scored below 10, you have an excellent resistance to stress. If your score was over 30 you are vulnerable to stress in your life; a score of over 50 indicates you are seriously vulnerable to stress, and you should begin making some changes in your life.

Take a look at the items on which you scored '3' or higher, and begin trying to modify your behaviour. For instance, if you scored '4' on Number 19, you can cut your consumption of caffeine-rich beverages, and reduce your vulnerability to stress. Tackle the easy-to-change items, before the more difficult ones.

Work is a major source of stress for many people. Again, while normal work pressures can stimulate performance, a stress overload at work can lead to serious health problems. In the UK a recent stress study found that many factors influence stress ratings. A job can rate low stress on autonomy[2], high on physical danger, financial insecurity, time constraints or legal accountability[3]. One job that was omitted from the study was that of housewife/mother. Other studies have shown that housewives experience significant stress, something that will be no surprise to those who fall into that category.

Fighting stress in the workplace requires the co-operation of employee and employer. Far-sighted companies are providing sports and exercise facilities for employees, day-care or nurseries for working mothers, drug and alcoholism counselling. Job design is changing, too, in this age of dual-career families. More and more firms allow 'job-sharing', or work at home.

Employees can protect themselves from the effects of stress in simple ways. Taking a walk at lunchtime can help, as can simply getting up from the desk occasionally. Winston Churchill was wont to retire for a nap every afternoon, declaring that it enabled him to 'press a day-and-a-half's work into one'. John F Kennedy was another famous afternoon napper who calmed his mind and boosted energy with an afternoon snooze. Not all of us are able to take siestas, but there is sound evidence that a 10-minute to one-hour nap will do much to renew energy and relieve daily stress. The best time for a stress-busting nap? Mid-afternoon.

Mary Trevelyan Hodder

Reproduced by kind courtesy of Asia Magazine

[2]*autonomy* – freedom to make one's own decision

[3]*accountability* – responsibility

MULTIPLE CHOICE QUESTIONS
▶ Paper 1, Part 3

STRATEGY

4 **Finish reading the text and then answer the questions below by choosing the right answer A, B, C or D according to the information in the text.**

- Skim the text fairly quickly for general meaning. Try to ignore any difficult vocabulary at this stage – you may not need to understand it in order to answer the questions.

- Look at each question and try to answer in your own words **before** you look at the possible answers A–D.

- Find the key parts of the text and read these very carefully in order to choose the correct answer.

1 What general advice on reducing stress is given?
   A To drink less coffee and tea.
   B To try not to work quite so hard.
   C To make gradual changes in your lifestyle.
   D To check your stress levels regularly.

2 Some employers are described as 'far-sighted' because
   A they want their companies to succeed internationally.
   B they provide facilities which will have long-term benefits.
   C they don't think enough about things happening at present.
   D they have extensive knowledge about the subject of stress.

3 Who wouldn't be surprised to hear that housewives can suffer from stress?
   A   a housewife
   B   a husband
   C   a manager
   D   a child

4 'Dual career families' are families where
   A   one partner has two different jobs.
   B   one partner has changed jobs.
   C   each partner has a job.
   D   each partner has two different jobs.

5 What did Winston Churchill and John F Kennedy have in common?
   A   They both went to bed very early.
   B   They both survived on very little sleep.
   C   They both worked extremely hard.
   D   They both rested during the day.

Focus on Listening 1 *Causes of Stress*

▶ Paper 4, Part 1

You will hear Peter, a solicitor, talking about the stress in his life. As you listen, fill in the missing information in the sentences below with up to four words. You do not have to use the exact words on the tape.

You will hear the recording twice.

The two main areas of stress in Peter's life are _____ and _____	**1**
He often dictates work on tapes which may last _____	**2**
Recently he spent _____ **3** dictating important documents.	
What caused him stress was that he had to do _____ **4** again later.	
Another source of stress in his work is _____	**5**
It's also stressful to handle matters which are _____ **6** to a client.	
His clients are usually at _____ **7** point in their lives.	
However, he finds his work _____	**8**
At home it's stressful when his children are _____	**9**

Focus on Grammar 1 *Expressing Cause and Effect*

1 a Stress can have a number of harmful physical effects. Read this short text and try to fill in the gaps without looking at the Study Box below.

One (1) ...... of stress is to lower the body's resistance to infection, making it more susceptible to colds and other minor ailments. Painful stomach ulcers can also be (2) ...... by stress. More seriously, prolonged periods of stress can (3) ...... to an increase in blood pressure, and may also (4) ...... in 'hardening' of the arteries, which is a major (5) ...... of heart disease.

b Consult the Study Box and check your answers.

2 Write sentences to link the following ideas. Try to use a variety of cause and effect expressions.
Example:
hypermarkets/local shops closing down
The new hypermarket will take away a lot of trade from the town centre and this may lead to local shops closing down.

1 accidents/black ice

....

2 regular exercise/more energetic

....

3 disco opposite the hotel/lack of sleep

....

4 stress/poor time management

....

5 watching last night's midnight movie on TV/ oversleeping/arriving late for work

....

3 Work in pairs and discuss the causes and effects of stress in your life. Think about home, work, daily travel, study, friends, family. Be prepared to report back to the class briefly on what **your partner** said.

STUDY BOX ▶ *Expressing cause and effect*

Nouns

Work is a major   *source* / *cause*   of stress for many people. (Text 1)

One   *effect* / *result*   of stress is to increase the risk of heart trouble.

Verbs

A stress overload at work can   *lead to*   serious health problems. (Text 1)

A sleepless night can   *cause* / *result in*   stress. (Listening 1)

Serious health problems can   *result from*   a stress overload at work.

Links

High blood pressure can be   *caused by* / *due to* / *the result of*   stress.

Stress has increased   *as a result of* / *because of*   our modern lifestyle.

Text 2

PREDICTION

1 How can you overcome the effects of stress? Is it best to do something quiet and relaxing or should you be more energetic? Work with a partner and make a list of ideas.

SCANNING

2 You are going to read about six people's methods for overcoming stress. Quickly scan the article opposite and underline any method they mention. Be careful, they may mention more than one method!

MULTIPLE MATCHING
▶ Paper 1, Part 4

3 a In this task you have to read a text with several short sections, each referring to a different person. The questions test how quickly and correctly you can find the information about each person. Remember to use scanning skills to find the key information first and only read the important parts in detail.

STRATEGY

- For each question, check through the activities you have underlined (see Exercise 2 above).

- Occasionally you may find the same word in the text and in the question (e.g. *humour* in Questions 9/10). More often you need to look for a parallel expression in the text (e.g. Question 3).

- Sometimes a key part of the text may contain a word you don't know (e.g. *drudgery* in section D). In this case, use the context to guess the meaning.

b Now answer questions 1–12 by writing the correct letter(s) A–F in the spaces. Notice that sometimes there are two correct answers.

According to the information, which person:		
likes to relax in the open air?	**1** **2**	**A** Advertising Agency Chairman
feels more energetic after their method of relaxation?	**3**	
doesn't have any special method of relaxation?	**4**	**B** Member of Parliament
relaxes in a way other people wouldn't enjoy?	**5** **6**	
likes to discuss the day's events?	**7**	**C** Business Executive
likes to think over what's happened during the day?	**8**	
mentions humour as part of the way they relax	**9** **10**	**D** Bank Executive
doesn't find gardening a good way of relaxing?	**11**	**E** TV Editor-in-Chief
has a method of relaxation which can make them absent-minded?	**12**	**F** Marriage Counsellor

A ADVERTISING AGENCY CHAIRMAN

I unwind in a way that other people would find most unrelaxing – by writing. It's completely absorbing, and you can forget the outside world while you're wrestling with adverbs. A lot of what I write is light-hearted and there's nothing I enjoy more than penning a sentence that I think is funny. New phrases occur at inappropriate moments, so I have a pen and pad in the car and make notes when I stop at traffic lights. I once thought someone was tooting me, then realised it was me, leaning on the steering wheel.

B MEMBER OF PARLIAMENT

I usually travel back to my constituency on the 8 am train on Friday morning. I have a house right on the front and, if it has been a hard week in London, I do one of two things – either lie in bed and look out over the sea, or go for a walk along the beach, preferably at night, and watch the waves. The sea is the most relaxing thing of all, because it makes you realise there are things beyond you which you can't have any impact on.

C BUSINESS EXECUTIVE

I've always believed in keeping your personal and business lives separate and I think if you can do that, then you don't need to do anything else to relax after work. Everybody has times when they are under a lot of stress, but if you keep a sense of perspective – and a sense of humour – then you shouldn't have to do anything extra to wind down. In addition, if you have a family you can immerse yourself in, that is usually enough to forget all about the problems at work.

Stress Busters

From walking on the beach to washing the kitchen floor, Alexander Garrett discovers how people under pressure unwind.

D BANK EXECUTIVE

Domestic tasks are my way of switching off. Tasks that other women might consider drudgery – such as washing the kitchen floor – I find very satisfying. Ironing is especially good for mulling over the events of the day, and it's also satisfying, because at the end you can see a result – a neat pile of pristine clothes.

E TV EDITOR-IN-CHIEF

I have two ways of unwinding. There is a gym in our building, and in the evening I go to a group event where about a dozen of us do circuit training as well as aerobics and weights. I have a problem with things that don't involve concentration, such as gardening, because my mind drifts back to work. But the thing about working in a group is that there is a competitive element, so it helps to focus your mind on what you are doing. At 5.30 I feel quite tired, but if I go to the gym from 6–7 pm, it suddenly gives me a new burst of life.

Also on Monday mornings I do yoga at 7.30 am before setting off for work. Although the physical exertion is less, the teacher makes you focus on every part of your body, so there's a physical and psychological effect – a little bit of a high, a sense of well-being.

F MARRIAGE COUNSELLOR

Work ends quite late, but one of the things I do to relax is try to cook a reasonable meal, often enjoying a glass of wine as I do so. Sharing a meal with your partner is a chance to talk about the horrors of the day, and we try to build in time for that. We don't watch much television. Often we'll do the cooking together, and sometimes I'll listen to the radio or just some music at the same time, so that my mind switches off. In the summer I garden in the evenings – it's only a town garden, but it's full of wonderful plants, and there is nothing more relaxing than to be outside in the fresh air.

Focus on Grammar 2 *-ing Forms and Infinitives*

1 *-ing* forms after prepositions and conjunctions

a Look at these examples from Text 2 and underline the *-ing* forms. What type of word comes in front of them?

> I unwind by writing.
> Domestic tasks are my way of switching off.
> I've always believed in keeping your personal and business lives separate.
> I do yoga before setting off for work.

-ing forms are always used after prepositions. Note that *to* functions as a preposition in the expressions *look forward to, be/get used to, object to*.

-ing forms can be used after these conjunctions: *before, after, when, while, on, despite* and *since*.

b Complete the following sentences by adding the correct preposition or conjunction and the *-ing* form of a suitable verb.

1 I like to have a hot drink ...... to bed.
2 Why do you always insist ...... an argument?
3 He's never apologised ...... so rude to my friends.
4 She didn't try to prevent him ...... a fool of himself.
5 I'm interested ...... for the post of Personal Assistant.
6 I congratulated Joan and Alan ...... engaged.
7 You can save time at work ...... interruptions.
8 I feel much better ...... yoga.

2 *-ing* forms and infinitives after verbs and other expressions

Some verbs can only be followed by an *-ing* form, e.g. *mind, enjoy*.

> I don't mind helping.
> Do you enjoy watching sport on TV?

Note: An *-ing* form after the verb *need* has a passive meaning.

> The carpet needs cleaning. (= needs to be cleaned)

-ing forms are also used after certain expressions like *can't bear* and *no use*.

> I can't bear watching thrillers.
> It's no use crying about it.

Some verbs can only be followed by an infinitive form, e.g. *want, promise*.

> I don't want to see you again.
> She promised to bring it back.

Complete the following sentences with a suitable verb in the *-ing* or infinitive form.

1 Some people spend too much time ...... about work.
2 It takes me a long time ...... when I get home from work in the evenings.
3 The company is planning ...... sports and exercise facilities for its employees.
4 If you suffer from stress, I recommend ...... yoga.
5 Taking a break at lunchtime helps ...... energy so you can get more done in the afternoon.
6 Consider ...... a holiday away from it all if you're tired and run-down.
7 You can choose ...... a stand-by ticket if you don't mind not ...... if you can travel until the last minute.
8 I can't help ...... that if he continues to do so little work he deserves ...... the exam.
9 It's not worth ...... him to the party. He hates ......
10 How did she manage ...... her boss ...... her a salary increase?

Check your answers by referring to the Reference Lists in the Grammar File, on page 154.

3 *-ing* versus infinitive with difference in meaning

a The following verbs can be followed either by an infinitive or an *-ing* form depending on the meaning: *come, continue, dread, forget, go on, mean, regret, remember, stop, try*.

Compare these pairs of sentences. What is the difference in meaning?

1 a I remember thanking her for her gift when we met last month.
  b John, you must remember to thank Aunt Sue for her lovely present.
2 a She tried to swallow it, but her throat was too sore.
  b She tried swallowing menthol syrup, but it didn't help her sore throat.
3 a The driving was tiring, so he stopped to drink some coffee at a service station.
  b He stopped drinking coffee while he was on a diet.
4 a After finishing his first degree, he went on to study medicine.
  b He went on studying medicine despite failing the first year exams.
5 a I can't find my passport. I think I forgot to bring it!
  b I'll never forget losing my passport when I was on holiday in the States.

b Complete the sentences using a suitable verb in the correct form.

1 Elizabeth is going on ...... translation when she finishes her Advanced exam.

2 I'll never forget ...... the lottery. It was the best day of my life!

3 We arrived rather late because Steve kept stopping ...... photographs.

4 I can't remember much about the accident. I certainly don't remember ...... that wall.

5 'I've tried ...... smoking, but it's impossible.' 'You should try ...... nicotine patches – they certainly helped me.'

6 I haven't told my parents that I'm giving up my studies. I dread ...... what they'll say.

7 She went on ...... to him for years, although he never once replied.

8 I wouldn't mind changing jobs, but not if it means ...... to another city.

9 You won't forget ...... the plants while we're away, will you?

10 I'm terribly sorry, I really didn't mean ...... you any trouble.

11 You can't go on ...... this hard, you'll have a nervous breakdown.

12 Several people came ...... to help when they saw what had happened.

c Now complete these sentences using an appropriate verb in the correct form.

1 'I just can't seem to lose any weight.' 'Have you tried ...... ?'

2 I don't really regret .... I think it was all for the best.

3 I didn't like ...... at first, but now I've come ....

4 I'll never forget ...... for the first time. It was such an enjoyable experience.

5 You must remember ...... when you go on holiday.

6 When I've finished this course, I mean ....

Focus on Vocabulary 1 *Word Formation: Verbs*

1 a Sometimes verbs can be formed from another part of speech by adding a *prefix* like *en-* at the beginning of the word or a *suffix* like *-ify* at the end of the word. Look at these examples from texts in this unit:

We can learn to *modify* our behaviour in ways   *mode* (*n*)
that *lessen* the harmful effects of stress.   *less* (*determiner*)
... it *enabled* him to press a day and a half's work into one. *able* (*adj*)

Here is a list of the main affixes (suffixes and prefixes) which can be used to form verbs:

Suffixes	
+ **en**	e.g. less, fright: less*en*, fright*en*
+ **ise/ize**	e.g. central, terror: central*ise*, terror*ise*
+ **ify**	e.g. simple, beauty: simpl*ify*, beaut*ify*
Prefixes	
en +	e.g. able, courage: *en*able, *en*courage

b Complete this table by adding the opposites of the adjectives.

strong	*weak*	short (of time/distance)	......
wide	......	thick	......
tight	......	sharp	......
hard	......	light (of colours)	......

c Now make verbs from each adjective and its opposite (16 in all).

2 The wrong affixes have been used to make verbs in the following sentences. Make the necessary corrections.

1 Would you be able to *largen* this photograph for me?
2 This could be a lovely house if you are prepared to *modernify* it.
3 If you paint all the walls white it will *enlight* the whole room.
4 As a company we aim to *maxify* our profits.

3 Complete these sentences with suitable verbs formed from the words below.
standard   sure   fresh   solid   false

1 Pour the hot fat into a bowl and wait for it to cool down and ....
2 The bathroom's upstairs if you'd like to ...... up before lunch.
3 He's been accused of ...... some of the company's official documents.
4 Please ...... that you take all your belongings with you when you leave.
5 They're going to ...... the entry qualifications for all similar courses.

Focus on Listening 2 *A Company Fitness Centre*

▶ Paper 4, Part 1

You will hear Roger Blake, the Fitness Manager at a company's fitness centre, giving employees an introduction to the centre.

• Before you listen, read through the notes below and try to predict what kind of information is missing. As you listen, fill in the missing information for questions 1–10 using up to three words.

• You will hear the recording twice. Use the second listening to check your answers.

Opening hours: [**1**]

To avoid possible health problems, must complete health
[**2**]

Personal exercise programme worked out to suit
[and **3**]

Treadmill – use first as [**4**] activity.

Back problems? Talk to Roger before using [**5**]

Cycling machine – for comfort/safety [**6**] saddle before use.

Weightlifting machines help to [**7**] muscles.

Minimum number of sessions recommended per week: [**8**]

Don't exercise for [**9**] after light lunch.

Exercise helps you manage stress and [**10**]

Focus on Writing *Leaflet*

▶ Paper 2, Part 2

TASK

> You work in a fitness centre. The centre would like to encourage more business people to use its facilities after work. There are many companies in your town which have English-speaking employees and you have been asked to prepare the text for a leaflet aimed at them.
>
> You should:
> 1 introduce the fitness centre and its facilities.
> 2 emphasise the benefits of regular exercise.
> 3 give brief general advice on ways of avoiding stress in daily life.
>
> Write the text for the **leaflet** using about 250 words.

CONTENT

1 Work in pairs or groups to do the following.

a Draw up a list of possible exercise and other facilities (such as a shop, café, etc.).

b Make notes about the benefits of regular exercise (and the dangers of inactivity).

c Discuss possible points to include in the 'general advice' section.

ORGANISATION/LAYOUT/ STYLE

2 Look at the notes on the **layout**, **organisation** and **style** of leaflets in the Writing File on page 163. Then make your personal decisions about these features:
1 What heading(s) should there be?
2 How can you catch the reader's attention and keep him or her reading?
3 How should the information be organised, and how can the text be divided up to be easy and attractive to read?

KEY STRUCTURES

This is an opportunity to use some different expressions of *cause* and *effect*. (See Focus on Grammar 1, page 55.)

Focus on Vocabulary 2 *Idiomatic Expressions*

a The following sentences contain idioms describing stressful conditions. Choose parts of the body from the list to complete them.

neck   teeth   blood   feet   hands   eyes

1 When my boss takes the credit for work I've done, it makes my ...... boil!
2 Pete's really got his ...... full with all the wedding preparations.
3 I'm fed up to the back ...... with all your criticism.
4 I'd like to help but I'm afraid I'm up to my ...... in work at the moment.
5 I nearly broke my ...... to get there and then they told me the meeting had been cancelled!
6 She tried to work from home but the children kept getting under her ....

b Use some of the idioms above to tell a partner about stressful situations that you have experienced. Your partner should give you appropriate advice on what to do in each situation.

English in Use I *Developing Skills: Lexical Cloze*

▶ Paper 3, Part I

1 Discuss this question: What kinds of things can make car driving stressful?

2 a Read the following advertisement quickly to find out how the idea of stress has been used to sell a car.

   b Now read the text more carefully and choose the answer (A, B, C or D) which you think best fits each space. The first answer has been given as an example.

Think of it AS LESS OF A test drive,

AND MORE OF A REST DRIVE

Imagine a traffic jam (**0**) .... over 122,000 km from nose to (**1**) .... . If motoring experts have got their (**2**) .... right, that's how much of Britain's roads will be (**3**) .... by the year 2005. And let's (**4**) .... it, the situation is bleak enough already. According to a recent (**5**) .... , 49% of business executives find travelling by car the most stressful way of getting from A to B. At the (**6**) .... of sounding alarmist, we'd like to (**7**) .... out that too much worry isn't good for you. (**8**) .... stress has been (**9**) .... to heart attacks, strokes and high blood pressure. Ironically, what every motorist needs to do is *slow down*.

Maybe you should start by choosing a car that helps you to stay calm, and relaxed, a car where you can (**10**) .... from the hubbub of traffic, yet still feel comfortable and in control, a car like the Vauxhall Omega.

Being in a cramped, confined space is the last thing that (**11**) .... to a feeling of well-being. That's why we've made the Omega even more roomy than its predecessor. It isn't just your engine that can overheat when you're stuck in a jam. When temperatures (**12**) .... , so do tempers. Your concentration lapses and you become more accident-prone. That's when air-conditioning becomes less of a luxury and more of a (**13**) .... . Fortunately we've included it as a standard (**14**) .... on every Omega.

Call our helpline: If you'd rather drive a car that reduces stress instead of one that (**15**) .... to it, give us a call.

▶ **Question I**

From head to foot describes a *vertical* measurement. This describes a *horizontal* measurement.

▶ **Question 5**

Only one word exactly describes the process of getting information like this.

0	A passing	B lasting	(C) stretching	D going
1	A tail	B foot	C end	D toe
2	A additions	B accounts	C measurements	D calculations
3	A congested	B massed	C dense	D stuck
4	A accept	B face	C imagine	D agree
5	A discovery	B experiment	C survey	D inspection
6	A danger	B risk	C chance	D worry

▶ **Question 10**

You can probably guess *hubbub* is something to do with noise. Two words don't fit grammatically – which are they?

▶ **Question 12**

Only one of these verbs can be followed by the preposition *to* in this sentence.

7	**A** speak	**B** set	**C** make	**D** point
8	**A** Excess	**B** Extensive	**C** Extra	**D** Exclusive
9	**A** united	**B** linked	**C** joined	**D** attached
10	**A** avoid	**B** remove	**C** depart	**D** escape
11	**A** causes	**B** develops	**C** contributes	**D** assists
12	**A** ascend	**B** advance	**C** grow	**D** rise
13	**A** necessity	**B** demand	**C** need	**D** minimum
14	**A** equipment	**B** feature	**C** section	**D** piece
15	**A** increases	**B** builds	**C** adds	**D** expands

English in Use 2 *Developing Skills: Register Cloze*

▶ Paper 3, Part 5

1   *Register* is the style of language used in a particular situation. It depends on the relationship between the writer and reader, the kind of writing – official letter or friendly note, for example – and also the subject matter. Register can be formal or informal, for example, or it can be more specialised or technical according to a particular profession.

Each pair of sentences below deals with the same topic but this is expressed in two different *registers*. For each pair of sentences:

• think about the context. Who could have written the first sentence?

• notice the differences in vocabulary and structure between the two sentences.

1   a   Kindly send your payment in respect of the enclosed invoice by return of post.
b   We've got to pay that bill right away.
2   a   You are invited to attend a meeting which will be held on Saturday 24th March.
b   They've asked me to go to a meeting they're having next Saturday.
3   a   We regret to inform you that your application has not been successful.
b   They went and appointed someone else!

2   In this task you have to use information from one text to complete another text, which has been written for a different audience and purpose, in a different register.

Read the advertisement for a health farm on page 64 and use the information to complete the gaps in the informal letter. Write one or two words in each gap, using the guidance notes to help you.

Note: The words you need do not occur in the advertisement.

ADVERTISEMENT

Feeling stressed? Worn out? Need to wind down?
Relax in luxury at beautiful Blandings Manor

Superb accommodation, delicious cuisine and a range of activities which is quite simply unrivalled.

Blandings is for everyone, male or female, young or old, active or inactive. There is no pressure as to how you spend your time. Our highly-trained staff will be happy to advise but we want you to get what *you* want from your stay.

Special All-Inclusive Weekend Offer: £80∗ (normal rate £180)

- Accommodation – all rooms look on to the magnificent gardens

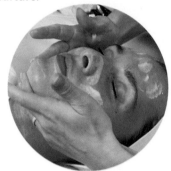

- All meals from dinner on arrival to lunch on the day of departure. Complimentary tea, coffee and mineral water served throughout the day
- A choice of daily treatments: sauna, spa bath, or steam treatment
- Personal programme to meet your individual needs
- Unlimited use of all sports and leisure facilities
- A choice of over 20 daily activities

Selected dates only. Call for information.

INFORMAL LETTER

► **Questions 1/2**

Make sure you use the right prepositions.

► **Question 9**

You need a verb which is followed by the infinitive without *to*.

► **Question 10**

How many more treatments? What is an informal expression for that number?

► **Question 12**

Compare the normal and special offer prices.

Dear Gill,

Do you remember me telling you about a health farm I'd seen advertised? Well, I've looked at the ad again and I must say it looks fantastic. Now I'm hoping to persuade you to join me there for a weekend!

The rooms you (**0**) ..stay in.. sound really luxurious and apparently they all have a (**1**) .... the gardens. The meals are all (**2**) .... the price and you can also get (**3**) .... whenever you want.

The brochure says that what you do is entirely (**4**) .... to you. You can have a whole programme specially designed to (**5**) .... you, or you can just ask staff to make a few (**6**) .... about activities to do. You can use (**7**) .... of the sports and leisure facilities for as (**8**) .... as you like, and the brochure also mentions loads of other activities every day. But don't worry, nobody will (**9**) .... you do anything. You could just spend the whole time relaxing in the sauna if you wanted (or there are a (**10**) .... of other treatments you could choose instead if you prefer)!

There's a terrific offer on at the moment with weekends costing (**11**) .... half the normal price although that only (**12**) .... certain dates. Anyway, let me know what you think.

Best wishes

Sue

Questions 1–3
Write **two** words in each gap.

Questions 4–10
Write **one** word in each gap.

Questions 11/12
Write **two** words in each gap.

Language Focus 3 *Coherence/Cohesion*

Coherence: A piece of writing is *coherent* if it is clearly organised and has a logical sequence of ideas.
Cohesion: A paragraph or section of text is *cohesive* if the sentences are well constructed and well linked together, and there is no unnecessary repetition.

1 Which of these paragraphs has a problem with coherence? Which has a problem with cohesion?

A

The book I would choose to take to a desert island is a book called 'Gulliver's Travels'. It's an amazing book about a man called Gulliver who travelled to different places. Every place Gulliver went was unusual, unexpected, unbelievable. In one place horses could talk and think like people. People lived like primitives. Gulliver lived with horses for a couple of months. He learned many things from horses. In the horses' society everyone was equal to each other. There was justice. No one had any advantages.

B

There are many good bookshops for students in my town. If I was going to live on a desert island, I would take a book on wildlife. That book gives you advice about how to survive in a desert place. It's a beautiful island with sandy beaches and palm trees. You probably have many questions such as where you could live, what you can eat and how. You will read a real story of 15 children who were lost on a desert island until they finally succeeded in making a new society for themselves.

Writers use a variety of methods to make a text cohesive. These include the use of:

- **reference words** like the relative pronouns *which* and *that*, the personal pronouns *he, it, them, her* or expressions like *the one, the person* or *the company* to avoid repeating names
  Note: There is more information on reference links after Text 1 in Unit 5.
- **linking devices** like *and, although, while* and *however* to provide a logical link between sentences and paragraphs
- **synonyms and parallel expressions**
  e.g. people/human beings

- **ellipsis or omission** – leaving out part of a sentence to avoid repetition. e.g. John got 98% in the exam but I only got 70. (= I got 70% in the exam); I didn't want a big wedding, but my parents did. (= my parents did want a big wedding)

2 Find three linking devices from the following list to match each of the headings below:

while   because   although
during (that time)   so as to   in addition to
despite (the fact that)   since   finally
owing to (the fact that)   as well as   whereas
in order to   both ... and   however
on the other hand   so that   as soon as

Addition   Concession   Cause
Contrast   Purpose   Time

You can check your answers in the Writing File, page 170.

3 Now combine the following sentences using suitable linking words and expressions from the list above.

1 Peter's going to have to leave early. He wants to get to the bank before it closes.
2 I've got a huge overdraft. I had all that work done on the roof last month.
3 You've already had three warnings. Your work hasn't improved at all.
4 We put out all the picnic things. It began to pour with rain.
5 The new 600 model looks fantastic. It drives like a dream.
6 I prefer classical music. My husband loves modern jazz.

4 Rewrite Text A using reference words and linking devices to link the sentences more successfully and avoid unnecessary repetition.

EXAM SKILLS ▶ Papers 2 and 3
Understanding cohesion and coherence is important for several tasks in the CAE exam. Both features are taken into consideration in your written work for Paper 2, of course, but in addition they are tested in Paper 1, Part 2 (gapped text), and in Paper 3, Parts 2 and 6 (structural cloze and discourse cloze). So make sure you are familiar with a good range of link words and that you know how to use them correctly.

Learning Focus 3 *Editing Skills 1: Revising your Draft*

1 What is editing?

This is when you look through what you've written with a critical eye, so as to make any changes which you think will improve your work. If you have left out any important information, or if there are problems with the organisation, sentence structure or spelling, for example, it will make your writing less effective and may cost you marks in the CAE exam, so it's worth working to improve your editing skills.

2 What is the first stage of editing?

Once you've produced the first draft of your written work (or a plan and detailed notes), read it carefully so that you can make any necessary changes to your final version. Check particularly that:

- it's **complete**, i.e. you have included all the necessary information

- it's **coherent**, i.e. you have organised the information in the clearest, most logical way

- it's **cohesive**, i.e. the paragraphs are well-constructed

- the **layout** is correct for the type of writing

- the **register** – neutral, formal or informal – is appropriate for the type of writing

- And finally, ask yourself if it is likely to have the intended effect on the reader, e.g. Will they be persuaded to do something? Will they understand something clearly? Will they be entertained?

3 Read the following instructions for a writing task and the two draft compositions which students have produced and discuss these questions.

a Which of the two pieces of writing:

1 did you find easier to read? Why?

2 is more cohesive, with better constructed sentences?

3 has more interesting or helpful suggestions in your opinion?

b What changes should these students make when they revise their work?

> You have been asked by a college magazine to write an article entitled 'How to enjoy yourself without spending a fortune'. Write your article in approximately 250 words.

A

> Are you in Patras to study and you don't have enough money available to amuse yourself? Then this article is written just for you!
>
> If you don't want to spend any money at all, the best solution is to go with your friends to one of Patras' many squares. Patras has a variety of different squares. The most amusing square is, as you would expect, 'Psila Alonia'. You can also go to King George's Square which is just in the centre of Patras.
>
> Perhaps, if you drink coffee you would like to go to one of the beautiful cafés. Our city has a lot of them, fortunately. There is one on every corner and coffee isn't ~~too~~ very expensive. It costs around 500 drachmas. Or, if you don't drink coffee, you could drink a coke. Or something else. There's a big variety of drinks.
>
> Why don't you have a party? Meet your friends in a flat, bring some CDs and drinks and start the dance. A party is a very interesting thing. You can have fun, you can gossip with the 'friends' that you don't like and meet new people without spending anything.
>
> Lastly, another thing you can do is to stay home alone and listen to your favourite music or watch your favourite TV programme. Call your best friend to join you and play cards or study together. This can also be amusing. You never know!

B

> Everyone knows that if someone wants to have a good time with his friends, has to spend a lot of money. Today, unfortunately, entertaining yourself can be extremely expensive. On the other hand, there ⟨are places where someone can enjoy ~~hisself~~ himself without having to spend a fortune. Our city has many sports centres which have tennis courts or basketball courts. For the low costX of buying tennis racquets or a basketball someone can go there and spend his free time in a more healthy way. You don't have to pay in order to play in these courts, and if you can't afford the money to buy the special equipment needed you can always borrow the things you need from someone else. Something else very important and inexpensive is going to a cinema or a theatre. There are many cinemas or theatres each one presenting a different movie or a play. It isn't absolutely free of course, but the tickets aren't very expensive. Watching a good movie, especially a good comedy can cause a lot of fun, you know. Apart from cinemas and theatres, you can always go and visit the biggest cafeteria called 'Galaxy'. It isn't an ordinary cafeteria. It has many elements that all the other cafeterias in the city don't have. You pay an admission ticket when you enter, and then you do what every you like. You can watch a movie on a high screen TV, listen to music, play a computer game and of course drink your coffee. You can⊁ do all these things for just paying an inexpensive ticket. So, as you can see there are many way of enjoying yourself without spending a fortune That's why next time you go out, think about these places first.

5 ▶ Globe Trotting

'If you look like your passport photo, in all probability you need the journey.'
Earl Wilson, 1961

Lead-in

Work with a partner to answer as many of these questions as possible.

Travel Quiz

1 Which countries fly these flags?

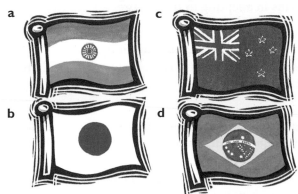

a
b
c
d

2 In which country can you see these festivals?

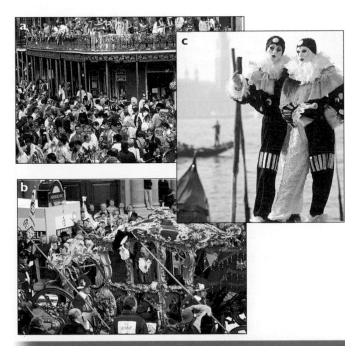

a
b
c

3 Where would you be given change in
   a roubles?
   b pfennigs?
   c rupees?

4 Can you name
   a the world's smallest state?
   b the busiest metro system?
   c the largest state in the USA?

5 Where do they eat
   a smorgasbord?
   b sushi?
   c enchiladas?

6 Beautiful beaches – but where are they?
   a Ipanema
   b Bondi
   c Waikiki

7 To which countries do the following airlines belong?
   a Varig
   b Sabena
   c LOT

8 Which places are also known as
   a the Big Apple?
   b the Windy City?
   c the Eternal City

You can check your answers on page 233.

Text 1

1 Skim-read the text opposite to answer these questions as quickly as possible.

1 What exactly is 'Servas'?
   A a travel agency which arranges cheap holidays
   B a charity which arranges for people to do voluntary work overseas
   C an organisation which arranges for travellers to stay with local people

2 Who can travel with 'Servas'?
   A only students
   B young people generally
   C people of all ages

3 How did the travellers mentioned in the article get on?
   A They all thoroughly enjoyed the experience.
   B Most of them enjoyed the experience.
   C Several had problems in adapting to the culture.

SCANNING

2 Now scan the text to find the answers to these questions.
   1 The travellers' names are printed in dark type. How many are there?
   2 Which countries did they visit?

MULTIPLE MATCHING
▶ Paper 1, Part 1

3 In this task, you have quite a long text to read. However, the questions are quite straightforward. The aim is to test how quickly and correctly you can find the information.

STRATEGY

• Look through the questions and underline the key words e.g. *progress/local language* in Question 1, *present* in Question 2.

• Remember, the questions often paraphrase and summarise the text, so you need to look for synonyms (e.g. Q 2) or expressions that say the same thing in different ways (e.g. Qs 4, 9).

• For each question, check the names highlighted in the text. Read those parts of the text carefully to find the answer. Ignore **all** the other parts of the text.

Answer questions 1–14 by choosing from the list of travellers (A–H) on the right below. Some of the choices may be required more than once.

Which traveller(s) ...		
made progress in speaking the local language?	**1**	**A** Rachel
brought a present for their host?	**2**	
had difficulty in adjusting to the local conditions?	**3**	**B** Andrea
spent longer with a family than originally planned?	**4**	**C** Irv
didn't travel by public transport?	**5**	**D** Joyce
had unusual tastes in food?	**6**	
learnt something about women's concerns?	**7** **8**	**E** Bridget
introduced local people to a new game?	**9**	**F** Johannes
was willing to make themself useful in the house?	**10**	**G** Mary
found they had been mistaken about one aspect of the culture?	**11**	**H** The Ruarks
had an embarrassing arrival?	**12**	
adapted their behaviour in some way to fit in with the local culture?	**13** **14**	

When the locals are friendly

Free accommodation with plenty of surprises... Servas is a cheap – and enlightening – way to see the world, says Patricia Cleveland-Peck.

When **Rachel** arrived in Bangladesh, her host, Ujol was waiting for her at the railway station. Rachel was looking out for a middle-aged man. Ujol was not expecting a woman.

Ujol, 25 and his family live in a two-bedroom flat. His original plan had been for himself and 'Mr Rachel' to sleep on the big bed in his room. 'Mr Rachel' ended up having the large room to herself, while Ujol and his family slept in one room. She stayed four nights in the end, as her plans to move on after two days were met with dismay. 'Once we had all got over our initial shyness', says Rachel, 'it was wonderful to live as part of an ordinary family'.

Living as part of the family is a key factor in an unusual organisation which enables its members to travel without the usual trappings of the tourist industry. Servas (the name means 'we serve' in Esperanto) is a non-profit-making organisation dedicated to promoting 'peace and international understanding'. It operates in 80 countries around the world through a network of hosts who are willing to open their homes to visitors free of charge for two nights and sometimes longer. It is *not* a travel agency offering a cheap travel option, but is intended for the traveller who wants to get to know individuals and their culture by sharing their activities for a short time.

Last summer I went to the local station to pick up my first Servas visitor. A tiny girl carrying a backpack almost as big as herself, **Andrea** from Budapest was planning a month's tour of England, staying two nights with 14 different hosts (for each of whom she had prepared a gift of a cassette of Hungarian music). She was a charming guest, offering to help with the washing-up. Andrea phoned me before leaving England to tell me how successful her exhausting circuit had proved.

This sort of travel suits the young but is by no means restricted to them. Last year **Irv** from the US, aged 64, hitch-hiked round Britain, spending 22 nights with 12 Servas hosts; 72-year-old **Joyce** from New Zealand travelled alone through Russia by rail – 'All across the country, 9,000 miles. I taught the Mongolians to play Snap and learned to tell my life story in Russian'. Sometimes it is the only way to find out what goes on behind closed doors in countries not renowned for their openness to visitors.

Bridget and Bill from England stayed in Fez, Morocco. Their Servas host was a young, out-of-work waiter, through whom Bridget and Bill learned how serious a problem unemployment is in Morocco for the university educated. Receiving Servas visitors offers them some contact with an outside world which they are unlikely to gain visas to visit.

'Men and women lead very separate lives,' Bridget discovered. 'I covered my head with a scarf to gain respect among the men – but they found it unusual that I wanted to join in the discussions and they tended to avoid eye contact. As I could also go to the kitchen and talk to the women about their lives and problems, I had the best of both worlds'.

Such visits are bound to break down prejudices. Before visiting Japan, **Johannes** from Germany was under the impression that Japanese women didn't talk much. Now he knows that this is not so. 'The women who talked about their young children were extremely worried about them, much more so than I feel Europeans are. The school system in Japan seems to put children under enormous pressure'.

Johannes also learned when to hold his tongue. 'It is not easy in Japan to discuss difficult or controversial topics. I had to stop asking questions when I felt a barrier'. So what did they make of Johannes? 'They all *seemed* to enjoy our time together'.

You must be flexible: things will be different. **Mary**, travelling in India, was proudly told by her Indian host, 'we have water'. This turned out to be cold water for short periods, twice a day. The lavatories she found 'difficult', as well as the fact that she came across hot water only twice in seven weeks.

On the other hand, sometimes western visitors prepare themselves for the shock of poor hygiene and poverty only to find the most wonderful hospitality. Not only may your hosts feed you meals they can ill-afford but they may also insist that you then take their bed while they sleep on the floor.

Sometimes the Servas official two-nights-maximum rule is a godsend, as when your guest shows no interest in you or your life but is simply out to use your home as a free hotel and to consume as much of your food as possible before getting you to drive him/her to the next sucker on the list. It happens. Prepare also to be perplexed by the habits of different nations. What was I to make of the **Ruarks**, a middle-aged American couple who would eat only raw green weeds gathered from the hedgerows, and preferred to sleep on the floor rather than on the bed I had made up for them?

Rupert from San Francisco, a regular host, says 'I have no agenda for my guests. If they want to stay one night or one month – they are welcome. If they want to spend most of their days doing the tourist thing, I will support that. If they just want to hang out with me – fabulous!'

> **'I taught the Mongolians to play Snap and learned to tell my life story in Russian.'**

Focus on Grammar *Past/past perfect simple/continuous*

1 Past simple/continuous

a Look at these examples and underline the finite verbs. Say what the tenses are in each case. Then complete the explanations below with the name of the correct tense.

1 When Rachel arrived in Bangladesh, her host Ujol was waiting for her at the station.

2 As soon as she arrived, he took her home to his two-room flat and introduced her to his family.

3 While she stayed in his home, she slept in the large room.

4 The sun was just rising as she left the house and set off on the next stage of her journey.

- The ...... is used to describe a series of events in a narrative.

- The ...... is used to describe the background to an event or story.

- The ...... is used to describe two events that happen at the same time.

- The ...... is used to describe a longer action or event which was interrupted by a shorter one.

b Complete these sentences with the correct forms of the verbs in brackets.

1 A friend of mine ...... (fly) from Heathrow to Boston when he ... (be take) violently ill.

2 As his temperature ...... (soar), he ...... (begin) to lapse into unconsciousness. The steward said he would look for a doctor.

3 A stewardess ...... (give) my friend emergency oxygen by the time the steward ...... (return).

2 Past perfect simple/continuous

a Underline the finite verbs in these examples and say what tense they are in. Then complete the explanations below.

1 Ujol's original plan had been for himself and 'Mr Rachel' to sleep in his room.

2 'Once we had all got over our initial shyness, it was wonderful to live as part of an ordinary family.'

3 Andrea had been planning her trip to Britain for months. She intended to stay with 14 different hosts, for each of whom she had prepared a gift.

- The past perfect refers to an action or event which happened ...... another action in the past. It is used to make the ...... of events in a narrative clear. It is often used to set the scene at the start of a story.

- It is not necessary to use the past perfect if the ...... is clear from the context or from the use of words such as ...... or ....

- The past perfect continuous tense is used when the first action or event ...... for some time or was unfinished.

b Underline the most suitable tense form in the following sentences.

1 We *had taken/took* the dog to the kennel before we set off for the airport.

2 Charles *worked/had been working* for the company for years before he finally got a pay rise.

3 I *tore up/had torn up* his love letters and then I smashed his photograph.

4 John had to rush home because he *forgot/had forgotten* to turn off the stove.

5 Mandy's face was quite red because she *sat/had been sitting* in the sun all morning.

3 Put the verbs in the following text into the appropriate tense.

Thomas Cook – the 'inventor' of package holidays

The inventor of the 'package tour' was Thomas Cook. Born in Leicester in 1808, Cook was a preacher who **1** ...... (go) around the country telling people about the evils of alcohol. He **2** ...... (believe) that people would be less tempted by drink if they could get out of the cities and into the countryside on their days off.

In 1841, while he **3** ..... (travel) around the North, he **4** ...... (have) a brainwave. He **5** ...... (reserve) an entire train to go from Leicester to Loughborough and back again in one day. Cook **6** ...... (organise) lots of activities for his customers, and the tickets, which he **7**...... (sell) for one shilling (five pence), included everything – travel, food and entertainment. The 'excursion' as he called it **8** ...... (be) a great success – he **9** ...... (sell) more than 500 tickets.

As the railway network **10** ...... (spread) across Britain, Cook's excursions **11** ...... (become) more ambitious. By the mid 1840s, he **12** ...... (conduct) tours to Scotland, Liverpool, Newcastle and London. By 1855 Cook **13** ...... (organise) tours for almost fifteen years and felt that he **14** ...... (have) enough experience to start venturing overseas. He **15** ...... (begin) with continental Europe, but soon **16** ...... (extend) his tours to North America, Egypt and India.

By the time of his death in 1893, the name Cook **17** ...... (become) synonymous with guided tours and what **18** ...... (begin) as a modest day-trip to the countryside **19** ...... (turn) into a worldwide business.

Focus on Speaking 1 *What kind of traveller are you?*

1   Work with a partner. Imagine you have booked a two-week package tour together, staying in a foreign seaside resort. Discuss the following questions and mark the answers which **your partner** chooses.

1 There is no sign of your luggage when you arrive at your destination in the middle of the night. Do you:
a   think what a terrible start to the holiday and decide to stay at the airport until it turns up?
b   take a telephone number and ring back in the morning?
c   do nothing and wait for the courier to sort things out?
d   grab a taxi and tell the driver to take you to the nearest all-night discotheque?

2 At the hotel, you are shown a room which has neither the balcony nor the sea view which you've asked for and paid for. Do you:
a   take what you're offered for the moment, but determine to get what you want in the morning?
b   refuse to accept the room and camp in the lounge?
c   smile and turn up the volume on your personal stereo (you knew things would go wrong)?
d   take the room, certain you'll be able to swap it later?

3 The restaurant at your hotel turns out to be ridiculously expensive. Do you:
a   eat without worrying because, after all, you *are* on holiday?
b   pay up, but moan continuously?
c   decide to go on a diet for the duration of the holiday?
d   find a cheaper restaurant a couple of streets away?

4 The weather is awful. Do you:
a   see if there's any chance of an earlier flight home?
b   stay in your room and listen to music on your personal stereo?
c   organise trips to museums and art galleries until it gets better?
d   make for the beach anyway? (You once read an article that said the sun can tan you even through thick clouds.)

5 Doing the accounts at the end of the day, you realise that you handed over a 200 instead of a 20 denomination note as a tip for lunch. Do you:
a   go back to the restaurant, certain they'll give you a refund once you explain what's happened?
b   curse all foreigners and never leave another tip all holiday?
c   shrug your shoulders and write it off to experience?
d   have an enormous meal at an expensive restaurant to show that you won't let your holiday be spoilt by a little thing like money.

6 Having tried all the restaurants, you are forced to acknowledge that the local cuisine is appalling. Do you:
a   feel thankful that at least the fruit and salads are delicious, and resolve to stick to them?
b   complain bitterly, and eat lots of ice-cream and sweets between meals – even though neither is particularly appetising?
c   give up on the local cuisine and go on a crash diet?
d   reckon you've just been unlucky so far, and give the restaurants another try?

7 You go on a whole-day coach trip with regular stops for drinks, meals and sightseeing. The rest of the party don't look like the sort of people you'd mix with at home. Do you:
a   talk only to your holiday companion and feel glad you both brought books?
b   bitterly regret your mistake and spend the day in a bad mood?
c   single out anyone who looks in the least bit 'your type' and see if you can start a conversation?
d   make yourself the life and soul of the party?

8 When you go away on holiday, do you:
a   hardly think about what's going on at home from the moment you arrive until the moment you return?
b   know there's absolutely no point in worrying about things at home because there's nothing you can do about them?
c   wake up most mornings worrying about how on earth they are managing at home without you?
d   send postcards to a few close friends during the second week?

INTERPRETATION

2   There are at least four different ways of behaving on holiday. From the four possible answers to each question in the questionnaire on page 71, can you tell what they are? Discuss your ideas with your partner. Then find out the answer by turning to page 233.

Focus on Vocabulary *Phrasal Verbs*

1   There is at least one phrasal verb in each of the eight sections of the questionnaire on page 71. Underline the ones you can find and then compare your answers with another student's.

2   Eight of the phrasal verbs from the questionnaire are needed to complete the sentences below. Use a verb and a particle from the following lists to fit the meaning in brackets at the end of each sentence.

| *make* | *pay* | *single* | *sort* |
| *stick* | *turn* | *turn* | *write* |

| *up* | *to* | *off* |
| *out* | *for* | |

1   We had to wait 20 minutes before the coach .... (arrived)
2   The travel agent managed to .... the problem about my tickets. (solve)
3   When you arrive, ... the centre of town and you should find a hotel quite easily. (go in the direction of)
4   For some reason, the customs officer ...... me ...... from the rest of the group and examined every bit of my luggage. (separated from a group)
5   They can fine you on the spot for speeding, and if you don't .... , they arrest you! (give the money that you owe)
6   They ...... the music ...... so loud that we couldn't hear each other speak. (increased the volume)
7   I don't like spicy food so I'm .... salads and fruit. (eating only)
8   The travel company won't refund the deposit we paid so I'm afraid we'll just have to ...... the money .... (accept that you won't get it back)

STUDY BOX ▶ *Three-word phrasal verbs*

Do you *give up* on the local cuisine and go on a crash diet? (Questionnaire)

The general meaning is 'have no further hope for'.

Other common three-word verbs include:

get away with   to avoid punishment for doing something wrong

get on with   have a friendly relationship with someone

look out for   to watch carefully in order to spot someone or something

put up with   to tolerate something unpleasant without complaining

Note: These (and almost all other three-word phrasal verbs) are inseparable.

Complete these sentences using three-word phrasal verbs.

1 I don't think George is difficult to deal with at all. I've always ....

2 I decided to leave when the drummer moved in upstairs – I just couldn't ....

3 He had problems at school but luckily there was one teacher who never ....

4 She hasn't paid any tax in years – how does she manage to ...... ?

5 If you visit my home town, you must ....

Focus on Listening 1 *Sun Facts*

▶ Paper 4, Part 2

You will hear part of a radio holiday programme in which the benefits and dangers of the sun are discussed. As you listen, fill in the missing information for questions 1–9. In the exam, you will hear the information **once** only. Try to answer all the questions during the first hearing, but listen again if you need to check your answers.

SUN FACTS

Benefits

Improves blood circulation.

Good for skin problems.

Helps produce [**1**] which is essential for health.

Good psychological effects.

Doctors recommend spending [**2**] a day in daylight during summer.

Dangers

Sunlight is the cause of [**3**] % of skin cancers.

80% of sun damage is caused before the age of [**4**]

Skin cancer risk is doubled every [**5**] km nearer the equator.

Ultraviolet light can pass through water, [**6**] and thin clothing.

Protection

The skin is naturally protected from [**7**] % of ultraviolet light.

Use a sun screen for increased protection.

A tanned skin is [**8**] more protected than an untanned skin.

A tan lasts approximately [**9**] days.

Focus on Speaking 2 *Visual Prompts*

▶ Paper 5, Part 2

1 Work in pairs. In this activity, Student A and Student B will each talk about a different photograph showing some of the negative effects that tourism can have. For this task, you need to:

- **describe** the scene in the picture fairly briefly, suggesting who could be responsible, e.g. careless tourists, an irresponsible tour operator.

- **comment** on the problem this represents for the local people and for the environment, e.g. plants, wildlife, rivers, sea, air. If you can think of any way of tackling the problem or at least lessening its impact, mention this too.

Turn to page 234. Student A should talk about photograph A.
Student B should talk about photograph B.

You each have one minute to describe your photo. There is no need to hide your picture from your partner.

2 When you have both finished speaking, you should comment on what your partner has said, saying if you agree or disagree.

Text 2

1   Many people take out travel insurance when they go on holiday just in case things go wrong. What kind of things can go wrong when you travel? Work with a partner and make a list.

2   Each sentence below can be completed by adding a word to do with insurance. The first and last letters are given and, if you need more help, unscramble the letters on the right to find the answers.

1   The document which contains details of the insurance is the
    p........y.   LYPICOL
2   The money you pay to buy insurance is the p..........m.   MURPIME
3   When something goes wrong and you ask for money
    from an insurance company, you make a c..........m.   LICAM
4   A person who arranges insurance for you is an
    insurance b...........r.   KERBOR
5   The protection you receive is called insurance c.............r.   VECRO

UNDERSTANDING TEXT STRUCTURE
▶ Paper 1, Part 2

3   This is an introduction to the gapped text task in the CAE. In this task, a number of paragraphs are removed from a text and presented in a jumbled list. You have to decide where each paragraph fits.

STRATEGY

a   Before you try to do the task, it's important to know what the article is about. Ignoring the gaps for the moment, read the article and answer these questions.
1   What is the main subject of the article?
2   Where does the information come from?
3   What do you think the phrase *stark raving bonkers* (para. 1) means?
(Think about this again after you've completed the task.)

Holiday claims too hot to handle

Debbie Hill

MOST of us go a little crazy when we jet off on holiday but some, it would seem, go stark raving bonkers.

| 1 | |

These are just some of the claims the company has received in the past 12 months. The director, Jonathan Biles, said: 'One of our policy holders skied into a tree while on holiday and made a claim for injuries'.

| 2 | |

But what if you were in the Mediterranean in August and had had enough sun for the day? Take a dip in the pool, sit in the shade for a while – or phone your insurance company requesting repatriation because you are feeling 'a bit hot'?

| 3 | |

Some get into trouble even before making it to their destination. One policyholder made a claim because he and his wife had missed their flight. He failed to mention that his wife had been banned from boarding because she had a baby pig in her hand luggage.

| 4 | |

b Now choose from the missing paragraphs (A–D) to fill each gap. Look for grammatical or logical **links** between the paragraphs. To help you, there are key words or phrases in italics in the missing paragraphs.

A A holidaymaker, who was staying in a Spanish resort, chose *the last*. Not surprisingly, his claim was refused.

B According to *Mr Biles*: 'What *he* omitted to mention was that he was blind and in the process of testing a new radar system for blind skiers.' The company did pay out for his injuries but has since adapted the policy to exclude reckless endangerment.

C *Another couple* cancelled the holiday of a lifetime because their pet dog was feeling unwell. Their claim was accepted.

D *They* see giant rats eating through their luggage, let belly dancers stamp on their ribs and even lose their mother-in-law in the back of a stolen caravan. So says *World Cover Direct*, the holiday insurer.

TASK ANALYSIS

4 a Check your answers with another student.

b In paragraph D, *They* refers to *some* (short for *some people*) in line 1. This sort of link is called a **reference link**. Say what the other words or phrases in italics in paragraphs A–D refer to.

Recognising reference links like these is an important reading skill and is essential for the CAE Paper 1.

STUDY BOX ▶ *Common reference links*

		First reference		Later reference
1	Personal Pronouns			
	he, it, them, etc.	e.g.	*A holidaymaker*	He /It/They
2	Articles	e.g.	*a* new computer	**The** computer ...
3	Names/ titles	e.g.	*Jonathan* Biles	Mr Biles
4	Contrasts	e.g.	*One* holiday	**Another** ...
5	Parallel Expressions	e.g.	*Mr and Mrs Smith*	**The** couple
			World Cover Direct	**The** company

Focus on Writing *Letter of Complaint*

TASK

> You have just returned from an extremely disappointing holiday booked through Cheapotours Ltd. Read the holiday details opposite, the letter from the company which you received shortly before your departure, and the postcard you sent to a friend.
>
> Using the information, write a **letter** of complaint to the travel company, describing the problems you experienced. You should use your own words as far as possible.
>
> Write about 250 words. Do not include the addresses.

UNDERSTANDING THE TASK

1 The Part 1 writing task in the exam is based on two or three pieces of written information, which you must read very carefully. Read the instructions and underline the points you'll need to remember.

CONTENT

2 Now read the three pieces of information carefully and make a list, in your own words, of the things you need to complain about. If possible, compare your list with another student's to make sure you haven't forgotten anything.

Be clear about the **purpose** of your letter. What do you want the company to **do**? Would you like some form of compensation (e.g. a sum of money or a discount on your next holiday) or would you be content with an apology?

ORGANISATION

3 Decide the best order in which to mention the things on your list. You could decide to deal with them chronologically, for example, starting with the change to the flight. Alternatively, you could deal with them in order of importance. Think about grouping similar things (like hotel problems), so they can be mentioned together logically, e.g.
Among the problems at the hotel were ...

If you find yourself short of words, *don't leave anything out* – just find a way of saying things more briefly.

PERSONALISING

4 Add a few details, such as the country and town you went to, the name of the local representative and the cost of the taxi, to make your letter more realistic.

STYLE/REGISTER

5 The notes and the postcard contain some abbreviations, incomplete sentences and informal expressions, which would not be appropriate in a formal letter. Make sure you 'translate' the information you need into correct, more formal, English.

Examples:
rep	*representative*
took taxi	*I had to take a taxi*
cost an arm and a leg	*was very/terribly expensive*
food disgusting	....
(the local rep) is worse than useless	....

HOLIDAY INFORMATION

ITINERARY

14 Aug

changed

Depart 08.00 on Flight RX791.
Please report to check-in no later than 07.00.

Arrive 10.00
You will be met at the airport by the Cheapotours representative, who will escort you to your hotel.

rep didn't turn up! took taxi

14 – 20 Aug

only if you give yourself neckache!

7 nights at the Hotel Bella Vista. Standard room with <u>sea view</u>. Breakfast included
Escorted visit to flower market.

21 Aug

Depart 18.15 on Flight RX792.
Arrive 20.15

Hotel: Bella Vista

- 30 mins from the airport by car
- Lift to all floors. *broke down almost daily*
- Cable TV in all rooms
- 24 hour coffee shop serving snacks and light meals
- Swimming pool *food disgusting!*
- Watersports available at small extra charge, including windsurfing, sailing and snorkelling *cost an arm and a leg!*
- Optional sightseeing tours arranged

Dear Jan,

Greetings! As you can see from the picture, it's a lovely spot -- just wish I could say the same about the hotel! Loads to complain about and unfortunately the local rep is worse than useless. I think she goes into hiding when she sees me coming now! <u>Never</u> book through Cheapotours – they even switched the flight at the last minute so I ended up losing a day. Can you believe it?
Hope you have a better time on your hols. See you when you get back.
Love

Booking Reference: OXY 342D

Dear Holidaymaker.

We have pleasure in enclosing the airline tickets and hotel coupons for your forthcoming holiday. Please note that for operational reasons it has been necessary to make the following change to your travel arrangements.

Flights: Your outward journey will now be on Flight RH793, which leaves at the later time of 20.15 (arrives 22.15). The details for the return flight are unchanged.

We would like to take this opportunity of wishing you a very pleasant holiday.

Yours sincerely,

A. J. Thomas

For and on behalf of Cheapotours Ltd.

LAYOUT

6 Begin your letter:

> Dear Sir,
> I have just returned from a holiday in ......, staying at the Bella Vista Hotel, and I am writing to complain about a number of points.

For more guidance on the layout and structure of this kind of letter, and for some examples of useful language, see the Writing File pages 159 and 160.

Focus on Listening 2 *Customer Complaints*

▶ Paper 4, Part 3

You will hear David B Porter, one of the Customer Services Managers for the airline Qantas, talking about letters of complaint and praise that the airline receives. As you listen, complete the sentences by filling in the missing information with up to three words. You do not have to use the same words as the recording. You will hear the recording twice.

When the airline receives a letter of complaint [   ] and [   ] **1** take place.

From the reservations record system it is possible to find out which [   ] **2** handled a customer's bookings.

The airline can also find out what happened and why by checking records of actual [   ] **3**

In the case of a very serious complaint, [   ] **4** may be arranged.

Lately the most common complaint has been in connection with [   ] **5**

Another frequent complaint is about the performance of [   ] **6**

Mr Porter describes the case of a businessman travelling to South America to give a series of [   ] **7** and lectures.

On arrival at his destination, he found that his [   ] **8**

When letters of praise are received, the [   ] **9** concerned are interviewed positively.

English in Use 1 *Developing Skills: Register Cloze*

▶ Paper 3, Part 5

1 Can you complete this definition of register? (It was given on page 63.)

> Register is the .... of language used in a particular situation and it depends on the relationship between the .... and the .... , the kind of writing and also the subject matter.

2 Match the informal words and expressions on the left to the more formal ones on the right.

1	a little bit	a	depart
2	pricey	b	mad
3	lots of	c	rather unpleasant
4	roomy	d	slightly
5	bonkers	e	convenient
6	handy	f	a wide variety of
7	set off	g	spacious
8	pretty nasty	h	expensive

TASK

3 In this task you have to use information from one text to complete another text, which has been written for a different audience and purpose.

You work for a travel company. A colleague of yours has recently written an informal report on some new accommodation which your company intends to include in its new brochure. You have to complete the brochure.

a Read through the informal report and the brochure descriptions. What is the **purpose** of each piece of writing? How are they different in **style**?

b Use the information to complete the brochure descriptions by writing the missing words in the spaces provided on the right. Use no more than **two words** in the first description, and **one word** in the second. The words which you need do not occur in the informal report.

CONFIDENTIAL REPORT

The Palm Hotel

Quite a nice hotel, if a bit on the small side, in the new town. Handy for the shops and it only takes 7 minutes to walk to the beach (I timed it!). The rooms have twin beds and most have a balcony. You get a glimpse of the harbour from the terrace (if you've got good eye-sight!) There's no hotel restaurant as such, but you only have to walk a short way to find plenty of local eateries. The one drawback I think it's worth mentioning is that with all the restaurants and bars, the centre of town does get pretty noisy at night (and into the early hours).

Seagull Studios

Three self-catering studios for the budget end of the market. They're down the road a bit from the Palm, so it's a bit of a trek into town if you miss the bus (every 60 mins). Every studio has twin beds (with toilet and shower) and a tiny balcony (looking on to the road). The so-called kitchenette has a mini cooker and fridge, and not much else – so make sure you warn people that they shouldn't expect to do any gourmet cooking!

Signed:

T Rowland

Palm Hotel

A pleasant, small hotel, which (**0**) .... in the newer part of town, a convenient (**1**) .... the shops and the beach. There are 15 rooms, all (**2**) .... are twin-bedded, and most have balconies with a (**3**) .... the picturesque harbour. Although the hotel has no restaurant, there is a wide (**4**) .... places to eat, all (**5**) .... few minutes' walk. (**6**) .... its central position, we do (**7**) .... this accommodation for those looking for peace and tranquillity.

0 *is situated*
1 ....
2 ....
3 ....
4 ....
5 ....
6 ....
7 ....

Seagull Studios

A little (**8**) .... down the road from the Palm Hotel, three twin-bedded self-catering studios, (**9**) .... with its own en-suite toilet and shower, and also a private balcony. The kitchenettes are basically (**10**) .... with a small cooker and fridge but are not (**11**) .... for preparing full-scale meals. There is an (**12**) .... bus service into town.

8 ....
9 ....
10 ....
11 ....
12 ....

English in Use 2 *Developing Skills: Structural Cloze*

▶ Paper 3, Part 2

1 **Read the text quickly and answer these questions.**
   1 What is the text about – in one word?
   2 What mistake do a lot of people make?
   3 Why is this a mistake?

STRATEGY

2 **Complete this advice on tackling this task. (The answers are on page 233.)**
   1 Think about the ...... of word which is needed in each space.
   2 Make sure your answer is ...... correct and makes ...... in the context.

3 **Complete this newspaper article by writing one word in each space. The first answer has been given as an example.**

It's in the bag – but does it need to be?

Now that the holiday season is **(0)** ......*under*...... way, airport travellers can be entertained **(1)** .... one of the summer's most familiar sights: revolving swimwear. Many of the enormous suitcases on luggage carousels give up the struggle to stay closed, spilling **(2)** .... contents across the moving rubber belt. The standard weight allowance **(3)** .... most flights is 20 kg for checked-in luggage, plus **(4)** .... further 5 kg as hand baggage. **(5)** .... is more than enough for a two-week supply of T-shirts and paperbacks.

(6) .... millions of us persist in a back-breaking exercise that involves emptying almost **(7)** .... entire wardrobe into a suitcase, paying porters and taxis to transport our luggage, hunting desperately **(8)** .... trolleys at busy airports, and arguing with cabin crew **(9)** .... how much **(10)** .... be carried on board. And that's before we have to work out **(11)** .... to carry back the souvenirs we buy on holiday.

Large stuffed animals, life-size sculptures and birds in cages are just **(12)** .... of the more challenging items that passengers **(13)** .... attempted to bring back from holiday, says a spokesman **(14)** .... the International Air Transport Association.

The best advice is old but trusty: take half as much luggage and twice as much money as you think you **(15)** .... need. You can always wash your shirt abroad, but you won't find a branch of your bank.

▶ **Question 6**

A linking word is needed here. Should it show addition or contrast?

▶ **Question 8**

This is a dependent preposition – find the verb, which appeared earlier.

▶ **Question 13**

Think carefully about the tense which is needed here.

6 ▶ Language Matters

'A man who is ignorant of foreign languages is ignorant of his own.'
Johann Wolfgang von Goethe (1749–1832)

Lead-in

How much do you know about these languages? Answer the questions by choosing from the languages in the box. Some languages may be chosen more than once, and some may not be chosen at all. Check your answers on page 233.

Which language ...
1 is spoken by the greatest number of people as their first language or mother tongue?
2 is the official language for most people?
3 is only one of 15 major languages (and 830 other languages and dialects) spoken in one country?
4 can be written vertically or horizontally?
5 has 63 forms of the present tense and different words for falling snow, newly fallen snow and snow on clothes?
6 has no irregular verbs?
7 has 283 irregular verbs?
8 is spoken in parts of the USA, Canada, Russia and Greenland?

Hindi
English
Spanish
Eskimo
Esperanto
Chinese
Russian

Focus on Listening I *Which Language?*

▶ Paper 4, Part 4

Five people were asked the question: If you had the chance to learn a language you had never studied before, which one would you choose?

For **TASK ONE** match the extracts as you hear them with the languages, listed A–G. Write the correct letter in each box. Two options will not be needed.

A French   **E** Spanish
B Japanese   **F** Chinese
C Irish   **G** Greek
D Arabic

1		4
2		5
3		

For **TASK TWO**, match the extracts as you hear them with the reasons each person gives for choosing their particular language, listed A–G. Two reasons will not be used.

A to help their career
B because it would be a challenge
C for tourism
D to learn about the politics of a country
E because the language is attractive
F to understand the culture of a country
G to study classical literature in the original

6
7
8
9
10

Text 1

PREDICTION

1 Before you read the text, try to answer these questions. (The answers are on page 233.)

1 How many languages are there in the world today?
   a 40   b 400   c 4,000

2 Two hundred years ago, was the number
   a more?   b fewer?   c the same?

UNDERSTANDING TEXT
STRUCTURE
▶ Paper 1, Part 2

2 This is another example of the gapped text task that you were introduced to in Unit 5. Remember to find out what the text is about before you start the task. Read the main part of the article, ignoring the gaps, and answer these general questions.

1 Which language has recently died? Where was it spoken?
2 Who was its last speaker? Who still understands it?
3 Why are so many languages dying?
4 Why should we care about the death of a language?

The Day a Language Died

This week another language died; Carlos Westez, more widely known as Red Thunder Cloud, the last speaker of the native American language Catawba, died of a stroke at the age of 78. With him passed away the Catawba language.

Those who want to hear the war songs, the hunting songs and the religious chants of the Catawba can apply to the Smithsonian Institute where, back in the 1940s, Red Thunder Cloud recorded a series of them for posterity. Some earnest folk might even take the trouble to learn some of them by heart. But Catawba as something that lived and breathed and developed organically is gone for good.

Of the creatures alive on the planet, only Red Thunder Cloud's dog, which survived him and understood commands in no other language, still presumably has the sounds of Catawba rolling around his brain.

1 ☐

Less obvious, but no less harmful is the impact of one powerful culture upon our languages and ways of life. We are witnessing the spread of English, carried by an American culture, delivered by Japanese technology. We are also witnessing the increasing dominance of

a few great, transnational tongues: Chinese, Spanish, Russian and Hindi.

2 ☐

One of *those under threat* is Aore, the language native to Vanuatu in the Pacific. Like Catawba (until this week) it is spoken by that island's only remaining native inhabitant. So *it*, too, *is bound to die out.*

3 ☐

In the Americas too, 100 languages, each of which has fewer than 300 speakers, are on their last legs. North America, which once had hundreds of languages, has only about 100 languages left.

4 ☐

He was not actually born into the Catawba tribe, and the language was not his mother tongue. But he was a frequent visitor to the reservation in South Carolina and immersed himself in the language. The songs he recorded for the Smithsonian helped to start a craze for native American music.

5 ☐

Now *he* is gone and the language is dead – but what does it mean for the rest of us when a language disappears? To be the last remaining speaker of a language, like Red Thunder Cloud, or like Dolly Pentreath, who died in 1778, the last person to speak Cornish as her mother tongue, must be a peculiarly lonely destiny, almost as strange and terrible as to be the last surviving member of a dying species. But what the rest of us lose when a language dies is the possibility of a unique way of perceiving and describing the world.

6 ☐

His theory lacks scientific proof but one's own experience as a language learner is that to speak another language is to become another person. Anyone who has learned to speak another language moderately well will have had the sensation of discovering a new personality, with new facial expressions and gestures to match.

3   Now choose which of the missing paragraphs (A–F) fits each of the numbered gaps (1–6) in the article.

Look for a grammatical or logical link with the paragraph before, the paragraph which follows, or both. To help you, there are key words and phrases in italics.

A   Many other languages will share *its fate*; a large proportion of the languages of Ethiopia are used by tiny numbers of people. Two speakers of the Ethiopian language Gufat were fine until a well-intentioned language researcher took them out of their native jungle, whereupon they caught cold and died.

B   *For* speaking a language is a complex accomplishment. Understanding how we do it has occupied experts throughout the 20th century. Recently, Mark Pagel, a biomathematician in the Zoology department of Oxford University, has claimed that learning a language brings about permanent changes to one's brain.

C   It has become clear to all of us, over the past 20 years, how much damage modern industry can inflict on the world's ecology; how the destruction of the rainforest also brings about the death of untold species of plants and insects.

D   In *his* attempt to spread word of the tribe's language and culture, he came as far as Britain where, in 1992 he erected a tent in Edinburgh and gave demonstrations of story-telling.

E   With *their rise* as tools of culture and commerce has come the deaths of hundreds of other languages which are the losers in the competition for linguistic survival.

F   It was *for this reason* that Red Thunder Cloud's death this week made news around the world; if native Americans face a peculiar and formidable threat to their languages, Red Thunder Cloud was one of the first to recognise this and to try to do something about it.

TASK ANALYSIS

4   **a**   Compare your answers with another student.

b   Explain how the expressions in italics make links between paragraphs. For example, in paragraph 3, *Less obvious but no less harmful* refers back to the well-known problems mentioned in paragraph C: the *damage* (caused by modern industry), *the destruction of the rainforest* and *the death of plants and animals*.

VOCABULARY: PARALLEL EXPRESSIONS

5   Synonyms or parallel expressions are often used as a way of linking texts. Find two partners with similar meanings for each word or expression below.

1   under threat
2   rapid increase
3   harmful effect
4   attempt (*n*)
5   extensive
6   present problems (*v*)
7   disappear
8   important matter

vital concern	effort	cause trouble
pass away	at risk	wide-ranging
chief thing	vanish	bid (*n*)
destructive influence	swift rise	speedy growth
damaging impact	in danger	
lead to difficulties	broad	

Focus on Grammar 1 *Relative Clauses*

1 Relative pronouns

a Underline the relative pronouns in the following sentences.

1 Only Red Thunder Cloud's dog, which survived him, still has the sounds of Catawba rolling around his brain. (Text 1)

2 I'd like to hear the recording that they made of Red Thunder Cloud's war songs.

3 The Smithsonian Institute, where the recordings are kept, has an excellent library.

4 North America is a continent whose inhabitants used to speak more than 100 languages.

5 Her grandmother, whom we never met, is the only surviving speaker of Aore.

6 Anyone who has learned to speak another language will have had the sensation of discovering a new personality.

b Relative pronouns can be the subject or object of verbs. Say whether each relative pronoun in 1–6 is a subject or an object.

c Relative pronouns usually come immediately after the noun they refer to. Which of the relatives you underlined in the sentences above can only be used before a noun?

2 Defining and non-defining relative clauses

a Relative clauses, which come after the noun they refer to in a sentence, give extra information about a person or thing. Answer these questions about the relative clauses in the sentences in Exercise 1.

1 In three of the sentences, the relative clauses make it clear who or what is being talked about. They are essential to the meaning of the sentence and are called defining relative clauses. Which sentences are they?

2 In three of the sentences the relative clauses give extra information which is not essential to the meaning of the sentence. These are non-defining relative clauses. Which sentences are they?

3 Commas are normally used with one kind of relative clause. Which is it?

4 Can the relative pronouns in sentences 1 and 5 be replaced by *that*? Why/why not?

5 In one of the sentences the relative pronoun can be left out. Which sentence is it? Is it defining or non-defining? Is the relative pronoun an object or subject?

Check your answers by referring to the Grammar File on page 146.

b Make eight complete sentences by matching the sentence halves. Use a relative pronoun **where necessary**.

1 It's useless keeping a guard dog
2 She's the best friend
3 Don't make a promise
4 It's not a job for anyone
5 Don't worry, it's in a place
6 You're just the person
7 It's the film
8 I demand to speak to the person

| *who* | *which* | *that* | *where* |

a he'll never think of looking.
b won all those Oscars last year.
c I was hoping to bump into.
d is in charge here.
e can't stand heights.
f anyone could have.
g you know you can't keep.
h wouldn't hurt a fly.

c Complete the following sentences with a suitable relative clause, adding commas where necessary.

1 The car ...... will be the winner.
2 The hotel has no lift, so is unsuitable for old people ......
3 Anybody ...... will receive a reward.
4 The incident happened at a time of day ...... people around.
5 One of the best forms of exercise is swimming ......
6 The film ...... was really excellent.
7 There are lots of reasons ....
8 Unfortunately, I had to take a taxi ....

3 Reduced relative clauses (participle clauses)

a Look at these examples. The parts in italics are participle clauses, which have a present or past participle instead of a finite verb.

1 We are witnessing the spread of English, *carried by an American culture*.
2 Mark Pagel, *working at Oxford University*, claims that language learning alters the brain.
3 Carlos Westez, *known as Red Thunder Cloud*, died of a stroke at the age of 78.

They are a simpler, reduced, version of these relative clauses:

1 which is carried by an American culture
2 who works at Oxford University
3 who was known as Red Thunder Cloud

In the three examples, which type of participle has an active meaning and which has a passive meaning?

b Look at these sentences and decide if the verb in each relative clause is active or passive. Then rewrite it using a suitable participle clause.

1 The only surviving record of the language is the songs, which were recorded in the 1940s.
2 The film, which stars two of my favourite actors, has won the Palme d'Or at Cannes.
3 His car, which had been driven into a ditch by his brother, was a write-off.
4 The jury listened carefully to the witness, who stood nervously in the witness box.

c Complete the following sentences with a suitable reduced relative clause.

1 Examination answers ...... in pencil will not be marked.
2 Anyone ...... the door will set off the alarm.
3 Cars ...... will be towed away.
4 People ...... the plane were furious when they heard about the delay.

STUDY BOX ▶ *like v as, alike*

Like is a preposition meaning *similar to* and is used before a noun or pronoun:

> *Like* Catawba, Aore is bound to die out. (Text 1) Stop behaving *like* a child.

As can be a preposition meaning *with the character or function of*, e.g.

> Catawaba, *as* something that lived ...... is gone for good. (Text 1) He is thought of *as* an expert.

... or a conjunction and introduce a clause:

> Do exactly *as* I say. He got the job, *as* I thought he would.

Note: In American English, and in informal spoken British English, *like* can be used before a clause:

> Let's do it, *like* we agreed.

Alike can be an adjective or an adverb. It is used:

after a verb: The twins are so *alike* it's hard to tell them apart. *(adj)* All the students were treated *alike*. *(adv)*

after a noun: The new tax laws will affect rich and poor *alike*. *(adv)*

Fill in the gaps with *as*, *like* or *alike*.

1 Why do you always treat me ...... an idiot?
2 Gary bought her some flowers ...... he had promised he would.
3 He works ...... an interpreter for the United Nations.
4 Talk about clumsy! He was ...... a bull in a china shop!
5 The British and Japanese are rather ...... in their respect for tradition and good manners.

Text 2

Bill Bryson

1 Read this quotation from George Bernard Shaw, the British playwright (1856–1950). What do you think he means?

'England and America are two nations separated by the same language.'

2 Do you know the British English equivalents of these American words? If you need help, the answers are jumbled up below.

1 automobile	7 the fall	13 sidewalk
2 candy	8 flashlight	14 subway
3 closet	9 french fries	15 traffic circle
4 cookie	10 garbage	16 vest
5 drapes	11 gasoline	17 vacation
6 elevator	12 rest room	18 zero

> rubbish   lift   waistcoat   petrol   autumn   sweets   torch
> Underground   car   holiday   pavement   chips   nought
> curtains   roundabout   biscuit   cupboard   WC

MULTIPLE CHOICE QUESTIONS
▶ Paper 1, Part 3

3 Read the following book review and then answer the multiple choice questions 1–6 on the next page.

US and them

KEITH WATERHOUSE thanks America for some fine words

MADE IN AMERICA
by Bill Bryson, Secker

It is just not true that Britain and America are two countries separated by a common language – we are separated by two different ones. For, while Americans are mistaken in believing that we pronounce 'potato' differently from them, we do say a good many things they don't say, and vice versa. Every English writer who has ever had a book published in the US has suffered his *lifts* being altered to *elevators*, his *cars* to *automobiles*.

We have been assimilating American words and expressions into our vocabulary ever since the first settlers arrived in New England in the 17th century – and often without our being conscious of where we picked them up.

That is the argument Bill Bryson puts forward in this fascinating ride along the highway of the American language.

For example, did you know that when we *hold our horses, face the music* or *bark up the wrong tree* we are talking American? On the other hand, there are a fair number of old English words still much in use across the Atlantic, but now thought of as Americanisms here – *the Fall* for *autumn, zero* for *nought, closet* for *cupboard*.

The fun of this book is that it follows America's social progress alongside the development of the nation's language. For the two are inseparable. Each vigorous leap ahead – air conditioning, central heating, the skyscraper, the telephone, radio, television – brought its own crop of colourful new words.

Thus with the birth of the Model T Ford, terms like *traffic jam, rush hour*, and *gridlock* could not be far behind. When the railways pushed out into the suburbs, the suburbs became – new word – *suburbia*, and the business types riding into town became – new word – *commuters*.

Bryson's book is full of facts that not a lot of people know. The term 'Dixie'

(as in Dixieland jazz), for example, comes from the French *dix* on southern $10 bills.

It has to be said that, although the Americans put colour into the language, one of the colours was grey. Following the pioneers – who gave us such words as *department store, shopping mall* and *supermarket* – came the men in suits with their vision of *optimal positional isochromes* (good sites). Bryson has little to say on the American business school tendency to talk gobbledygook (an American word) like this or to use the longest form of a word available, such as *transportation* for *transport*.

He touches briefly but amusingly on the question of political correctness. It seems that last year someone noticed that Maryland's motto *Fatti maschii, parole femine* ('manly deeds, womanly words') was blatantly sexist. The problem was that the words were expensively carved into a lot of civic buildings and monuments. The ingenious solution reached by Maryland's legislators was to change not the motto but the translation. *Fatti maschii, parole femine* came to mean 'Strong deeds, gentle words'.

1 According to the reviewer, Americans
   A don't realise how different British and American English are.
   B can't understand British English when they hear it spoken.
   C have some inaccurate ideas about British English accents.
   D insist on making changes to the grammar in British books.

2 What does Bill Bryson say about the British?
   A They try to avoid using American expressions if possible.
   B They aren't always aware that they are using American expressions.
   C They find all kinds of American expressions fascinating.
   D They tend to use rather old-fashioned American expressions.

3 One of the book's important features is that it
   A describes how many American expressions came from French.
   B has a large section on the development of road transport.
   C includes a large number of colour illustrations.
   D shows the link between language and new technology.

4 The reviewer seems to dislike the American habit of
   A using complicated expressions where simple ones would do.
   B inventing so many different words to do with shopping.
   C constantly changing the words and expressions they use.
   D introducing so many slang expressions into business language.

5 What was the problem about Maryland's motto?
   A It was a difficult idea to translate from the Latin.
   B The original translation had been incorrect.
   C The original translation was no longer acceptable.
   D The new translation had to be carved on so many buildings.

6 What is the reviewer's general opinion of Bill Bryson's book?
   A He disagrees with the book's main argument.
   B He thinks the book is very readable but not completely accurate.
   C He doesn't think the book covers the subject in enough detail.
   D He finds the book enjoyable and informative.

Note: For the exam, you don't need to know American English or American spelling. However, if you learnt American English, you can use it, provided you do so consistently.

Focus on Vocabulary

IDIOMS

1 **The following idioms occur in the texts in this unit. Use them to complete the sentences below, making any necessary changes, and then match them to the meanings on page 88.**
   to be on one's last legs (Text 1)   to hold your horses (Text 2)
   to bark up the wrong tree (Text 2)   to face the music (Text 2)

   1 If my tutor ever finds out that I've been skipping lectures so I can rehearse with the band, I'll really have to ....
   2 ...... ! What's the rush? I haven't even told you how to get there yet.
   3 I need to replace my car. The engine's ....

4 If the police think I had something to do with the burglary, they're ....

a to direct one's efforts in the wrong way; have the wrong idea about something

b about to die, stop functioning

c to face up to blame or punishment for your actions

d to stop or wait before acting hastily

PHRASAL VERBS

2 a The phrasal verbs below come from the texts in this unit. Use them to complete the sentences.

bring about   put forward   pick up   die out   think of   touch on

1 Can you think of any traditional customs from your culture that have ...... in recent years? (disappeared)

2 Who is ...... as a modern hero/heroine in your country? (considered)

3 Which piece of modern technology has ...... the biggest changes in our lives? (caused to happen)

4 In your culture, is it acceptable to ...... the subject of religion in general conversation? (mention briefly)

5 What are the best ways of ...... a language if you don't want to study formally? (learning)

6 Can you ...... any arguments for abolishing examinations completely? (propose, suggest)

b Discuss the questions with another student.

Focus on Speaking 1 *Proverbs*

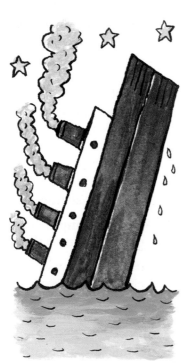

Work in pairs to do these exercises.

a **The seven proverbs below come from different cultures. Discuss what each one means. If you and your partner speak different languages, tell each other about any similar proverbs in your own language.**

1 A word is not a bird; once flown you can never catch it. (Russian)

2 The other man's bread tastes sweeter. (German)

3 When the ship has sunk everyone knows how she could have been saved. (Italian)

4 Talk does not cook rice. (Chinese)

5 Don't judge a book by its cover. (English)

6 Never promise a fish until it's caught. (Irish)

7 To the bad driver, the mules are always to blame. (Greek)

b **Choose two of the proverbs and think of real life situations to illustrate them. Do not use the same words as the proverb. For example:**
You can't make an omelette without breaking eggs. (English/French)
'If you reorganise the company to make it more efficient, some people will unfortunately lose their jobs.'

c **Take it in turns to describe one of your situations to other students in the class and see if they can identify the proverb it illustrates.**

Focus on Grammar 2 *Comparison*

I Underline the expressions of comparison in these extracts from Texts I and 2.

1 In the Americas, 100 languages have fewer than 300 speakers.
2 To be the last remaining speaker of a language ... must be a destiny almost as strange and terrible as to be the last surviving member of a dying species.
3 Less obvious, but no less harmful, is the impact of one powerful culture upon our languages and ways of life.
4 ... the American tendency to use the longest form of a word available, such as *transportation* for *transport.*

2 Comparatives and superlatives

Do the following exercise to test yourself. Then check in the Grammar File, page 137, where the rules and exceptions are explained.

Correct the mistakes in these sentences.

1 Oxford boasts the ancientest university in England.
2 Learning English is more easy than learning Japanese.
3 People seem to travel more and more far these days.
4 He did more badly than me in the exam.
5 Andalucia is the dryest region of Europe in summer.
6 Less people speak Portuguese than Spanish.

3 Qualifying comparisons

The following expressions can be used with comparisons to qualify comparatives.

> *hardly any   slightly   (quite) a bit   a lot*
> *considerably   a great deal   far   (very) much*

Complete these sentences using a suitable qualifier and adjective so that they express the ideas given.

1 Your written work has improved since last term, but not by much.
   Your written work is only *slightly better than* .... last term.
2 Frank is 61, and his new wife is 43.
   Frank's new wife is ...... him.
3 Tom is a fantastic actor, but John is terrible.
   John is a ...... Tom.
4 The train costs £90 and the plane costs £95.
   The train is ...... the plane.
5 It would be useful to learn Japanese, whereas Catawba wouldn't be useful at all.
   Japanese would be a .... Catawba.

6 The USA has a population of over 200 million compared with Britain's 60 million.
   Britain has ...... people than the USA.

4 *as (adjective/adverb) as ...*

a This structure can be used to compare things that are alike in some way, e.g.

> He was as busy as me. / He was as busy as I was.

The negative form is *not as ... as* or *not so ... as*, e.g.

> Learning Japanese wasn't as/so hard as I expected.

The structure can be used with *much/many*, e.g.

> We weren't given as much time as we needed.
> Japanese hasn't got as many irregular verbs as English.

A special word order is sometimes used with nouns, e.g.

> This is as good a time as any.
> It's not such an easy language as I was led to believe.

The following expressions can be used to qualify comparisons with *as ... as*:

> *just   (not) nearly   not quite   twice/five times,* etc.

e.g. His latest film isn't nearly as good as his last one.
There are 10 times as many speakers of X as there are of Y.

b Work in pairs. Compare each pair in Column A according to the topic in Column B. Make true sentences using *(not) as ... as ...* .

A	B
1 You/a member of your family	tidiness
2 Two animals	lifespan
3 Your language/English	the sound of the language
4 Reality/your expectations	a test/exam you've taken

5 Use structures from Exercises 3 and 4 to compare each pair in A, according to the topics in B.

A	B
1 Two films you've seen recently.	plot; production
2 Two subjects at school.	difficulty; relevance
3 Two places you know well.	beauty; things to do
4 Two sports/hobbies you've tried	challenge; disadvantages
5 Present/past	your appearance; your abilities

Focus on Speaking 2 *Visual Prompts*

▶ Paper 5, Part 2

1   a   Work in pairs. In this activity, Student A and Student B will each look at a different cartoon. The two are related in some way. You each have one minute to describe what your cartoon shows. (Don't show them to each other.)

         Student A should turn to the cartoon on page 236.
         Student B should turn to the cartoon on page 239.

     b   When you have both finished, discuss a) what is similar about the situations and the problem in the two cartoons and b) what are the differences.

2   a   Now look at each other's cartoons and talk in more detail about what message each cartoon is trying to convey. One cartoon has an important message for language learners. What is it?

     b   Have you ever had an experience like either of the situations in the cartoons? If so, tell your partner about it.

Focus on Listening 2 *Critics' Choice*

▶ Paper 4, Part 3

     a   You will hear part of a discussion between a group of film critics about three recently released films based on plays. Read through the sentences before you listen. What do you know about the plays that are mentioned? Have you seen any of them?

     b   For questions 1–10, complete each of the statements using up to three words. You will hear the recording twice.

Alan thinks the film version of *Hamlet* works [**1**] the play.

Two aspects of the film that impressed him are the acting and the [**2**]

However, he criticises the [**3**] which he feels is too intrusive.

Although *The Crucible* is about an event that took place 300 years ago, Beryl thinks it still has [**4**]

Arthur Miller wrote the original play of *The Crucible* in response to [**5**] in America in the 1950s.

Beryl praises the director for obtaining [**6**] from a young cast.

Charlotte thinks that re-releasing old films like *His Girl Friday* is [**7**]

In this film, the hero's first main problem is to stop his ex-wife [**8**] an insurance salesman.

The added complication is that he needs her to continue working [**9**]

Charlotte believes the film has probably survived so well because of [**10**]

Focus on Writing *Review*

▶ Paper 2, Part 2

TASK

> You have been asked to write a short film review for a school/college magazine. Choose any film which you think might be of interest to your fellow students. The film can be in any language and it can be of any type: comedy, thriller, science fiction, romance, historical drama, etc.
>
> Your brief is to include a clear description of the story/contents, to comment on what you think the most successful and least successful features are, and to give an overall recommendation. Write about 250 words.

CONTENT

1 a Make a list of three or four possible films. They don't have to be new films though it is helpful if you have seen them recently, and you don't have to have enjoyed them. Sometimes it's easier to pinpoint what you don't like about something than what you like!

  b Work with one or two other students. Take it in turns to describe the films on your list and say what you like or dislike about them. This should help you decide which it will be easiest to talk about. Ask your colleagues which film they'd be most interested to read about.

ORGANISATION

2 a Having chosen a film to review, look at the instructions again and underline the three parts of the task.

  b Read the notes on reviews in the Writing File (pages 167–168), and study the example film review and Useful Language section. Highlight expressions and topic vocabulary that you might want to use.

  c Make notes for each of the main sections, and when you're satisfied that you've covered all the main points and given a balanced account of the film's strengths and weaknesses, begin the final version.

STYLE/REGISTER

3 Look through all the example reviews in the Writing File and notice the slightly different styles. Think about the **readers** of your review (age? interests?) and try to speak directly to them. Make sure you start and finish in a clear, memorable way.

KEY STRUCTURES

This is an opportunity to use relative and participle clauses, structures which are typical of reviews. (See Focus on Grammar 1, page 84.)

English in Use I *Developing Skills: Spelling & Punctuation*

▶ Paper 3, Part 3

1 In this task you have to find a number of spelling and punctuation mistakes in a text. Don't forget the general task procedure:
  • Read the text quickly for general understanding.
  • Read it again very carefully, line by line, so you don't miss any mistakes.

2 Make sure you know the rules of punctuation in the Study Box on page 92.

STUDY BOX ▶ *Punctuation*

Basic features to check for:

1 Capital letters at the beginning of sentences

for the names of people, cities, days, months, etc.

2 Full stops/Question marks at the end of sentences

3 Commas to separate words, e.g. *a long, hot, exhausting walk*

to separate phrases, e.g. *In the meantime, let's sit down*

to separate clauses, e.g. *As I was late, I took a taxi.*

4 Apostrophes to indicate a missing letter, e.g. *it's; can't*

to show possession, e.g. *John's car; The teachers' staffroom*

(but **note:** *The cat is in **its** basket.*)

These punctuation marks always come in pairs. Check **both** are present.

1 Commas around non-defining relative clauses, e.g. *John, who's ill, stayed away.*

around phrases/clauses in the middle of sentences, e.g. *The suspect, a 40-year-old man, is in custody. It's best, I think, to wait and see.*

2 Quotation marks indicating direct speech, e.g. *'Have you seen my bag?' she asked.*

3 Brackets containing extra, non-essential information, e.g. *Myanmar (formerly Burma)*

---

3 In most lines of this text there is either a spelling or a punctuation error. For each line (1–16), write the correctly spelled word or show the correct punctuation in the space on the right. Three lines are correct. The task begins with three examples.

TYPOGRAPHY

Have you ever wondered why you have stopped reading something?	**0** ✓
It might not neccessarily be that the content is boring, but that the	**0** *necessarily*
layout of the type is not designed effectively causing your eyes	**0** *effectively,*
to tyre. Whilst reading, we concentrate on the content of the	**1** ......
words and rarely consider the seperate letters, yet the way these	**2** ......
letters are formed and are spaced is important. If all the letter	**3** ......
forms were different they would become hard to read. Therefore,	**4** ......
letters of the alphabet are formed into sets called *typefaces* which	**5** ......
have the same characteristics.	
• Try taking a peace of paper and covering the bottom half of	**6** ......
the line of type. You should be able to read it quite clearly.	**7** ......
If you cover the top half, it is not quiet so easy. Studies have	**8** ......
shown that the readers eye travels along the top of the characters	**9** ......
and it is for this reason that lines set in upper case (large letters	**10** ......
are harder to read.	
• The widht of a line should average 50–70 characters for	**11** ......
maximum readability.	
• Too much type and not enough white space have the affect of	**12** ......
making the page more difficult to read.	
These are just three of the rules of type It is important that any	**13** ......
document you send out, whether it is a personal letter or a glossy	**14** ......
advertising brochure conveys the message you wish to get across.	**15** ......
Effective use of type will insure that your message gets read.	**16** ......

English In Use 2 *Developing Skills: Lexical Cloze*   ▶ Paper 3, Part 1

1 Talk to a partner. What is 'body language'? What examples of body language can you think of?

2 Read the text quickly and answer these questions:
  1 When can our body language be a disadvantage?
  2 The text describes a situation when changing one's body language could be helpful? What is it?

3 Now read the text more carefully and choose the word A, B, C or D which you think best fits each space. The first answer has been given as an example.

Body Language Get your message across – without saying a word!

Have you ever wished you could (0) .... someone's mind? Well you can – by watching their body movements. Body language has been studied since the 50s, when US scientist Ray L Birdwhistell began writing about 'kinesics' – the study of body movements. He filmed conversations and then (1) .... them back in slow (2) .... to examine gestures, expressions and (3) .... . Every day we use our bodies to send messages – nodding instead of saying 'yes', or (4) .... to say 'hello'. But even when we don't want people to know how we're feeling, certain things may still (5) .... the truth. When we (6) .... a lie, our bodies often give the (7) .... away when we blush or (8) .... eye contact, swallow or cover our mouth with our hand.

You can also use body language to your (9) .... . For example, if you're always the last to be picked for a sports team, take (10) .... of these tips.
- Stand with your feet slightly (11) .... and with your hands on your hips. This will make you look stronger, fitter and much more athletic.
- (12) .... jogging on the (13) .... or limbering up – it gives the message that you can't wait to get on the pitch.
- (14) .... your team mates right in the eye and smile. But don't (15) .... them a huge fixed grin or they'll think you're desperate.

▶ **Question 4**

All these words can be used to describe movements of the hands. Check the exact meanings, then note them each down in a phrase.

▶ **Question 7**

This is part of an idiom meaning 'to reveal a secret'. Guess the answer if necessary.

▶ **Question 10**

Only two of these words combine with *take .... of*, and only one has the correct meaning.

▶ **Question 14**

Only one answer can be used with the sense of 'facing someone directly and without fear'.

0	A see	B hear	C read	D know
1	A turned	B rewound	C showed	D played
2	A motion	B speed	C time	D movement
3	A standing	B figure	C posture	D position
4	A shaking	B wagging	C clapping	D waving
5	A discover	B reveal	C inform	D explain
6	A say	B make	C commit	D tell
7	A game	B sport	C trick	D play
8	A removing	B avoiding	C escaping	D ignoring
9	A interest	B favour	C advantage	D reward
10	A note	B care	C attention	D advice
11	A away	B apart	C ajar	D aside
12	A Try	B Go	C Make	D Play
13	A place	B spot	C point	D ground
14	A See	B Watch	C Look	D Observe
15	A make	B do	C offer	D give

93

Language Focus 4 *Vocabulary Skills 2: Making the right choices*

Good vocabulary skills include:

- choosing the right word or expression to fit the meaning and register of the context
- making sure the word grammar and spelling are correct
- not overusing certain general words when more precise or interesting expressions would be better
- not using too many words when there is a clearer and simpler way of saying something
- only using slang or idiomatic expressions when you're sure they're absolutely appropriate

Work through the following tasks to practise your vocabulary skills.

I Frequently confused words

Choose the correct word to complete the sentences. Then compare your answers with another student and discuss the differences in meaning and use between the words.

Use a dictionary to check any you're not sure of and make a point of learning them.

1 The swelling should go down if you ...... (*bath/bathe*) it in cold water twice a day.
2 What other exercise do you get ...... (*beside/besides*) swimming?
3 Why don't you hang your ...... (*clothes/cloth(s)/clothing*) up in the wardrobe?
4 These measures are designed to tackle the current ...... (*economic/economical*) crisis.
5 Choices you make now will ...... (*effect/affect*) the rest of your life.
6 ...... (*At first/First of all*) I would like to thank everyone for coming tonight.
7 She has to ...... (*follow/attend*) language classes every morning.
8 Jane ...... (*proposed/suggested*) I wore my green dress but I thought it was too formal.
9 Her skin is highly ...... (*sensible/sensitive*) to the sun and she burns very easily.
10 It's a miracle no one was ...... (*wounded/injured*) in the accident.

Are there any other words which you sometimes confuse? Make a note of them.

2 Overused words

The words in italics tend to be overused in students' work. Suggest a number of alternative ways of expressing each idea.

e.g. We're looking for a *cheap* holiday (an inexpensive/a reasonably-priced/a bargain holiday; a holiday which represents good value for money)

1 He became *quite fat* in middle age.
2 They gave me an *expensive* present.
3 It's a *very interesting* subject.
4 Do tell us about your *journey*.
5 He's had many *problems* in his life.
6 Where can I *obtain* a student card?
7 I'm planning to *join* a course on car maintenance.
8 Give me a ring when you *reach* the station.
9 We *spoke about* our news for a few minutes.
10 *Maybe* I'll go to the cinema this weekend.

3 Redundant words

The following extracts from students' work contain words, expressions or longer sections which are unnecessary. Suggest how they could be rewritten more clearly and concisely.

A

> My cousin is a girl of eighteen years. She's got a round-shaped face with a pale complexion, and the colour of her hair is blonde. She's relatively short and normal concerning her weight. She has a wide range of varied interests including listening to music, figure skating and also drawing.

B

> In this essay I would like to talk about the kind of place that I would like to live in. Of course, one must first of all consider the various options in different places around the world. Personally, I must say that I would prefer to live in a quiet rural area rather than a city because it's important to me that I can see the sight of fields and trees from my window, and enjoy breathing the fresh air.

4 Wrong register

The following sentences contain expressions which are either too formal or too informal for the context. Identify the problem and suggest more suitable alternatives.

1 Have you met my beloved brother?
2 I'm really excited about this mystery tour we're going on. Anything could occur!
3 As a matter of fact, I'm writing to request further information about your training schemes.
4 The jobs he's currently considering are medicine and dentistry.
5 The salary is above average and the company will also provide travel expenses and perks.
6 She took me to a lovely restaurant situated in Oxford.

5 Common spelling errors

The following list contains the words which students most commonly misspell. Underline and correct the twelve which are wrongly spelt.

accomodation	guarantee	responsability
argument	immediatly	separate
begining	independent	specialy
committee	medecine	succesful
disappear	occured	therefor
embarassed	pronunciation	truly
fortunately	receive	wellcome
goverment		

Learning Focus 4 *Editing Skills 2: Polishing*

1 a What is the polishing stage?

This is when you look through the final version of your work in order to correct grammar and spelling mistakes and make any other final changes to improve your work.

b Why is it necessary?

It's not always easy to spot mistakes, especially if you are thinking about meaning rather than grammar. But careless mistakes will give the reader a bad impression and may cost you marks in the exam, so it's worth allowing time for a polishing stage.

c Improving your polishing skills

There are several things you can do to help yourself. In the first place, there are probably a few mistakes which you make frequently in your written work. It could be omitting definite articles, misspelling certain words, or misusing a particular tense, for example. Make a note of them and check these points first when you're reading through your work. Eliminate the predictable problems first!

After that, check your work systematically. What you look at will depend on the type of writing, but here are some suggestions:

CHECKLIST

Agreement	– Do all the verbs agree with their subjects?
Time	– Is your use of tenses correct for the context?
	– Is your use of tenses consistent (or do you sometimes slip from past into present in a narrative, for example)?
Articles	– Are definite and indefinite articles used correctly?
Sentence structure	– Are your sentences complete?
	– Have you used a variety of structures?
Linking	– Are pairs of clauses correctly linked?
	– Have you overused *and* and *but*?
	– Could you make more use of words and expressions like *while/whereas, despite, as a result* and so on to link ideas? Look back at Language Focus 3 to remind yourself about this feature.
Spelling	– Have you made any careless spelling slips? Check the rules for forming participles in the Grammar File, page 148 if necessary.
	– Have you used capital letters where necessary? (See the Grammar File, page 148.)
Punctuation	– Have you used commas, full stops, quotation marks, etc. correctly? (Check the rules in the Study Box in Unit 6, page 92.)

Vocabulary — Have you used the right word for the meaning you intend?
— Have you used more words than necessary to say what you want?
— If you've used an idiomatic expression, are you sure it's appropriate?

Register — Is the register – neutral, formal or informal – consistent throughout?

2 You have already had some practice editing other people's writing in exercises in the English in Use and Language/Learning Focus sections. The examples below, which all come from real life, contain a variety of types of mistakes. Use your knowledge and experience to identify and correct them.

A Wrong word!

1 Madonna arrived alone at the restaurant at 9 o'clock. She wore a nice red night-dress and showed a good suntan.

2 The Sydney Opera House is one of the most beautiful examples of modern agriculture in the world.

3 Applicants for this post should write enclosing a detailed post mortem.

(Language student's work, Australia)

4 Put the meat, smashed potatoes and vegetables into a ditch.

5 Thomas Edison was responsible for designing the electric lamb.

(Language students' work, Malaysia)

B Unintended meaning!

1 **If this is your first visit to Russia, you are welcome to it.**

(Hotel notice, Moscow)

2

JUST ARRIVED
Large Shipment of
WICKER FURNITURE
IT WON'T LAST LONG!!
Open 9–5 p.m. Monday to Saturday

(Nassau newspaper)

3 Underline the mistakes you find in the student's composition below, and then discuss with a partner the best way to correct them.

The Australian
The Australian is different from the Japanese and from my view there are both advantages and disadvantages in this. First, I remark advantages of the Australian.

When I lived in Japan, I was tiring after work every day because many Japanese companies compel us to work for many hours. But in most Australian companies employees finish work at 5 o'clock and only work five days a week. I believe that the Australian treasures each individual life and this is very important for the human beings.

Next, I remark disadvantages of the Australian. If I want to go shopping, I must go to a store till 5 o'clock. This is very inconvenient and it is one reason why there is no development of the country's economy. I think that personal freedom is very important in Australia and people insist to have time to enjoy their leisure activities.

Finally, I mentioned advantages and disadvantages of the Australian but I think the common factor between the two is that the Australian is a true individualist.

7 ▶ The Ages of Man

'Remember that as a teenager you are in the last stage of your life when you will be happy to hear that the phone is for you.'
Fran Lebowitz 1946–

Lead-in

1 a Look at the eight photographs below. How old would you say each person was? In his/her early/mid/late teens/twenties/seventies? (Each represents a different decade.)

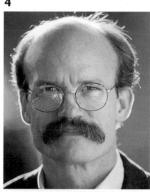

b Compare your guesses with other students. Were they quite similar? What factors did you take into account particularly? e.g.

skin, hair …

2 a What other changes does the process of ageing bring about? Think about:

*the senses (eyesight, hearing, smell, etc.)   appetite   posture
physical fitness and stamina   learning ability   memory*

b Are all these changes inevitable? Suggest ways of avoiding or disguising them.

3 We tend to expect certain types of behaviour from different age groups. What sort of behaviour and attitudes do you expect from

- a young person?
- a middle-aged person?
- an elderly person?

Text

SKIMMING

1 Read the first three paragraphs of the text quickly and answer these questions.
1 What is *taekwondo*?
2 Why are the pensioners learning it?
3 Have the classes proved popular? How do you know?

MULTIPLE MATCHING
▶ Paper 1, Part 1

2 a This task is similar to the one you did in Unit 5. You have to answer questions 1–12 by choosing from the list of names on the right listed A–G.

STRATEGY

Read through the questions and underline the key words. Remember that the questions often paraphrase words and phrases in the text. Before you read the text, think about the kind of information you need to look for.

List some examples of the following:
Question 1: security precautions in the home
Question 2: health problems that could be improved by doing *taekwondo*
Question 3: physical injuries that could occur while practising

Think of other ways of saying the following:
Question 5: street attacks
Question 7: concerned, anxious
Question 12: painful

b Skim the text quickly to get the general picture. You may be able to answer some of the questions at this stage.

c Scan the text to find the names listed A–G. Read these sections intensively to check the details.

Who ...		
has a lot of security precautions in their home?	**1**	
says taekwondo has improved a health problem?	**2**	**A** Master Vohra
has suffered a physical injury?	**3** **4**	**B** Yvonne
thinks the classes may reduce the number of street attacks?	**5**	**C** Sid
explains why the classes were first offered?	**6**	**D** Ethel
has a relation who was initially concerned about them taking part in the classes?	**7**	**E** Frank
mentions that they can break blocks of wood?	**8** **9**	**F** Ena
is said to be capable of fighting off a group of attackers?	**10**	**G** Doris
has only recently started learning taekwondo?	**11**	
mentions how painful it can be if you get hit while practising?	**12**	

DISCUSSION POINTS

3 Discuss these questions.
1 What was your first reaction to the idea of pensioners learning *taekwondo*?
2 How would you feel if an elderly relative of yours took up *taekwondo*?
3 Can you think of other solutions to the problem of attacks on old people?
4 Would you consider taking up *taekwondo*? Why/Why not?

Where old folks learn new kicks

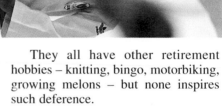

Andrea Waind meets Master Vohra and his taekwondo pensioners

Aaow! screams International **Master Vohra**, taekwondo black belt fourth dan (grade), who could demolish a house with his fists. Hey! answer the ranked warriors performing *chigi-chigi* – stepping forward, each shooting out a fist. Aaow! Hey! Aaow! Hey! **Sid**, 70, screams with a Korean accent, his extended fist shaking with the fearful force. And in the doorway, his dog trembles in Bill Baxter's arms. 'Don't worry,' says Bill, 'it's only Daddy.'

Taekwondo is The Way of the Fist and Foot. It turns fingertips into spearheads, the edge of the palm into a knife blade and feet into iron hammers. It is too dangerous to demonstrate upon human beings so practitioners smash bricks, wood and concrete, often as they fall through the air. There have been deaths in competition.

'We started the pensioners' class in response to a spate of attacks on old people here in Nottingham,' says Master Vohra's wife, **Yvonne** ('just a black belt second dan'), who regularly smashes concrete building blocks or roof tiles.' The pensioner classes are free – they pay only the cost of insuring themselves against injury – but some are so keen they also study for belts three times a week. **Sid**, **Ethel**, **Frank** and **Ena** are yellow belts.

'I use this fist, and my elbow to smash wood,' says **Sid**, sliding into the lotus position to rub his dog's ears. He admires his fist. 'Do you know, I was worried about tackling thugs but now I'd certainly use this.'

'You've got to be aggressive or it's no good,' says **Ethel**, 71, in her soft Norfolk accent. 'Oh, I'd use it on a mugger; give a good shout first to put him off his guard – Aah hoy! I used to be too scared to speak to people on trains. And it's done wonders for my arthritis.' She kicks Master Vohra in the groin and smiles; it is comforting to be able to make an International Master wince.

The shiny floor thuds to *ap-chagi* (kicking). The movements are thousands of years old, devised by peasants to knock armed noblemen off their horses. A speciality is the flying kick over ten bodies; pensioners start with two.

Ethel and her husband **Frank**, 67, are so keen they can't sleep before a grading and at 3 am are up practising techniques. **Frank** has a grazed arm which he explains he got by putting his elbow through a block of wood.

Ena has a plaster on the toe she hurt trying to break a wall. 'Sometimes we hit one other accidentally and it's agonising.' She prods the pressure point under Sid's nose. 'There are others just under the Adam's apple and the collar bone.'

They all have other retirement hobbies – knitting, bingo, motorbiking, growing melons – but none inspires such deference.

Doris, 68, who also does old-time dancing, has had two break-ins. 'I've got four bolts and chains, special locks, the windows screwed down. I'm a beginner – when I go out I take an alarm, but I want to dispense with that.

Families are stunned and delighted. **Ena**: 'My son was worried at first because he thought it was like karate, but it's not. It's fiercer.'

'I think this could have a direct effect on muggings,' says **Master Vohra**. 'They could kill. It's within their capabilities to get a black belt. When you can defend yourself you have an aura of confidence which deters muggers anyway,' says **Master Vohra**. 'We advise them to give up the purse – avoid a fight if possible – but they've got to the stage where they're scared of no individual and not worried about the gang of youths across the street. If three youths attacked **Ethel** she'd beat one or two and the others would be in shock.'

Frank and Ethel are just leaving. In their raincoats they look like ordinary pensioners, but underneath is indomitable spirit.

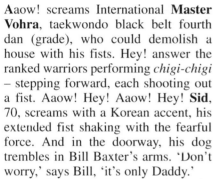

Focus on Writing 1 *Articles: An Introduction*

FEATURES OF ARTICLES

1 a 'You can't teach an old dog new tricks' is a saying in English. It means that as people get older they find it difficult to accept new ideas, fashions or inventions. The headline of the article on page 99 is a clever play on the words of this saying. What is the connection with the topic of the article?

b Now discuss these questions about the key features of the article on page 99.

Headline	1	What is the purpose of the headline? What are some of the ways writers try to achieve this purpose?
Sub-heading	2	What do we learn from the sub-heading?
Introduction	3	Where are we given information about the sport?
	4	What does the writer try to do in the first paragraph?
Paragraphing	5	When does the writer begin new paragraphs?
Ending	6	How does the writer round off the article?
Specific details	7	What specific facts and/or figures are given? Why do you think these have been included?
Quotations	8	How much use is made of direct speech? Why do you think this has been included?

STYLE/REGISTER

2 The style and register of an article depend on the type of publication it is written for, who the readers are and what the purpose is. Look at the text again and decide:

- who it was written for – a general audience, businesspeople, adults or teenagers.
- what the purpose is – to entertain, inform, persuade ...
- whether the tone is serious or humorous.
- whether the register is formal, neutral or informal.

VOCABULARY

3 The choice of vocabulary can help make an article more lively and readable. Try to use a precise word rather than a general one, and look for opportunities to use interesting expressions you know.

a Find the interesting expressions used in the text to express:
1 each *putting out* a fist
2 *several attacks* on old people
3 It's *had a good effect* on my arthritis.
4 Families are *surprised* and *pleased*.
5 When you can defend yourself, you *look confident*.
6 The pensioners have spirit which is *impossible to defeat*.

b Suggest more precise or interesting expressions for these words and phrases.
Example:
    a child: *new-born baby, infant, toddler, little darling, little terror,* etc.

1	a friend	3	go fast	5	tired
2	a good idea	4	be afraid of	6	angry

4 a Choose one of the following headlines and:
1 decide what the topic is, and who the article is aimed at.
2 write an explanatory sub-heading.
3 on a separate page, write an interesting introduction.

Why working-out may be bad for you

THE SECRET OF YOUTH CAN BE YOURS!

How to embarrass your children

Reaching for the stars

Your face could be your fortune

A little learning is a dangerous thing!

b Exchange your introductions with other students and see if you can match them to the correct headlines. Which introductions succeed best in catching the reader's attention and making him/her want to read on?

5 Write the rest of your article. Make sure that:
• the article is divided into at least three paragraphs.
• you develop your points clearly.
• you round off the article in a suitable way at the end.
• you include a few specific details and at least one quotation.
• you include some interesting vocabulary.

Focus on Vocabulary *Idiomatic Expressions*

1 a Divide these words into four groups according to whether they are:
1 part of the head/neck   3 part of the foot/leg
2 part of the hand/arm   4 injuries

*heel   Adam's apple   knee   sprain   skull   bruise   palm   elbow
throat   ankle   wrist   break   shoulder   chin   dislocation   thigh
jaw   nose   temple   funny bone   thumb   toe   graze   shin*

b The words in Group 4 can be used as nouns or verbs. For example:

Frank *grazed* (verb) his elbow.
The boy was covered in *grazes* (noun).

Use each injury as an adjective and match it to two parts of the body.

c Have you ever had any of these injuries? Explain what happened.

2 Choose parts of the body from Exercise 1 to complete the following idioms.
1 What's the matter? You've been giving me the cold ...... all week. Have I done something to offend you?
2 It's nothing to do with you. Stop poking your ...... into other people's business!
3 I tried to get her to sell her flat but she dug her ...... in and refused to move.
4 She was going to ask him to marry her on St Valentine's Day but she got cold ....
5 I wouldn't have gone to the theatre if my friend hadn't twisted my ....

STUDY BOX ▶ *used to + infinitive; be/get used to + -ing*

Look at these examples. The first is from the text on page 99.

> I used to be too scared to speak to people on trains. (Text)
> I didn't use to like jazz.
> I am used to working under pressure.
> You'll soon get used to driving on the left.

The verb *used to* only refers to the past and describes a habitual action in the past. In questions and negatives, the infinitive is *use to*.

The expressions *be/get used to* describe actions that are normal or customary. They are followed by an *-ing* form, and can refer to the present, past and future.

Find and correct the mistakes in these sentences. Some sentences contain more than one mistake.

1 Alvaro didn't used to speak any English.

2 Don't worry about me, I used to drive in these conditions.

3 Now that I work in an office, I use to wear a suit every day.

4 Did you used to playing football when you were a child?

5 Charles has become so rude, and he is used to being such a polite boy.

Focus on Grammar I *Present perfect simple/continuous*

1   The present perfect / past simple

a   Look at these sentences and underline the verb forms. Match each verb form with the correct use (a–e) below.

1 Taekwondo was invented more than two thousand years ago.

2 There have been deaths in competition. (Text)

3 It's done wonders for my arthritis. (Text)

4 There have been a lot of attacks on pensioners recently.

5 She's suffered from arthritis for years.

6 Before the Neighbourhood Watch scheme was set up, some old people felt too frightened to go out shopping.

a habitual actions and states in the past ......

b an action or event which was completed at a specific time in the past ......

c an action in the recent past with a significant result in the present ......

d an action or event in the past where the time is unknown or unimportant ......

e a habitual action or state which began in the past and still continues ......

b   Underline the correct form in each sentence.

1 Clara *lived/has lived* here until just recently.

2 *Did you see/Have you seen* that new teacher yet?

3 It *was/has been* a long time since we last *saw/have seen* each other.

4 I feel much better now that I *gave up/have given up* smoking.

5 Taekwondo *was used/has been* used in ancient Korea.

6 I *went/have been* there at least a dozen times so far.

7 I can't remember the last time that I *went/have been* to the theatre.

8 I *learned/have learned* to drive over ten years ago.

2   The present perfect continuous

a   Compare these pairs of sentences. Say what the differences in use between the present perfect simple and continuous tenses are.

1 a I've worked for this company since I left school.
   b I've been working for this company since March.

2 a He's typed three pages of his report this morning.
   b He's been typing his report this morning.

3 a We've gone there for our holidays every summer since we were children.

b We've been going there for our holidays every summer ...

4 a Dave has won several prizes this season.

  b Dave has been winning a lot of prizes.

5 a I've waited long enough! I'm going home.

  b I've been waiting for three hours!

b Which of the following statements are true about the present perfect continuous tense?

1 It emphasises activity rather than achievement or result.

2 It emphasises achievement or result rather than activity.

3 It suggests the completion of an action.

4 It does not make it clear if an action has been completed or not.

5 It tends to suggest recent activity where there is no time adverbial.

6 It is used with a time adverbial for repeated actions over a longer time period.

3   Practice

Rewrite these sentences using a present perfect form, without changing the meaning.

Example:

> We bought this house last year and we still live here.
> *We've been living here since last year/for a year.*

1 I go to judo classes every week. The classes started in September.

2 The last time we visited France was five years ago.

3 I'm a mess because I've just spent the morning painting the kitchen.

4 I have to write 250 words for this article. I've got 30 words to go!

5 I seem to spend a lot of time watching TV these days.

4   Stative versus dynamic verbs

a Can you explain what's wrong with these sentences?

1 That jacket is fitting you nicely.

2 These wall paintings have been surviving for more than 3,000 years.

3 When I was younger, I was preferring playing to studying.

Can you list any other verbs like these?

b Some verbs cannot be used in continuous tenses when they have a particular meaning. Compare these pairs of sentences and explain the differences in meaning.

1 a I'm thinking about next year's holiday.

  b I think that film's really boring.

2 a We're looking at wallpaper designs for the living room.

  b You look very slim in that dress.

3 a She's been feeling rather unwell.

  b I feel they're going to lose the election.

4 a We're having a party next week.

  b They have a beautiful Dresden dinner service.

5 a I'm seeing Caroline tomorrow.

  b I see what you mean.

There are reference lists of the verbs mentioned in **a** and **b** in the Grammar File, page 155.

5   The following text describes the feelings of Jason Hunter, a successful bond dealer, on reaching the age of thirty. Complete the text by putting the verbs in brackets into the correct tense. Choose from the present perfect simple or continuous, simple past or *used to* forms. Make any necessary changes to word order.

'I don't mind being 30 at all except that in work terms it does mean I pretty much **1** ...... (reach) the last stage of my career as a bond dealer. In the old days it **2** ...... (be) possible to carry on until you **3** ...... (be) 40, but in today's market people burn themselves out more quickly. The pressure on the trading floor is unbelievable and since my late twenties **4** ...... (find) it increasingly difficult to cope with the stress. And I don't really want to any more! Work **5** ...... (be) the most important thing in my life but that is changing as I get older.

For example, I **6** ...... (get married) recently and in fact I just **7** ...... (return) from my honeymoon in Europe. While we **8** ...... (be) there, we **9** ...... (go) to the opera and ballet several times and I **10** ...... (love) it. I **11** ...... (not have) much time for leisure and cultural activities up to now, but that's going to change from now on.

I also **12** ...... (change) in that I now try and see more of my parents than I **13** ...... (do) when I was younger. I hardly ever **14** ...... (see) my father when I was a child because he always **15** ...... (be) away at work, so in the last couple of years I **16** ...... (try) to make up for lost time.

When I **17** ...... (reach) my late twenties I **18** ...... (feel) the need to settle down and I **19** ...... (be) lucky enough to meet the right person. I really feel that I **20** ...... (mature) over the last couple of years and I think I can face the future with a reasonable sense of optimism.'

LANGUAGE CHECK ► *Word formation*

Fill in the missing parts of speech. All the answers come from the questions or text on pages 98 and 99.

	Verb	Noun			Noun	Adjective
1	......	demolition		8	......	secure
2	compete	......		9	pain	......
3	respond	......		10	aggression	......
4	press	......		11	......	special
5	retire	......		12	accident	......
6	defer	......		13	agony	......
7	......	deterrent		14	......	capable

Focus on Listening 1 *Attitudes to Age*

► Paper 4, Part 4

1   Five people, who each represented a different decade between teens and 80s, were asked how they felt about being the age they were.

For TASK ONE you have to decide how old each speaker is. Match the extracts as you hear them with the given ages, listed A–G. Write the correct letter in each box on the right

Which speaker is ...
A   in his/her eighties?
B   in his/her twenties?
C   in his/her teens?
D   in his her fifties?
E   in his/her early forties?
F   under ten?
G   in his/her late sixties?

	1
	2
	3
	4
	5

Discuss your answers and the reasons for them with a partner.

For TASK TWO, answer the questions by completing the boxes with the correct letter.

Which speaker ...
A   speaks most positively about their age?
B   seems surprised at how quickly they've aged?
C   has no regrets at all about growing older?
D   has noticed a change in other people's attitudes to them?
E   says they would like to change their age?
F   doesn't think they've changed much physically?
G   seems concerned about small changes in their appearance?

	6
	7
	8
	9
	10

Focus on Grammar 2 *Reported Speech*

For detailed information about reported speech, see Grammar File pages 147 and 148. There are also lists of reporting verbs on pages 154 and 155.

1 Reporting statements: verb + *that* clause

a Look at these examples of direct and reported speech. Underline the tense and vocabulary changes that occur in reported statements introduced by *that*. When is it not necessary to make any changes?

1 'I think this could have a direct effect on muggings.'
   Master Vohra said (that) he thought this could have a direct effect on muggings.

2 'You've got to be aggressive,' says Ethel.
   Ethel said (that) you've got to be aggressive.

3 'I've noticed the beginnings of a few wrinkles.'
   She said (that) she had noticed the beginnings of a few wrinkles.

4 'I'm taking the ferry so I won't be in Paris until tomorrow.'
   He told me (that) he was taking the ferry and wouldn't be in Paris until the following day.

b A variety of reporting verbs can be used to introduce a reported statement in place of *say*. Put each of the following statements into reported speech, using an appropriate verb from the list. Use each verb once only.

> *admitted   confirmed   boasted   announced*
> *explained   estimated   doubted   complained*

1 'This steak is as tough as old boots!' He complained that ...
2 'My husband is a superb cook.'
3 'We will definitely be getting married in June.'
4 'It'll cost at least £1,500 to fix the roof.'
5 'She's leaving to have a baby.'
6 'OK, I lied about where I was.'
7 'I don't really think that he needs help.'
8 'I couldn't finish my report because my computer crashed.'

2 Reporting questions

a Look at these direct and reported questions.

1 'Are you Turkish?'
   She asked me if I was Turkish.

2 'Are you taking the exam in June or December?'
   She asked me whether I was taking the exam in June or December.

3 'Where do you live?'
   He asked me where I lived.

Can you formulate rules for the following in reported questions?

- word order
- questions with *or*
- question marks
- sequence of tenses

b Carlos, a new student in your class, asked you these questions yesterday. Report them to a partner.

1 Where will we be taking the exam? *Carlos asked ...*
2 Have you been doing a lot of grammar in the class? *He wanted to know ...*
3 When did the new teacher take over?
4 Does he set a lot of homework?
5 Are you studying full-time or part-time?

3 Other reporting structures

To report orders, requests, suggestions and intentions, we use the structure appropriate to the reporting verb. The tense changes you noticed in reported statements do not apply.

a Match the verbs in A with the structures which can follow them in B. Some verbs can be followed by more than one structure.

A
1	He ordered	7	He advised
2	He recommended	8	He regretted
3	He asked	9	He insisted
4	He promised	10	He threatened
5	He suggested	11	He offered
6	He denied	12	He warned

B
a that I (should) do it.
b me (not) to do it.
c doing it.
d to do it.

b Change the following into reported speech, using an appropriate verb from the list above.

1 'I'll be more careful next time.'
2 'Don't touch that wire, it's dangerous.'
3 'I wish I hadn't got married so young.'
4 'Shall I give you a lift home?'
5 'You'd better put a bandage on that cut.'
6 'Don't be ridiculous! Of course I didn't lose the keys.'
7 'Why don't you leave the car at home and go by train?'
8 'You really must come and stay with us this summer.'

Focus on Writing 2 *Information Report*

▶ Paper 2, Part 2

FEATURES OF A REPORT	**1** Answer these questions by looking at the example report in the Writing File (**page 166**).

1 What do you notice about the way the report is organised?
2 The first section explains two things – what are they?
3 What is the purpose of the last section?
4 How would you describe the language used in the report?
   - personal or impersonal?
   - technical or non-technical?
   - formal or informal?
5 In the last section, underline three expressions which make the conclusions and advice a little less definite.

TASK

An English friend of yours is working on a series of articles called 'Young and Old Around the World' which looks at different towns and cities through the eyes of teenagers and senior citizens. She has written asking for your help, and this is an extract from her letter:

> What I want is some first-hand information about what it's like to live in your town from the point of view of the two different age groups. You would need to interview, say, ten people in each category on the main topics of public transport, entertainment and shopping, and write me a brief report. Could you also include a short introduction about your town and give a little summing up at the end?

Write your **report** in about 250 words.

CONTENT

2 Work with one or two other students to discuss the following points.
1 Look at the three topics you need to cover, and list as many facilities as you can think of which might be of interest to the two groups. Tick the ones available in your town.
2 Try asking other students a few questions about some of these facilities in their town. (There's no need to write these down.)

ORGANISATION

3 Remember these features of a report:
1 **Headings:** For the title, use 'Perspectives on (name of your town)'. The question gives you the three subheadings – what are they?
2 **Introduction:** (2 paragraphs) Say why you are writing the report, using expressions from the Useful Language section on page 167, and describe your town briefly (e.g. location, size, etc.).
3 **Conclusion:** This should provide a brief 'verdict' on your town, drawing on the main plus and minus points which have been expressed.

STYLE/REGISTER

4   Your report should contain a mixture of fact (e.g. what public transport services exist) and opinion (e.g. how reliable/cheap/convenient it is).

On the whole, it is best to avoid using the personal 'I' in a report. Instead of 'I think', use 'It seems to me', for example.

There are various ways of reporting your findings:

Your own observations: *There is a night club called X, which is popular with teenagers.*
Unfortunately, bus services stop at midnight.
A majority view: *Most elderly people felt/seemed to think …*
Individual comments: *According to X, aged 76, …*

For other useful expressions, see the Writing File on page 167.

Focus on Listening 2 *Young Achievers*

▶ Paper 4, Part I

You will hear part of a radio arts programme about child prodigies – children who have an exceptional gift or talent at an unusually young age. For questions 1–9, fill in the missing information.

You will hear the recording twice.

Vanessa-Mae's record sales are similar to those of _____ **1**

Her music combines _____ and _____ **2** and classical influences.

Vanessa-Mae appears to be extremely

_____ and _____ **3** in interviews.

She gave her first _____ **4** when she was 10.

A teacher said that, like Mozart, she has unusual

_____ **5** for her age.

Zara Long was the _____ **6** to compete in the
Olympic Games.

Zara now works as a _____ **7**

Many prodigies say they find it difficult to satisfy their

_____ **8**

Prodigies don't seem to be any more _____ **9** than
other children.

Focus on Speaking *Problem Solving*

▶ Paper 5, Part 3

1   What are the ideal ages for the following occupations? Work with a partner to match the occupations to the ideal age.

racing driver	14	
surgeon		25
gymnast	30	
marathon runner		30
judge	45	
airline pilot		50
footballer	65	

You can check the answers, given in a UK survey, on page 233.

2   Discuss with your partner the ideal ages for the following stages of life.
1   the age at which you start school
2   the age of majority – the age when you are legally an adult
3   the age at which you leave home
4   the age at which you have your first child
5   the age at which you retire from work

> Useful Language
> **Suggesting an opinion**
> *I think ...   I'd say ...   In my opinion ...   As I see it ...*
> **Agreeing**
> *(Yes) I agree with you (about that)*
> *That sounds right/reasonable   because ...*
> *(I think) you could be/may be/must be right*
> **Disagreeing**
> *I'm not sure I agree with you (about that)*
> *But surely that can't be right   because ...*
> *But don't you think that ...?*

English in Use 1 *Developing Skills: Discourse Cloze*

▶ Paper 3, Part 6

In this task, a number of phrases have been removed from a text. You have to choose the correct phrase or clause from the list below to fill each gap. Two of the suggested answers do not fit at all.

STRATEGY

a   First read through the text and answer these questions.
1   What is unusual about the village of Bama in China?
2   What explanation do local businessmen give for this?
3   What other reasons could there be?

b   Look at the example answer (0). Notice that it comes at the end of the sentence, following a comma, and gives extra information about the main facts. Question 1 is also like this. Remember that punctuation can give important clues about the kind of information to look for.

- Sections **between commas** give extra information. They may tell us more about the **subject** of the sentence in a relative clause starting with *who*, *which* or *that*, or in a phrase. They may also add a comment. Make sure you choose an answer which fits grammatically and logically (e.g. Q 2, 3, 5, 7).

- Sections **following a phrase in commas** are likely to be part of the main sentence. Check that this makes sense (e.g. Q 4).

- Missing sections **not following a comma** may complete a sentence. They may also be separate clauses – look for link words such as *and*, *but*, *when* (e.g. Q 6).

In remote spot Chinese guard the secret of youth

In Bama, in the Guanxi province of China, the concentration of centenarians, people more than 100 years old, is one of the highest in the world, (**0**) .I. . People in their 80s and 90s are also common, (**1**) .... , and still working in the fields.

Lan Boping, still going strong at 111, has some good news for those reluctant to forgo life's pleasures in the quest for long life. He has smoked heavily for decades, (**2**) .... , eats heartily and drinks a glass of fiery amber wine twice a day. Local businessmen are promoting this rice wine, which they call 'the spirit of longevity wine', (**3**) .... . But it is unlikely to catch on outside Bama since its ingredients include lizards and snakes as well as a secret blend of herbs and grasses.

Although Chinese researchers give a grudging nod of approval to the longevity wine, they also stress other factors that, (**4**) .... , are less exportable. The first is environment. The mountain air and streams are unpolluted (**5**) .... Heredity may also play a role. But the Bamans also offered a simpler explanation: plenty of exercise. Huang Masheng was born just 10 years after the invention of the telephone, (**6**) .... . She has always been active, still potters round in the garden and 'eats everything and anything'. She also makes sure her son, a mere 78, still does a full day's work in the fields. Huang now has a new job: helping look after her latest great-great-grandchild.

As for the 'spirit of longevity' wine, she says: 'I've never touched a drop of it in my life.'

A and the people of Bama face none of the stresses of modern life
B unfortunately for the enterprising wine producers
C unlike the beautiful scenery
D which has not yet reached her village
E as the key to long life
F most in robust health
G like other Bama centenarians
H which is one of the poorest regions in China

I according to official statistics

English in Use 2 *Developing Skills: Word Formation* ► Paper 3, Part 4

For questions 1–15, read the two texts below. Use the words in the boxes beside the texts to form one word that fits in the same numbered space in the text. The exercise begins with an example (0).

STRATEGY

In this task, it's important to establish:

- which **part of speech** you need to fill each space – noun, verb, adjective or adverb.

- what **meaning** makes sense in the context. For example, you may need to make an adjective negative, or you may have to choose between two possible suffixes -*ful* and -*less*.

► **Question 1**

You need to make two additions to this word so that the whole sentence makes sense.

► **Question 4**

Remember to make any necessary spelling changes.

► **Question 12**

You need to add a prefix here.

---

5 Five is a (**0**) *friendly* year. It is also a more serious, competent year. It is the age when special efforts are made to be (**1**) .... , but when there remains a (**2**) .... need for repeated contact with the (**3**) .... parent. The 5-year-old likes to help its parents and will (**4**) .... run simple errands for them. It innocently tells tales about its child companions, without realizing that it is being (**5**) .... to them. According to some schools of thought, 5 is age when childhood (**6**) .... deteriorates into adult sophistication. Clifton Fadiman wrote: 'All children talk with integrity up to the age of five, when they fall victim to the influences of the adult world. It is then they begin, (**7**) .... , to become actors. The product of this process is known as (**8**) .... , or you and me.'

6 Six is the year when reading becomes a (**9**) .... It is an (**10**) .... age, an age for thinking things out in one's head before performing an action. Books, stories, television and films suddenly become more (**11**) .... because of the child's expanding imagination. As so much more is going on inside the head of the 6-year-old, he or she often seems more (**12**) .... , compared with younger children; also more (**13**) .... and sometimes (**14**) .... . The 6-year-old sometimes dawdles where the 5-year-old would have rushed. Despite these changes, the 6-year-old child is still a (**15**) .... , if rather demanding, companion.

(0) FRIEND
(1) DEPEND
(2) POWER
(3) PROTECT
(4) HAPPY
(5) LOYAL
(6) BEHAVE
(7) CONSCIOUS
(8) MATURE
(9) PLEASE
(10) IMAGINE
(11) ABSORB
(12) OCCUPY
(13) APPREHEND
(14) HESITATE
(15) DELIGHT

8 ▶ Personally Speaking

'An optimist is a man who starts a crossword puzzle with a fountain pen.'
Anon
'A pessimist is a man who looks both ways when he's crossing a one-way street.'
L J Peter

Lead-in

1 a Work with another student to put the following words into three groups according to whether you think the word has 1) a generally **positive** meaning, 2) a generally **negative** meaning, or 3) a generally **neutral** meaning. Be prepared to explain your reasons.

adaptable	*ambitious*	*balanced*	*carefree*	*cautious*
cheerful	*considerate*	*contented*	*critical*	*disorganised*
enthusiastic	*generous*	*hard-working*	*imaginative*	*immature*
impatient	*inquisitive*	*insecure*	*irritable*	*lazy*
optimistic	*possessive*	*selfish*	*sensitive*	*shy*
stubborn	*tolerant*	*unfeeling*	*withdrawn*	

b Which adjectives in Group 2 have a negative prefix?

c How many adjectives in Groups 1 and 3 can you make negative using the prefixes *un-, in-* or *dis-*?

Focus on Listening *A Walk Through The Forest*

1 In this first activity, imagine you're going on a walk through a forest. Listen and read the following text. Be prepared to describe your forest to a partner.

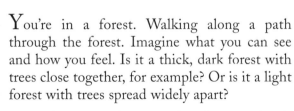

You're in a forest. Walking along a path through the forest. Imagine what you can see and how you feel. Is it a thick, dark forest with trees close together, for example? Or is it a light forest with trees spread widely apart?

Now what about the trees? Are the trees clearly separate from one another or are they growing in groups? Are they short or tall? Have they got lots of leaves or fruit or are they bare? Are you attracted to any one tree in particular? If so, describe it.

You continue down the path through the forest and suddenly you come across a bear. Think about this bear. What's it like? What colour is it? Is it large or small? Is it dangerous (perhaps a grizzly bear) or is it friendly?

Do you feel afraid? Do you face the bear or do you stay away?

Carrying on along the path, the next thing you see is a piece of pottery on the ground. What is it? A jug or a vase, maybe, or a bowl? Think carefully about the shape and the design. Is it plain or has it got a pattern on it? Is it whole or is it cracked or broken? Do you pick it up and take it with you or do you leave it where it is?

You continue on your way again and the last thing you see is a key on the ground. What's this key like? Is it new and shiny or is it old and rusty? How big is it? Again, do you pick it up or leave it lying there?

2   Work with a partner. Describe your forest and the things you saw there to each other. Listen to what your partner says and fill in the first column of the table below. You will be able to complete the second column after you have heard the excerpt from a radio programme which follows.

	Your partner's description	Interpretation
The forest	....	....
The trees	....	....
The bear	....	....
The piece of pottery	....	....
The key	....	....

Paper 4, Part 3

3   You will hear part of a radio programme in which listeners phoned in with their descriptions of the forest and what they had seen. The presenter then tried to interpret their descriptions and say something about their personalities.

When we join the programme, Dave, the presenter, is about to speak to the last caller, Chris. Complete the statements for questions 1–13 using a few words.

FOREST

Chris describes his forest as very [and | **1**] with a soft, friendly feeling to it.
According to Dave, this shows that Chris is [**2**] with his life. If things go wrong, he has plans he can fall back on.
The forest represents our life at the moment.

TREES

Chris saw a number of similar [**3**] trees with low-lying branches.
He probably has the sort of friends who are [and | **4**]
The trees represent our [**5**]

BEAR

Chris saw a grizzly bear, but it [**6**]
The bear represents a person's attitude to [and | **7**]
People who choose [**8**] tend to be very passive.

POTTERY

Chris described his piece of pottery as broken or misshapen.
Dave asks if he has experienced some [**9**] in his life.
The pottery represents our [**10**]
The more fancy in style the pot is, the more [**11**] we are.

KEY

Chris's key was old, long and heavyish.
This indicates that he's interested in the past and has a [**12**] which he enjoys using.
The key represents [**13**] we are.

4 Now look again at your partner's description of his/her forest in Exercise 2. Give your partner your interpretation of what they told you.

STUDY BOX ▶ *the ... the ... (comparatives)*

Look at these examples from the radio programme in Focus on Listening.

The smaller and *thinner* the pot, *the more* you would keep in your emotion.
The more elaborate the key, *the more* imagination you have.

This is a convenient and common pattern in English.

The + comparative word ... *the* + comparative word
   (more/less/-er)   *(more/less/-er)*

Notice that *the* **can be followed by both adjectives and adverbs.**

The faster he worked (*adverb*), *the more* mistakes he made (*adjective*).
The darker it became (*adjective*), *the more slowly* she drove (*adverb*).

Complete these sentences using the ideas in the radio programme.
1 The darker the forest, ... (unhappy/life)
2 The ... (small/cuddly) the bear, the more likely it is that you're non-aggressive.
3 The more fancy the pot, ... (romantic)

Focus on Vocabulary 1 *Phrasal Verbs*

The following phrasal verbs were used in the radio programme you heard in Focus on Listening. Match each phrasal verb to its definition (a–j).

1 If you *tune* in,

2 If you *pick out* one thing from a group,

3 If you *work* something *out*,

4 If you *fall back* on something that you know you can rely on,

5 If you *tick off* items on a list,

6 When you *put down* words or numbers,

7 If you *steer away from* a subject or an action,

8 If you *face up to* a difficult situation,

9 If you *fight it out* with somebody,

10 If you *eke* something *out*,

a you accept or deal with it.

b you use it when other things have failed.

c you argue or fight until one of you wins.

d you select it.

e you make it last as long as possible by using it carefully.

f you think about it and manage to understand it.

g you set the controls of a radio or TV so you can listen to a particular station or channel.

h you write them down.

i you avoid talking about it or doing it.

j you put a mark next to them to show that you have dealt with them.

Text: Part 1

PREDICTION

1   Read the statements below and try to decide if they are true or false. Discuss your ideas with another student.

1   Green dyes in sweets make people feel ill.
2   Food manufacturers think that colour dyes make their products more appealing.
3   The British like tinned vegetables to be a bright colour.
4   Both Americans and Britons like apples which are bright red.
5   There is no scientific evidence that colours can have an effect on the nervous system.
6   The colour blue can make us feel calm.
7   The colour red is used by fast food chains to encourage customers to stay in their restaurants.
8   People also judge a cleaning product like soap powder by its colour.

2   Now read the text and say whether the statements are true or false according to the writer. If you think a statement is false, be prepared to say why.

YOUR TRUE COLOURS

Seeing red can quite literally make you 'see red'. It can also make you eat faster. Colour influences the mind in mysterious ways, and those who wish to influence *you* – to make you buy their products, or work harder – often do so with colour. But you can make this process work to your advantage. Go through the spectrum with Paul Kerton and Deirdre McQuillan; then use our colour test to show you the finer shades of your personality and your temperament.

The marketing world is full of folklore about consumer reactions to colour: how, for example, too much green on a confectionery wrapper is a recipe for disaster. For years the food industry insisted that without its handy 'azo-' dyes the public would find processed produce unappetising. Yet colour preference can often sound like a mix of fad and cultural custom, especially when the French will eat grey tinned peas and beans, while the British will not, and we prefer green apples to the Americans' glossy red. However, there is more to colour than meets the eye.

This, at least, is the view of light researcher John Ott, who has discovered that colour may directly affect our nervous systems.

The idea that colour can affect the nervous system in some way seems strengthened by the fact that experiments have recorded raised blood pressure in red surroundings and lowered blood pressure in blue surroundings. Red evokes subjective reactions of increased energy and hunger; blue evokes tranquillity and relaxation. Whether knowingly or otherwise, the effects of seeing red have been cleverly exploited by fast food chains. As well as making people hungry, red and its close relation, orange, cause time to seem to pass more quickly and influence people to feel in a hurry. By using these colours, places like McDonald's create an atmosphere which increases the appetite but subtly dissuades the customer from hanging around for very long.

Colour has also been used to striking effect in the marketing of consumer products. A group of housewives was once asked to test samples of identical soap powder in three different boxes, one yellow, one blue and one a mix of blue and yellow. Extraordinary results ensued: the powder in the yellow packet was judged to be so powerful that some said it had damaged their clothes, while the blue was said to be so weak that it left stains behind: the powder in the mix of blue and yellow was assessed as just right. Yet the only difference was in the colour of the packet.

© *The Telegraph Sunday Magazine*

Text: Part 2

1 Read the instructions for the Colour Test below and then fill in the boxes with the names of your favourite colours.

BLUE **BROWN** **RED** **BLACK**

VIOLET **GREY** **GREEN** **YELLOW**

Test your personality

This is a shorter version of the full Lüscher Colour Test, developed over twenty years by Max Lüscher. The colours used were selected for their associations with physical and mental states. To find out what colour says about your personality, briefly study the colours above and then choose the colour which appeals to you most immediately. (Don't choose on the grounds of fashion or whether it does wonders for your hair.) Write this in the first box and then repeat the process with your second favourite colour in the second box, and so on until your least favourite colour is in the eighth box.

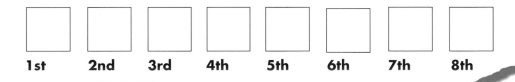

1st **2nd** **3rd** **4th** **5th** **6th** **7th** **8th**

© *The Telegraph Sunday Magazine*

2 Work with another student. Exchange your lists of colours and then turn to the main text on page 117. Read out the interpretation for your partner's two top colours and listen while your partner explains what your two favourite colours mean. Discuss how accurate (or not) these interpretations are.

MULTIPLE MATCHING
Paper 1, Part 4

3 Now answer questions 1–8 by choosing from the colours in sections A–H of the text. Some choices may be required more than once. When more than one answer is required, these may be given in any order.

Which colour ...	
represents health?	**1** ......
is often popular with teenagers?	**2** ......
indicates someone who wants to lead a quiet, untroubled life?	**3** ......
represents two contrasting characteristics?	**4** ...... **5** ......

Which colour are you likely to have towards the beginning of your list ...

if you are very energetic and ambitious?	**6** ...... **7** ......
if you are happy with your life as it is?	**8** ...... **9** ......
if you need other people's approval and recognition for what you do?	**10** ......
if you don't like joining in with other people?	**11** ......
if you need to feel safe in your surroundings?	**12** ......

Which colour are you likely to have towards the end of your list ...

if you have a realistic view of life?	**13** ...... **14** ......
if you are seriously discontented at the moment?	**15** ......
if you have been disappointed in your hopes and ambitions?	**16** ...... **17** ......
if you are *extremely* keen and ambitious?	**18** ......

A Red
B Yellow
C Green
D Violet
E Brown
F Grey
G Blue
H Black

Focus on Vocabulary 2 *Colourful Idioms*

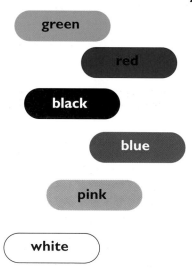

green
red
black
blue
pink
white

Choose the correct colours to complete each sentence.

1 When I see people dropping litter in the street, it really makes me see ....
2 If you keep your bank account in the ......, you won't have to pay any bank charges.
3 His sister's financial success and luxurious lifestyle makes him ...... with envy.
4 We used to be good friends but now I only see him once in a ...... moon.
5 Things are going very well for Brenda at the moment. When I saw her, she really looked in the ....
6 I'm afraid my account is in the ...... at the moment, so I can't afford a holiday.
7 That office block they built has turned out to be a real ...... elephant. They spent the earth on it and it's still unoccupied.
8 I was completely ...... when I first started my own business, and I had to learn some important lessons the hard way.
9 The sales figures are down again and the boss is screaming ...... murder.

Test your personality

A   Red

Red represents passion and energy. Red in the first position means you are impulsive, sexy and have a will to win. You are a good leader. You want to expand your horizons and live life to the full. Red in the seventh or eighth position means your desire for life and thirst for adventure have become less.

B   Yellow

Yellow represents happiness and relaxation. Anyone who chooses yellow in second, third or fourth place is a positive, optimistic person who always looks to the future – never backwards. You find life easy, and problems simply do not exist for you. Free from worry, you lead a carefree life; but this does not mean that you are lazy. You can be extremely hard-working, although not consistently. Yellow in first place means that you are ambitious and eager to please. When yellow is in the latter part of the spectrum you have had your hopes and dreams dashed and you feel isolated and disappointed, often becoming defensive and withdrawn.

C   Green

Green represents firmness and resistance to change. In first place, you are persistent, possessive and quite selfish. You are a high-achiever and an accumulator of 'things' – like a penthouse, a BMW, a Rolex, a holiday flat, a compact-disc player. You want to be recognised and need to impress but worry about the prospect of failure. If green is a later choice, your ego has been bruised and you have been humbled by the resistance to your progress. Consequently you can be highly critical, sarcastic and stubborn.

D   Violet

A mixture of red and blue, violet represents a conflict between impulsiveness and calm sensitivity, dominance and submissiveness. The person who prefers violet wants to find a mystical, magical relationship. Both mentally and physically immature, you are stuck in a dream world of wishful thinking and fantasy. Often violet is chosen by adolescents who still see the world through fairy-tale eyes. When violet appears in the latter part of the sequence, it indicates that the person choosing it is more mature and has outgrown the 'fantasy' vision of life, confronting harsh reality head-on.

E   Brown

Brown is the colour of physical well-being and is an indicator of how healthy you think you are. If you put brown in fourth or fifth place you are not very concerned about your health and body. This means that you are probably in good shape. Those worried about illness tend to put brown earlier in their sequence. If you choose brown as your favourite colour, you are restless and insecure. If brown is in eighth place, you don't care enough for your body: you may not be as healthy as you think. Placing brown early also indicates the importance of a secure environment: refugees often pick brown first.

F   Grey

Grey is a neutral and represents a point between two contrasting and conflicting motivations. Grey in the first position means that you want to shut yourself off from everything and remain uncommitted, so that you can swing with opinion and emotions. You hate joining anything with 'group' connotations and are an observer rather than a doer. Those who choose grey in the eighth position seek to join in with everything, eager and enthusiastic. Such people will try absolutely everything in their efforts to achieve their goals.

G   Blue

Blue represents calmness and loyalty. A person who favours blue is sensitive and easily hurt. You never panic and are in total control of your life and content with the way it is going. You desire to lead an uncomplicated and worry-free life and are prepared to sacrifice certain goals in order to achieve this. You need a stable relationship without conflict. Perhaps, as a side-effect of contentment, you tend to put on weight. The later blue appears in the sequence, the more unsatisfied you are and the more you feel the need to break from the ties that restrict you. But you probably aren't unfeeling enough to walk out on a family or job; instead, you will suffer in silence.

H   Black

Black is the negation of colour and means 'No'. Anyone who chooses it in the first position (which is rare) is in revolt against their fate. Chosen second, it means you are prepared to give up everything else to achieve what you want. It is normally put in seventh or eighth place, representing control of one's destiny and a balanced outlook. If yellow precedes black in the first two positions, then a change is on the way.

© *The Telegraph Sunday Magazine*

Focus on Grammar *The Passive 2*

1   The passive infinitive

a   Underline the passives in the following examples and complete the table below to show how they are formed.

1   You want to be recognized, but worry about the prospect of failure. (Text 2)
2   Watch out! You could have been run over.
3   This garment must be washed at 40 degrees.
4   I don't like being watched while I'm working.

Gerunds:	verb	+	being
Infinitives:	verb	+	......
Modals (present):	verb	+	......
Modals (past):	verb	+	......

+ past participle

You can check your answers by referring to the Grammar File on page 145.

b   Make sentences by choosing appropriate verbs from this list and putting the verbs in brackets into the passive.

enjoy   could   used to   might   ought
would like   want   must   should   forget

Example:
All entries for the June exam *must be received* (receive) before March 23rd.

1   Let us know if you ...... (meet) at the airport.
2   I'll never ...... (test) on my times tables every week at primary school.
3   All cheques ...... (accompany) by a cheque card.
4   It's not a good idea to pat a strange dog, you ...... (bite).
5   She's so good, she ...... (promote) soon.
6   Rooms designed to be relaxing ...... (paint) yellow or blue.
7   France ...... (rule) by a king.
8   Most parents ...... (involve) in their children's education.
9   I wouldn't sign that document; it ...... (use) against you in the future.
10   Everybody ...... (pamper) from time to time.

2   *make/let, cause/allow*

a   Look at the verbs in these examples and fill in the tables below to show the patterns they follow.

1   Seeing red can *make* you *eat* faster.
2   *Let* me *impress* you!
3   Red and orange *cause* time to seem to *pass* more quickly ...
4   Please *allow* us to *help* you.

make/let + ... + infinitive	cause/allow + ... + ...

What other verbs follow these patterns? (You can refer to the reference lists in the Grammar File, page 154.)

b   Now compare these pairs of sentences and complete the notes below.

1   a   The customs officer made us open our suitcases.
     b   We were made to open our suitcases (by the customs officer).
2   a   The teacher let the class leave early.
     b   The class was allowed to leave early.

When *make* is used in the passive, it is followed by the .... form.
In the passive, *let* is replaced by ....

c   Rewrite each of these sentences beginning with the words given and using the verb in brackets in the active or passive as necessary.

1   Many rivers have flooded as a result of heavy rain.
     Heavy rain .... (cause)
2   I was forced to do it by the commanding officer.
     My commanding officer .... (make)
3   They made us wear a really embarrassing uniform at my school.
     We .... (make)
4   Do they let candidates use a dictionary in the exam?
     Are .... ? (allow)
5   John allowed me to use his library ticket.
     John .... (let)
6   You can't come in if you are wearing jeans.
     No one .... (allow)

3   Uses of the passive

a   There are a number of reasons for using the passive rather than the active, for example when the agent is unknown or unimportant. Look at these sentences and try making them active. Say why you think the passive is used here. (You can find the uses of the passive listed in the Grammar File, page 146.)

1   The powder in the yellow packet was judged to be extremely powerful. (Text 1)
2   Blue is believed by many to be the most beautiful colour.
3   The MD is rumoured to have received a huge pay rise.

b The passive, often with an introductory *It* structure, is useful if you want to avoid mentioning the source of a piece of information, especially if it is confidential.

Read these notes made by a business journalist. Then use the information to write eight sentences about the situation at ABC Electronics using appropriate verbs from the list in passive constructions.

> judge   say   believe   feel   think   claim
> report   rumour

Examples:

> It is believed that the company is about to go bankrupt.
> The Director of Finance is felt to be responsible.

Trouble at ABC Electronics
I spoke to some of the staff today 'off the record' and made a note of their feelings. Most of them are convinced the company is about to go bankrupt. They feel the Director of Finance is responsible. Apparently, despite the company's poor financial position, she has just bought a private jet for the directors to use on foreign trips. And, amazingly, the directors have just received a 50% pay rise. One of the workers told me that a big overseas contract has fallen through. It seems that the clients decided the price of spare parts was too expensive. I heard that another important client has cancelled his contract in the last few days. The latest gossip here is that a strike is imminent at the main factory and tax inspectors are investigating the company's accounts.

Focus on Speaking *Selecting and Ranking*

Paper 5, Part 3

Work with a partner. For each of the jobs below choose six key skills or personal characteristics and put them in order of importance 1–6 (1 = most important).

Flight attendant

The right qualities for the job
good general education
good communication and interpersonal skills
sense of humour
patience
initiative
self-motivation
stamina
attractive appearance
good clothes sense
ability to speak at least one foreign language
ability to work under pressure
ability to work as part of a team
leadership qualities

TV reporter

Useful Language	**Interrupting**
See *Suggesting an opinion, agreeing and disagreeing* in Unit 7 (page 108).	*Sorry to interrupt but ...* *Yes, but hang on/hold on a minute, ...*
Asking for an opinion	**Seeking agreement**
*What do you think? Which would **you** choose?* *Which do you think is more important, X or Y?* *Where shall we put it, (first or second)?*	*Don't you think ... /Wouldn't you agree that ...?* *Shall we include it/leave it out?* *So you agree we should put it first/second?*

Focus on Vocabulary 3 *Word Formation*

The following adjectives and nouns can be combined to form compound adjectives with a metaphorical meaning.

tight   short   level   two   big   thick   warm

head   temper   skin   heart   face   fist

Fill in the gaps in these sentences with an appropriate compound adjective. Discuss the meanings with another student and check any you don't know.

1 He's extremely _short-tempered_ , so be careful not to annoy him.
2 In this job, you've got to be ...... enough to stay calm in a crisis – a wrong decision could cost lives.
3 ...... and generous, she was the most popular girl in the school.
4 The government's ...... policies towards the disabled are alienating those who think they deserve more money, not less.
5 Being a politician is a no-win situation – you're criticised whatever you do. You've got to be pretty ...... to take it all.
6 She's beautiful and talented yet she isn't the slightest bit ...... – it's amazing!
7 Don't trust him, he's so ....

Focus on Writing *Informal Letter*

Paper 2, Part 1

TASK

An English-speaking friend of yours is hoping to get a job in Britain, and has written to you, asking for advice on how to go about it. Your friend mentioned an interest in beginning a career in broadcasting. You notice the Candidate Column in a British newspaper and decide it would be a good idea for your friend to advertise in it. You think some of the advertisements in the column work better than others and you have made some notes on them. You have also spotted a short article on working in broadcasting, which you think your friend should read.

Read the information about the Candidate Column, the notes you have made on the advertisements, and the article. Using the information provided, write a **letter** to your friend explaining why you think they should advertise in the column, giving some advice on how to write the advertisement and saying why you are enclosing the article.

Write approximately 250 words. You should use your own words as far as possible. You do not need to include addresses.

CONTENT

1 a In Part 1 of the Writing paper, it's vital to follow the instructions precisely. If you leave something out, you'll lose marks. Read the instructions very carefully and underline the three key points you have to include in the letter.

   b Then read each piece of information, and highlight the important parts. Make notes on these, using your own words as far as possible.

ORGANISATION/LAYOUT   **2**   Deal with each of the key points in turn, beginning a new paragraph for each. You will also need a brief introduction (e.g. responding to the letter from your friend) and a suitable conclusion (e.g. wishing them luck).

Before you begin, check the notes on layout and language in the Writing File pages 157–158.

STYLE/REGISTER   **3**   This depends on your relationship with the reader and also on the subject matter. Decide if this is a close friend you've known for years or someone you know less well. Consider how seriously or light-heartedly to treat the subject.

CANDIDATE COLUMN

Calling all high-fliers

Have you tried the Candidate Column yet?

It allows you, the reader, to place a free advertisement on this page to sell your skills to potential employers. If you're looking for a first job, a step up the ladder to success, or if you want to so something radically different with your career, just fill in the coupon below and send it off.

You have a maximum of 50 words in which to describe your qualifications, abilities and ambitions before an audience of over two million professional business readers. To encourage your creativity, we'll also be offering a prize for the best ad published each month.

© The Observer

BROADCASTING

The major requirements in the industry are a capacity to cope with crises and, in television, physical stamina. From your armchair, the people on screen may look peaceful and quiet; in the studio, it will be hot, dirty and almost everyone will be on their feet.

Broadcasters get to the top by having practical ideas for good programmes. When the idea gets launched, said an ITV producer, 'you eat, sleep and dream the subject'. It may involve long hours and months away from home.

To get on, you need to be pushy and tough. But an openly harsh and aggressive approach will not work: television and radio depend on teamwork and you must be capable of getting on with everybody, including technicians.

© Times Newspapers Ltd

YOUNG enthusiastic Honours graduate, currently a research technician, requires a challenging post within 40 miles of Chester. I am efficient and I want to work hard! Box 490   *Clear and direct*

HI! I'm Kay. I'm determined, diligent, personable and I'm looking for a career with an international company. I have an Honours degree in languages and I'm successful in my present job. Write to me and find out! Box 220   *Nice chatty style (a bit too friendly?)*

SPANISH LAW GRADUATE (25) permanently in London, presently assistant in solicitor's office, seeks challenging post using linguistic and academic capabilities. Box 385   *Doesn't mention any personal qualities*

DYNAMIC female, 24, bilingual English/Spanish, with a degree in English, seeks interesting, creative job in the media or publishing. Box 622

ONCE YOU MEET ME you'll know you need me. I'm intelligent, charming and trustworthy and that's on a bad day. My CV says more. Let me impress you. Box 342   *Sounds big-headed! And what kind of work does he want?*

LAZY LIE-ABED seeks easy job with lots of money. Are you bored with all the cliches and boasts in the other ads? Hire me and you'll get imagination, initiative and intelligence. Honestly! Box 192   *Eye-catching (but a bit dangerous?)*

© The Observer

English in Use 1 *Developing Skills: Discourse Cloze* ▶ Paper 3, Part 6

For questions 1–6, read through the following text and then choose from the list A–J the best phrase or sentence given below it to fill each of the spaces. Write one letter (A–J) in the correct space. **Some of the suggested answers do not fit at all.** The exercise begins with an example (0).

How boring can you really get?

Instead of just *thinking* the person sitting next to you at dinner is the most boring person in the universe, you may be able to prove it. But beware, (0) ..J. that bores are more intelligent than their fascinating neighbours.

Psychologists have just completed a study of (1) .... . Professor Mark Leary, of Wake Forest University in North Carolina, has isolated those boring characteristics (2) .... (a condition marked by short attacks of extreme drowsiness) and assembled them in a league table:

- Negative egocentrism: the 'I'm a martyr to my varicose veins' syndrome – droning on about personal problems.

- Banality: talking about superficial things, repeating the same joke over and over again.

- Low affectivity: avoiding eye contact, keeping facial expression to a minimum and speaking monotonously.

- Tediousness: dragging conversations out.

- Passivity: conforming and (3) ....

- Self-preoccupation: talking about oneself.

- Seriousness: not smiling, taking everything seriously.

- Ingratiation: trying to win friends, being excessively funny or friendly.

- Distraction: being easily side-tracked or excited, engaging in too much small-talk or using a great deal of slang.

Leary asked 297 undergraduates to rate behaviour (4) .... from 'not at all boring' to 'extremely boring'. In another experiment, students (5) .... rated the participants on their friendliness, competence and strength. Bores were found to be less friendly, less enthusiastic, more impersonal, weaker and less reliable. However, (6) .... 'significantly more intelligent than interesting targets'.

A who listened to taped 'interesting' and 'boring' conversations
B to everyone's surprise
C reluctant to express opinions
D they were rated
E that revealed remarkable results
F which induce chronic narcolepsy
G on a five-point scale
H what makes people boring
I raising many questions

J for new research says

English in Use 2 *Developing Skills: Lexical Cloze*

Paper 3, Part I

Read the article below and circle the letter next to the word which best fits each space. The first answer has been given as an example.

Colour Sense

ICI colour consultant Jack Widgery painted one police interview room light green, and another (0) .... red. Subsequently, the police found that suspects (1) .... statements more quickly when they were in the red room, again enforcing the idea that too much red (2) .... a feeling of being pressurised. The soft green room was for (3) .... victims and their families, and there are many (4) .... of light colours being used to (5) .... feelings and encourage relaxation.

Some institutions in the USA have special pink areas to cool the (6) .... of angry prisoners, service recruits and patients. Soft blues, greens and beiges seem to be (7) .... and hospitals, schools and dentists are beginning to take this into (8) .... when choosing colour schemes.

An airline which (9) .... from a yellow and brown interior scheme to one (10) .... green and blue reported a forty-five per cent decrease (11) .... airsickness. But the workplace is the biggest challenge: (12) .... too much nor too (13) .... energy will do. The (14) .... fashion for grey with a few details in brighter colours may be a good (15) ....

© *The Telegraph Sunday Magazine*

0	A heavy	(B) strong	C lively	D sharp
1	A gave	B said	C admitted	D spoke
2	A makes	B leads	C has	D creates
3	A discussing	B interviewing	C requesting	D explaining
4	A ways	B occasions	C examples	D demonstrations
5	A play up	B play down	C run up	D run down
6	A tempers	B moods	C personalities	D senses
7	A sleepy	B leisurely	C tiring	D restful
8	A view	B mind	C account	D opinion
9	A changed	B turned	C adapted	D altered
10	A by	B for	C from	D of
11	A of	B in	C with	D about
12	A never	B nor	C no	D neither
13	A few	B small	C little	D low
14	A current	B nowadays	C actual	D instant
15	A result	B system	C solution	D way

9   Mind Your Manners

'Social tact is making your guests feel at home, even though you wish they were.'
Anon

Lead-in

Read these extracts, which describe what is considered the polite thing to do when invited to a social occasion in Britain. Discuss these questions.

1 Are any of the 'rules' the same in your country? Are any completely different?
2 Which of the rules seem sensible? Do any seem ridiculous?
3 Do you think rules like this are outdated, or do they serve any purpose?

A

If you are invited for 8 pm, you should arrive about 10–15 minutes later. In fact, it's impolite to arrive exactly on time.

B

It's not necessary to bring a gift for the hosts, but flowers or chocolates will always be appreciated.

C

The host should introduce you to other guests you don't know, but you can introduce yourself if he/she doesn't do this. A smile and 'Hello' is enough at an informal party – you don't have to shake hands.

D

Forks go on the left, prongs upward; knives (with blades facing inwards) and spoons on the right. The basic rule is to use the cutlery starting at the outside and working in.

E

It is not polite to refuse a course, unless you can't eat the food for some reason such as a health or diet problem. If you don't like the food, try to eat it anyway. If you can only manage a mouthful or two, eat lots of everything else.

F

Smokers should ask the host and other guests before lighting up at the table, and should be prepared to take no for an answer. No one should smoke until the end of the meal.

G

Say thank you, by telephone or letter, but say it promptly, within a couple of days at the most.

Focus on Listening *Bad Manners*

▶ Paper 4, Part 4

You will hear five people giving examples of behaviour which they consider to be bad manners. You will hear the recording twice.

1 TASK ONE lists the places where the examples of bad manners occur. Match the extracts as you hear them with the places, listed **A–G**. Write the correct letter in each box.

A in an office

B in somebody's home

C in the street

D in a restaurant

E in a shop

F in the street or on public transport

G in a shop or on public transport

	1
	2
	3
	4
	5

Sunday **14**

2 TASK TWO lists the things that the five speakers complain about. Match the extracts as you hear them with the topics, listed **A–G**. Write the correct letter in each box.

A somebody not talking at all

B somebody speaking too much

C somebody speaking rudely

D somebody not getting out of the way

E somebody allowing noise to go on during a conversation

F somebody who can't do their job

G somebody interrupting a conversation to talk to another person

	6
	7
	8
	9
	10

DISCUSSION POINTS

3 What do you consider to be 'the height of bad manners'?

4 a Discuss in pairs what it would be good manners to do in these situations.

1 You are sitting in the middle of a row of seats during a concert when you are overcome with coughs.

2 Someone starts to tell you a story they've already told you before.

3 A friend asks you to give your honest opinion of a new item of clothing they've bought. (You think it's awful.)

4 You have been invited to dinner but miscalculate the journey and arrive half an hour early.

5 You have invited friends to dinner but they arrive before you've finished cooking.

b When you've finished, compare your ideas with other students.

c Now compare your answers with the key on page 233. Do you agree or disagree with the advice given?

Text

PREDICTION

1 a Before you read the text on the next page, decide which of the following would cause offence.

1 Which gift would a Chinese friend consider to be in bad taste?

   a an alarm clock   b a lap top computer   c a calculator

2 Which gift could offend a Hindu colleague in India?

   a a silver pen and pencil set   b a cut glass vase   c a leather briefcase

3 Which gesture would cause offence in Greece?

   a tapping one side of the nose with the index finger

   b the US and British OK sign, thumb and finger touching in a circle

   c kissing the fingertips

4 Which way of calling the waiter is considered rude in Japan?

   a raising and moving the index finger towards you

   b moving the whole hand towards you, palm up

   c catching the waiter's eye and moving the head backwards quickly

b Read the first paragraph of the text on page 126 to find the answers to questions 1–3. Then read the rest of the text and the missing sections on page 127 for the general meaning and the answer to question 4.

GAPPED TEXT
► Paper I, Part 2

2 For questions 1–6, you must choose which of paragraphs A–G on page 127 fit into the numbered gaps in the following newspaper article. There is one extra paragraph which does not fit in any of the gaps.

STRATEGY

Remember to look for grammatical or logical links between paragraphs, including:

- **reference links** such as personal pronouns (e.g. *he, it, her*, etc.) or names/titles (e.g. *Ann Smith → Mrs Smith*). See list in Unit 5, page 75.
- **parallel expressions** such as *attempt → effort.* See examples in Unit 6, page 83.
- **linking topic vocabulary** such as *examination/enter/paper/answer/results.*

Must One Be So Polite That It Hurts?
By Sherry Buchanan
International Herald Tribune

NEW YORK – When in China, don't give a clock as a gift. It symbolizes death. When in Greece, don't make the OK sign, thumb and forefinger touching in a circle. It is an offensive gesture. When in India, don't give a Hindu a gift made of cowhide. It is sacrilegious.

1

Some visitors follow a rule of thumb. They weigh how much displeasing their host matters to them against their degree of personal discomfort.

'During our briefings, we help people develop respect for the country they are going to live in,' said Claire Stewart, who works for an organisation which teaches manners to people being transferred overseas by their companies or universities.

Letitia Baldridge, an authority on manners in the United States and the author of a book on the subject, said:

'Good manners are not elite, artificial or snobbish ways of behaving. Manners are a combination of common sense and consideration for others. It's 75 per cent

common sense and 25 per cent thinking about others.'

2

Her advice covers every aspect of social behaviour, including smoking manners, flag etiquette for banquets, writing letters of apology, and the proper form for business cards.

Everywhere, it has become extremely complicated to be polite. Not only are customs different but in many countries standards of behaviour have changed in recent years.

3

'I had the option of not going in, but you feel a bit of a fool if everybody else in there is naked,' said the banker, who decided to take the plunge. To make matters worse, he was attending the house party with his boss. The hot-tub session, during which business was discussed, lasted three hours.

4

Mrs Stewart said she believed that the banker had done the right thing, although he had an option. He could 'have had the sangfroid to decline with grace without making the Australians feel stupid,' she said.

5

Alexander Moorrees, a young American investment banker in London, was invited by some British friends to spend a weekend at their home in the country. The weather was below freezing. The manor house to which he had been invited had no central heating and the bedrooms had no fireplaces. 'I kept waking up every hour to make sure I was still breathing,' said Mr Moorrees. 'I was worried I was going to die of hypothermia.'

Finally, at 3 a.m., fearing for his health, he took all his blankets, went down to the main living room, built a fire in the large fireplace, and went to sleep in front of it. He has not been invited back.

6

▲ **Question 2**

Name/title link: which answer links the speaker in the previous paragraph and *Her* in the following paragraph?

▲ **Questions 3/4**

Topic vocabulary link: what do *not going in/ naked/take the plunge* refer to? The clue is in the last sentence.

▶ **Para. A**

Pronoun link: **what**
felt 'quite good'? The
clue is in the last
sentence.

▶ **Para. B**

Pronoun link: *He*
could refer to two
possible men. Make
sure you make the link
with the correct one.

A   'Even though it felt quite good, an
Englishman's reserve scarcely allows him to
feel comfortable in these circumstances,' he
said. 'Coming out is just as embarrassing. I was
all wrinkly.'

B   He could have followed Ms Baldridge's rule
No. 2 when visiting a foreign country:
'Become familiar with the dress code in that
country.' If so, he might have added long johns
and a ski mask to his wardrobe.

C   A young British banker recently found himself
at a house party in Sydney. After a barbecue,
the hosts invited everyone to climb into a large
bath tub to relax. The hosts' rule was that to
participate you had to take your clothes off.

D   The British use this gesture to call a waiter, but
in Japan it's considered rude to beckon a waiter
by moving the index finger. In Germany the

waiter might well respond by bringing you two
more drinks.

E   Knowing how to behave abroad can save
people from some major social gaffes.
However, etiquette writers and experts disagree
over how far people should go in complying
with foreign habits and customs that can create
great discomfort to the uninitiated.

F   In a business situation, 'short of doing
something unethical,' the best advice is usually
'to go along with whatever the foreign custom
is,' she added.

G   Ms Baldridge, who began her career as social
secretary to an ambassador and his wife at the
US embassy in Paris, now teaches manners to
international executives and charges thousands
of dollars a session.

DISCUSSION POINTS

3   Discuss in groups. If you were going to live abroad, what aspects of manners
and social behaviour would you consider it most important to know about?
For example, dress codes for different occasions, useful gestures (and gestures
to avoid!), table manners, handling business cards, choosing suitable gifts.

STUDY BOX ▶ *Inversion after negative introductions*

Not only are customs different but in many countries standards of behaviour have changed. (Text)

After the expression *Not only*, the verb is placed before the subject as a way of adding more emphasis or
dramatic effect. If there is no auxiliary verb, *do/does/did* or *had* are used, as in a question.

e.g. Not only **does** she work long hours but she also has two children to look after.

This inversion of subject and verb also happens after other negative introductions such as:

At no time ... Never ... Rarely ...	e.g. At no time *have I* made any such promise!
On no account ...	e.g. On no account *must you* tell anyone.
Not a (person/thing) ...	e.g. Not a single person *did I* see the whole evening.
No sooner ... than ...	e.g. No sooner *had I come* in than the telephone rang.

See the Grammar File, page 139 for more information.

Rewrite these sentences, beginning with the words in brackets.

1   He managed to offend everybody and then left without even saying goodbye. (Not only)

2   It's not often you see people in traditional dress like that these days. (Rarely)

3   As soon as we went to sleep the baby began to cry. (No sooner)

4   I forbid you to touch anything on this desk. (On no account)

5   I haven't heard a word from him since he left eight weeks ago. (Not a word)

Focus on Grammar 1 *Modal Verbs 2*

For more information about modal verbs see the
Grammar File, pages 142–144.

1   Obligation – present and future

a   Look at the sentences below and decide which ones:

- describe an obligation or prohibition (OP)
- describe absence of obligation or necessity (AO)
- give strong advice (positive or negative) (SA)

1   It's impolite to arrive exactly on time.
2   It's not necessary to bring a gift for the hosts.
3   It's important to go along with the foreign custom.
4   In future all applicants will be required to have a
    medical examination.
5   Taking photographs of military sites is forbidden.
6   Obtaining a visa is no longer compulsory for British
    visitors to the United States.
7   There's no need to shake hands at an informal party.

b   Rewrite the sentences above using suitable forms of
the following verbs. Use each verb at least once.

   must   have to   should   need   ought to

c   Complete the following sentences with suitable verb
forms expressing obligation or advice.

1   In China, you ...... (never give) a clock as a gift, as it
    symbolises death.
2   You ...... (write) or phone to thank your hosts after a
    dinner party.
3   You're overweight. You ...... (eat) so many sweets.
4   You ...... (tell) a soul what I've said. Promise!
5   Deborah ...... (work) a lot harder if she wants to do
    well in her exams.
6   You ...... (have) a medical certificate before you can get
    a work permit.
7   Don't worry, you ...... (be) especially fit to join the
    aerobics class.
8   You ...... (use) that word, children. It's rude.
9   Do I ...... (have) a receipt to get a refund?
10   You ...... (shout). I'm not deaf!

2   Obligation – past

a   Match each sentence in 1–4 with a suitable comment
a–d.

1   They wouldn't let me pay by credit card: they made
    me pay cash.

2   I took cash just in case, but they let me in for free.
3   I took my credit card, but they would only accept cash.
4   I didn't take any cash because I knew entry was free.

a   He should have taken cash.
b   He didn't need to take cash.
c   He needn't have taken cash.
d   He had to pay cash.

b   Complete the following sentences using a suitable
modal verb and the verb in brackets.

1   I'm sorry I'm late. I ...... (make) an urgent phone call.
2   You really ...... (apologise) to him at the time. It's a bit
    late now.
3   We ...... (take) a cab because Joe gave us a lift in his car.
4   Our flight was cancelled so we ...... (stay) the night in a
    local hotel.
5   You ...... (speak) to him like that; you really upset him.
6   We ...... (take) a tent with us because we never had a
    chance to use it.
7   The queue was quite short so I ...... (wait) very long.
8   I feel exhausted, I ...... (stay up) so late last night.

3   Permission: *can, may, might, could*

a   In the examples below, there is one incorrect
sentence. Which is it and why is it incorrect?

1   We were allowed to leave early yesterday.
2   Children could work at the age of 12 in the 19th
    century.
3   On my eighth birthday I could stay up until 9 o'clock.

b   Complete the following sentences with suitable verb
forms expressing permission.

1   'Do you think I ...... ask you a favour?' 'Yes, of course ......'
2   I apologise for interrupting, but ...... a suggestion?
3   Before 1969, you ...... in an election in the UK until you
    were 21.
4   They wanted to keep him at the police station for
    questioning but when his solicitor arrived, he ...... home.
5   In some societies couples ...... married unless they have
    their parents' permission.
6   If we get work permits, we ...... , so we won't have to
    take so much money with us.
7   When my grandfather was young, you ...... a car
    without even taking a test.
8   You've got such an interesting face. I wonder if I ......
    take your photograph?

Focus on Writing 1 *Article*

▶ Paper 2, Part 2

TASK

You have a friend who works for an organisation that arranges study exchanges for school and college students. The organisation produces a regular magazine, which features articles about exchange countries, experiences people have had abroad, etc. Here is part of a letter from your friend.

> there's been a big increase in the number of people applying for study exchanges to your country – nearly double last year's figures, in fact. Almost all will be staying with local families and, as it'll be the first time most of them have been to your country, we thought we ought to put an introduction to the basic customs in the next edition of our magazine. So I was wondering – you've guessed it! – if you could possibly write a short article on the topic. You could explain any special habits to do with greeting, eating, being a good guest, etc., and also include any points about family or social life which you think they should be aware of. I know you'd do a brilliant job and I'd be really grateful.
>
> Hope to hear from you soon,
>
> Love

Write your **article** in approximately 250 words.

TASK CHECKLIST

1 Read the instructions carefully and ask yourself these questions.
   - What **form** of writing do you have to produce? What special features does this have? (layout? language?)
   - Who are your **readers** going to be? (ages?/interests?/needs?)
   - What is the **purpose** of the writing?
   - What points do you have to mention?

CONTENT/ORGANISATION

2 a Discuss these possible titles with other students and choose the best one.

   Notes for visitors to ...   WELCOME TO MY COUNTRY!

   When in Rome, do as the Romans do   How to be a popular guest

   b Try to think of another, better title. You could add a touch of humour, for example, with a slightly unusual angle: 'How to be an unpopular guest'.

   c Make a list of the topics suggested in the question and jot down any ideas you have for each one. Imagine yourself as a visitor to your country and your family. What would seem strange? What mistakes might you make?

   d Decide on the best order for the topics.

STYLE

3 Make your article readable. Remember your readers' ages. How can you get their attention to begin with? How can you keep them reading? What would be a good ending? (See Unit 7, page 100.)

Focus on Vocabulary *Collocation*

VERB + NOUN

1 **a** Match verbs from Column A with phrases from Column B in each of the two boxes below.

	A		B
1	throw	a	a problem
2	take	b	a question
3	raise	c	an explanation
4	make	d	regret
5	give	e	the opportunity
6	cause	f	a party
7	express	g	an excuse

	A		B
1	pay	a	somebody good
2	give	b	somebody's eye
3	put	c	somebody's attention
4	do	d	something up to date
5	catch	e	somebody right (about something)
6	bring	f	something priority
7	attract	g	somebody a compliment

VERB + ADVERB

b Match each adverb on the right with two of the following verbs.

apologise   complain   congratulate somebody
thank somebody   welcome somebody   regret

bitterly   profusely   warmly

ADJECTIVE + NOUN

c Match each adjective with a noun.

1 glowing   4 keen
2 heartfelt/deepest 5 disgraceful
3 generous/lavish   6 invaluable

a interest	d hospitality
b advice	e sympathy
c behaviour	f praise

2 Complete these sentences with collocations from Exercise 1.

1 I'm writing to say how much we enjoyed our stay and to thank you for your ....
2 Why don't you take a short break away? I'm sure it would ...... you ....
3 The ...... which nobody has ...... yet is: How are we going to pay for it?
4 Although I ...... for arriving so late, I'm not sure they'll invite me again.
5 All the reviews of your book were full of .... You must be delighted.
6 Didn't you see me? I was shouting and waving to ...... your ....
7 He ...... some feeble ...... about why he was late, but nobody believed him.
8 She likes travelling alone but she .... about having to pay a supplement for a single room.

LANGUAGE CHECK ▶ *Negative prefixes*

Make the following nouns and verbs negative by adding the correct prefix, *dis-*, *mis-* or *in-*.

1	agree	5	calculate	9	obey	13	convenience	17	comfort (*n*)
2	conduct (*n*)	6	respect (*n*)	10	action	14	honesty	18	print (*n*)
3	please	7	ability	11	represent	15	understanding	19	accuracy
4	justice	8	pronounce	12	approval	16	attention	20	spell

Focus on Grammar 2 *Type 3 and Mixed Conditionals*

1 a Look at these examples of conditional sentences and underline the verb forms in the *if* clause and the result clause. Then answer the questions.

1 If Alexander Moorrees <u>had taken</u> the right clothes, he <u>wouldn't have felt</u> so cold in the unheated house.
   Did he take the right clothes?
   Did he feel cold?

2 If Letitia Baldridge hadn't spent many years working as an ambassador's secretary, she wouldn't be an expert on international etiquette now.
   Did she work as a secretary?
   Is she an expert on etiquette now?

3 The young banker could have offended his hosts if he hadn't joined them in the bath tub.
   Did he join his hosts in the tub?
   Did he offend his hosts?

4 I might be doing more business if I had bothered to learn about local customs when I first arrived.
   Am I doing more business now?
   Did I learn about local customs?

b Sentences 1 and 3 are examples of a type 3 conditional. Sentences 2 and 4 are examples of mixed conditionals. Complete these notes about each type.

1 *Type 3 conditionals* are used to talk about something which could .... in the past, but ....
2 In a *type 3 conditional*, the .... tense is used in the *if* clause, and *would have*, *should have*, *could have* or *might have* + ... are used in the main clause.
3 A *mixed conditional* is used to talk about the .... result of a past condition.
4 In a *mixed conditional*, *would be* or *might be* are used in the .... clause, and the past perfect tense in the .... clause.

Check your answers by referring to the Grammar File on page 138.

Note: Other tense and time combinations are also possible in mixed conditionals, for example:

   If John spoke Japanese, his company might have sent him to Tokyo.
   Does John speak Japanese?
   Did his company send him to Japan?

In this example, the *if* clause refers to an unreal condition in the present, and a hypothetical result in the past.

2 Put the verbs in brackets into the correct tense in the following sentences.

1 He ...... (not be) so unpopular if he ...... (remember) to bring some gifts for his hosts.
2 If I ...... (not persuade) someone to lend me some money, I don't know how I ...... (get home).
3 What on earth ...... (you do) if you ...... (be) in the same situation that night?
4 The company ...... (not make) so much money now if it ...... (not carry out) the restructuring programme last year.
5 She ...... (feel) much fitter now if she ...... (join) that aerobics class when it started.
6 I ...... (not become) an actor if my parents ...... (not force) me to go to the theatre when I was small.

3 a Read the story and answer the questions below.

Now living in Japan, Steve Dorland works for *Hi-Tech*, an American technology magazine. A couple of years ago *Hi-Tech* opened a small office in Tokyo and they sent Steve out there. After the long flight from Boston, Steve arrived in Tokyo tired and hungry. He took a taxi into the centre and stopped at the first restaurant he saw. Although Steve spoke no Japanese he was able to order by pointing to the dishes he wanted in the window display. At the end of the meal a bill arrived. Anxious to find a hotel for the night, Steve left a pile of yen on the table, remembering to add a 15% tip to the total, and rushed out into the street. Suddenly he heard shouting behind him. Looking around, he saw an anxious-looking waiter running towards him with a fist full of cash. 'Oh no,' thought Steve, 'How embarrassing. I didn't leave a big enough tip.'

1 What do you think happened next?
2 Was Steve right? Why did the waiter run after him?
3 What are the tipping customs in a) Japan, b) the USA, c) your country?

b Now complete these conditional sentences.

1 Steve wouldn't be working in Japan now if .....
2 If Steve had travelled abroad before .....
3 He wouldn't have rushed out into the street if .....
4 If Steve had known about Japanese customs .....
5 If the waiter had known about American customs .....

Focus on Writing 2 *Report*

► Paper 2, Part 1

TASK

You are studying in a college which has both British and overseas students. The college recently held an International Day, with events organised by the students themselves, with the aim of increasing staff and student awareness of other countries and cultures.

As a student representative on the Staff–Student Committee you have received the letter below from the Principal. Read the publicity poster for the event, the Principal's letter and the notes you made at a students' meeting. Then, using the information given, write the **report** which the Principal requests.

You should use your own words as far as possible. Write approximately 250 words.

PUBLICITY POSTER

Want to make new friends? learn about other cultures?
Don't miss INTERNATIONAL DAY!

- See slide shows and videos
- Listen to short presentations
- Watch cookery demonstrations
- Enjoy international cuisine
- Listen to music from around the world
- Join in the dancing!

and much more!

Friday 17th February

PRINCIPAL'S LETTER

Dear Student Rep,

Thank you for your help in organising the recent International Day.

As you know, this was the first event of its kind which has been held in the college. If we are to hold similar events in future, we need to assess how successful the day proved to be and to take note of any problems which occurred. We will also be considering the possibility of increasing the budget available for future events.

I would be grateful if you could carry out a survey amongst the students who attended the event and prepare a short report on their reactions. Please include some general recommendations based on your findings.

Your help in this matter is appreciated.

R Dearing

R. Dearing

Principal

NOTES FROM STUDENTS' MEETING, 24TH FEBRUARY

INTERNATIONAL DAY
Survey of Student Opinions

GENERAL
– Very interesting, informative
– Food excellent! Dancing good fun
– Maybe a bit overambitious for a first event
– Definitely worth doing again

PROBLEMS
Planning: – rather last-minute, a few people
                ended up doing all the work
Organisation: – people didn't know what was
                happening when
Events: – one or two presentations a bit
                boring – went on too long
                – not enough music from different
                countries
Equipment: – slide projector got stuck
                – music wasn't loud enough
                – rice cooker not available
Rooms: – not really enough space for
                dancing

SUGGESTIONS FOR FUTURE EVENTS
– Form Planning Committee (at least 1 month in advance)
– Programme/timetable of events needed
– Training needed in giving presentations and using audio-visual equip
– All equip (audio-visual + kitchen) to be checked
<u>College could:</u>
– build up collection of suitable CDs
– provide free soft drinks/coffee and maybe help towards cost of food

---

TASK CHECKLIST

1 Read the instructions and think about these questions.
- **Form:** How should a report be laid out and organised? Are there any special language features?
- **Target reader:** What is the appropriate style for addressing the Principal?
- **Purpose:** What exactly do you want to achieve?

CONTENT

2 a Read the instructions again very carefully and underline the key points.

   b Read each piece of information and make your own notes, using your own words as far as possible.

ORGANISATION/LAYOUT

3 Refer to the example report and the notes in the Writing File (pages 165 and 166). Remember to include a brief introduction. You can include your recommendations in your concluding section.

STYLE/REGISTER

4 Refer to the example report and Useful Language section in the Writing File.

English in Use 1 *Developing Skills: Structural Cloze*

▶ Paper 3, Part 2

1 **Read the newspaper article quickly and answer these questions.**
   1 What is a 'cabbie'?
   2 What is going to happen to Mr Gunduz?
   3 Why?

2 **Complete the text by writing one word in each space. The exercise begins with an example (0).**

▶ **Question 1**

The negative introduction points to a special point of grammar. See Study Box, page 127.

▶ **Question 3**

This is a way of quoting which you will find in the Writing File (page 167) if necessary.

▶ **Question 9**

Notice the commas. This is an expression of concession. Check the list of linking devices in the Writing File (page 170) if necessary.

NEW YORK CALLS IN ITS WORST CABBIE

It takes some doing to earn the title, (0) <u>among</u> 30,000 cabbies, of the worst taxi driver in New York. On no subject (1) ..... New Yorkers heap more criticism than on their taxi service. But the authorities have nominated Mr Vehbi Gunduz and are taking steps to revoke his licence.

Mr Gunduz, aged 34, has committed an unusually large number of offences, even (2) ..... the standards of local taxi driving. (3) ..... to the Taxi and Limousine Commission (TLC), Mr Gunduz has received 88 separate summonses over the past five years and been convicted (4) ..... breaking TLC rules 119 times. The offences (5) ..... from over-charging and reckless driving, to verbally abusing passengers and expelling them (6) ..... his cab. He has

also been (7) ..... to throw (8) ..... suitcases of unwelcome passengers on to the road.

Mr Gunduz has, (9) ..... , a champion in the shape of Michael Stone, his lawyer. The driver, conceded Mr Stone, is 'an individual who apparently has many, many problems', but at (10) ..... 'he has never attacked a member of the public'. That defence is accurate, says the TLC, (11) ..... when Mr Gunduz threatened murder recently, (12) ..... was against the person of an airport taxi dispatcher.

(13) ..... strict new TLC rules, a cabbie may lose his licence if he gets three convictions (14) ..... using violence or harassing his passengers. It (15) ..... Mr Gunduz just three days to achieve the required number of violations.

English in Use 2 *Developing Skills: Register Cloze*   ▶ Paper 3, Part 5

In this task you have to use information from one text to complete another which has been written for a different audience and purpose.

For questions 1–12, read the following Guest Comment Card and use the information to complete the numbered gaps in the formal memo to staff. Use **no more than two words for each gap**. The words which you need do not occur in the Comment Card. The exercise begins with an example (0).

Guest Comment Card

We would appreciate your opinion and suggestions for improving our services.

Reception

Obviously reception staff have never heard of 'service with a smile'! Any question we asked was treated as an annoying interruption.

Doorman/Porters

Their uniforms were a disgrace! Doesn't the hotel have irons? Staff were usually too busy having a quick puff on a cigarette (surely this can't be allowed?) to be of any help.

Housekeeping

The bedspread was torn, which we mentioned on the first day, but the Housekeeper seemed totally uninterested and nothing was done about it.

Restaurant

Service unbelievably slow, and when the food finally came there was a mix-up with our order on two occasions. Even that would have been alright if we had once heard the word 'sorry'.

Any other comments

My husband and I have stayed at the hotel on many previous occasions and have never had cause to complain before, but we were extremely disappointed by the service we received this time.

▶ **Question 1**

Two words: Look for information in the last section of the Guest Comment Card and make sure your answer combines with the preposition *to*.

▶ **Question 6**

Two words: What is the problem if something is *an annoying interruption*?

▶ **Question 9**

One word: Why was there a *mix-up* with the order? Your word must combine with *made* later in the sentence.

▶ **Question 12**

Two words: Think of a word which means *pay no attention to*. The subject of the clause is *the matter* – what kind of structure is needed?

From: General Manager
To: All Staff 13 June

MEMO

We have received a number of complaints from a (**0**) *couple* who are (**1**) .... to the hotel, and I shall be investigating these thoroughly.

One of the points raised concerned the untidy (**2**) .... of staff and I take this opportunity to remind you all that uniforms must be (**3**) .... and properly ironed on a daily basis. There was also a suggestion that some staff were seen to (**4**) .... while on duty, which is, of course, strictly prohibited.

These guests were also unhappy about the unfriendly (**5**) .... the reception staff, who apparently gave the impression that they were (**6**) .... to deal with any requests (**7**) .... .

I am aware that recent problems in the kitchen have led to some (**8**) .... in serving meals in the restaurant. However, it appears that (**9**) .... with orders were also made. In these circumstances, the least our guests could have expected was (**10**) .... .

Finally, it is disturbing to hear that although the guests reported that a bedspread needed to (**11**) .... , the matter (**12**) .... by Housekeeping staff.

This hotel prides itself on the quality of its service and I cannot emphasise too strongly the importance of maintaining the highest standards in your work.

Grammar File

Comparison

I Comparatives and superlatives

1.1 Adjectives

One-syllable adjectives add -er and -est.

e.g. *strong, stronger, strongest*

If the adjective ends in -e, -r and -st are added.

e.g. *wise, wiser, wisest*

If the adjective ends in a consonant -y, this changes to -ier, -iest.

e.g. *dry, drier, driest*

If the adjective ends in a single consonant after a single vowel, the consonant is doubled.

e.g. *hot, hotter, hottest*

The following have irregular forms:

good, better, best
bad, worse, worst
far, farther (or further), farthest (or furthest)

Two-syllable adjectives which end in -y add -er and -est.

e.g. *funny, funnier, funniest*

Most other two-syllable adjectives take *more* and *most*.

e.g. *ancient, more ancient, most ancient*

The following two-syllable adjectives can form superlatives with either the endings -er/-est or with *more/most.*

common   cruel   gentle   handsome   likely   mature
narrow   pleasant   polite   shallow   simple   stupid

Adjectives of more than two syllables take *more* and *most*.

e.g. *interesting, more interesting, most interesting*

1.2 *few* and *less*

fewer (the comparative of *few*) is normally used before plural nouns.

e.g. *fewer people, fewer opportunities*

less (the comparative of *little*) is normally used before uncountable nouns.

e.g. *less time, less money*

In informal English, however, *less* is often used with plural nouns.

e.g. *There were less people than I expected.*

1.3 Adverbs

Most adverbs form comparatives and superlatives with *more* and *most*.

e.g. *easily, more easily, most easily*

Adverbs with the same form as adjectives form comparatives and superlatives in the same way as adjectives.

e.g. *fast, faster, fastest*
hard, harder, hardest
early, earlier, earliest

The following have irregular forms:

well, better, best
badly, worse, worst

1.4 Qualifying comparatives

He's	no	older/more intelligent, etc.
	hardly any	
They go	a little/slightly	faster/more smoothly, etc.
	(quite) a lot	
	lots	
People have take	much/far	less free time now. far fewer days off.

2 as ... as ...

2.1 This structure can be used with adjectives and adverbs, and also with *much* and *many* + noun. The second *as* can be followed:

a	by a noun, noun phrase or object pronoun	He's as tall as his father. He thinks nobody knows as much as him.
b	by a clause	He's as tall as his father is. He thinks nobody knows as much as he does.
c	by *possible, ever* or *usual*	I'll stay as long as possible. He looked as handsome as ever.

The negative is formed with *not as ...* or *not so ... .*

e.g. *She's not as careful as she should be.*
He didn't do as well as he had hoped.
We haven't had so much rain as last year.

2.2 Qualifying comparisons with *as ... as ...*

A	is	just	as hard-working as B (is).
		almost	
A	works	nearly	as hard as B (does).
		quite	
		twice	
A	is	not nearly	as hard-working as B (is).
		not quite	
		not half	
A	doesn't work	nearly	as hard as B (does).
		quite	
		half	
X	requires	half	as much energy as Y (does).
		twice	as many players as Y (does).
		five times	

2.3 Special word order: *as* + adjective + *a/an* + noun + *as ...*

e.g. *A is as hard a worker as B.*

This is an alternative and slightly more formal way of expressing the meaning of *A works as hard as B*. In this structure, it is essential to place an indefinite article before the noun. The negative is formed with *not as ...* or *not such ...*

e.g. *That was as fine a game as I've ever seen.*
It wasn't as windy a day as had been forecast.
I'm not such an expert player as you are.

Conditionals

1 Summary of forms

Type 0: Conditions which are always true

| If | present form | + | present form or imperative |
| When | | | |

e.g. *When you put salt on ice, it melts.*
If you see her, give her my love.

Type 1: Conditions which are very probable in the present or future

| If | present form | + | future form or imperative |

e.g. *If I leave now, I'll miss the rush hour.*

Type 2: Conditions which are improbable or impossible in the present or future

| If | past simple/continuous | + | would, could, might + infinitive |

e.g. *If you met the President, what would you say to him?*
If they lived a bit nearer we might see them more often.

Type 3: Unreal conditions in the past

| If | past perfect simple/continuous | + | would/should/ could/might or have + past participle |

e.g. *If the telephone hadn't woken me, I'd have been late for my appointment.*
She could have gone to university if she'd wanted to.

Mixed conditionals

The conditional types above can be combined in several ways. The most common are:

Unreal conditions in the past with an unreal present or future result.

| If | past perfect simple/continuous | + | would/should/ could/might + infinitive |

e.g. *If you had driven faster, we could be there by now.*
If she hadn't decided to change jobs, she would be going to China next month.

Unreal conditions in the present with an unreal past result.

| If | past simple/continuous | + | would/should/ could/might have + past participle |

e.g. *If I didn't trust him, I wouldn't have let him look after the baby.*
If I spoke Japanese, I might have got that job.

2 Special points

2.1 Conditional links

Apart from *if*, the following links can be used to introduce conditional clauses:

unless   *as/so long as*   *suppose/supposing (that)*
providing/provided (that)   *on condition (that)*

2.2 Punctuation

When the *if* clause comes first in the sentence, it is followed by a comma. When the main clause comes first, no comma is used.

2.3 *Should*

In type 1 conditionals *should* + infinitive (without *to*) in the *if* clause makes the condition less likely.

e.g. *If you should need any help, just let me know.*

2.4 *Were* + infinitive (with *to*)

In type 2 conditionals *were* + infinitive with *to* in the *if* clause can be used in formal contexts.

e.g. *If we were to accept your conditions, would you be prepared to increase the loan?*

2.5 Inversion with *should/were* + infinitive

In very formal situations *should* + subject (in type 1 conditionals) and *were* + subject + infinitive with *to* (in type 2 conditionals) can replace *if*:

e.g. *Should you need any help, please don't hesitate to contact me.*
Were we to increase the loan, would you guarantee repayment?

Emphatic structures

1 Inversion

The following expressions can be placed first in a clause in order to give more emphasis or a more dramatic effect. The subject and verb are then inverted. If there is no auxiliary verb, *do/does* or *did* are used, as in a question.

Rarely/seldom ...	*Nowhere (else) ...*
Never ...	*Not (a soul/ a thing, etc.) ...*
At no time ...	*Not only ... but also ...*
Under no circumstances ...	*Hardly/scarcely ... when ...*
On no account ...	*No sooner ... than ...*
Nobody ...	*In vain ...*

e.g. *Never **have I seen** such an awful sight!*
*Under no circumstances **must you interrupt** the meeting.*
*Not a single word **would he say** on the subject.*
*Not only **does he drop** ash on the carpet, but he also spills his tobacco.*
*Hardly **had I sat down** when the doorbell rang.*
*No sooner **did she hang out** the washing than it began to rain.*

The following additional expressions can also be used in this way in certain circumstances.

Only before adverb of time (*now*, *later*, etc.) or when qualifying an introductory phrase.

e.g. *Only now **do I understand** why you behaved as you did.*
*Only in Cornwall **can you buy** real Cornish pasties.*

Little, few, so, such when not followed by a noun.

e.g. *Little **do you know** what's in store for you!*
*So strong **was the wind** that I could not control the car.*
*Such **is** fate!*

2 Cleft sentences

Cleft (or divided) constructions can be used to highlight particular items of information in a sentence by putting them into a separate clause of their own. They are used in both speech and writing, but are especially useful in writing, where emphasis cannot be indicated by intonation. There are two main types of cleft construction.

2.1 *What/The thing*, etc. + clause

This structure is used to place special emphasis on the subject, object or complement of a sentence.

e.g. *She wants to hear evidence that he cares.*
***What she wants to hear** is evidence that he cares.*
(emphasis on the object)
Lack of communication causes most problems.

This kind of cleft sentence often uses general terms like: *the person (who)*, *the thing (that)*, *the place (where)*, *the reason (why)*, etc.

e.g. ***The thing that** causes most problems is lack of communication.* (emphasis on the subject)
*Lack of communication is **the thing that** causes most problems.*

This structure can also emphasise the verb, by using *do/does* or *did* as a substitute in the *what* clause.

e.g. *She applied for another job.*
***What she did** was (to) apply for another job.*

There is usually an implied contrast with something that was said previously.

> e.g. *I can't help you find a husband.* **What I can do** *is help you make the most of your looks.*

2.2 It + be + that

This type of cleft structure can put emphasis on most elements of the sentence, except the verb. Like the *what* type, it implies a contrast with a previous statement.

> e.g. *What you say isn't important, but how.*
> **It isn't** *what you say* **that's** *important, but how.*
> (emphasis on the subject)
> *The differences lie in the way men and women talk.*
> *It's in the way men and women talk* **that** *the differences lie.* (emphasis on the adverbial)

Infinitive

1 The *to* infinitive

The *to* infinitive is used:

1.1 to express purpose.

> e.g. *There's a reporter here to interview you.*
> *I go swimming to try and keep my weight down.*

1.2 after certain verbs (there is a list of the main ones on page 154).

> e.g. *We can't afford to go out much.*
> *Don't hesitate to contact me if you need help.*

1.3 after the objects of certain verbs (there is a list of the main ones on page 154).

> e.g. *You surely don't expect me to come with you?*
> *Could you remind me to post this letter?*
> *Red causes people to feel in a hurry.*

1.4 after the auxiliary verbs *be* and *have*.

> e.g. *Does she have to be so aggressive all the time?*
> *The police are to start towing away vehicles soon.*

1.5 after adjectives.

> e.g. *They're bound to be hungry when they arrive.*
> *Fortunately, it's not likely to happen.*

1.6 after *too* + adjective and adjective + *enough*.

> e.g. *It's just too hot to eat.*
> *Are you fit enough to take part in the race?*

1.7 as the subject of a sentence.

> e.g. *To spend so much money would be foolish.*
> *To err is human, to forgive divine.*

2 Infinitive without *to*

The infinitive without *to* is used:

2.1 after modal verbs.

> e.g. *We could telephone to see how she is.*
> *Why can't you be more considerate?*

2.2 after the objects of certain verbs.

a *make*, *let* and sometimes *help*

> e.g. *She wouldn't let me pay for the damage.*
> *You can't make me go.*
> *The porter will help you carry your cases.*

b *hear*, *see*, *feel*, *notice*, *watch* when used in the sense of perceiving a complete action. (When part of an action is perceived, an *-ing* form is used.)

> e.g. *Didn't you hear me shout?* (Compare: *I heard a tap dripping so I got up.*)
> *I saw him go into the building.* (Compare: *I saw him talking to someone.*)

2.3 after *would rather ...*, *had better ...* and *why not ...?*

> e.g *I'd rather speak to you in private.*
> *You'd better hurry up.*
> *Why not take a break?*

3 Perfect and continuous infinitive

3.1 The perfect infinitive (*to* + *have* + past participle) is used to refer to the past.

> e.g. *It's useful to have had some experience in the field.*
> *I'd like to have known him better.*

3.2 The continuous infinitive (*be*/*to be* + *-ing* form)

a is used for actions which are or were happening at the time of speaking.

 e.g. *It's nice to be talking to someone who knows their subject.*

b can be used with modal verbs.

 e.g. *We could be lying on the beach instead of sitting in this traffic jam.*

See Grammar File, page 145 for passive infinitives.

-ing forms

1   *-ing* forms as nouns

-ing nouns, or gerunds, can be used with an article, with a possessive adjective, and with other determiners that go with uncountable nouns such as *this/that, some/any, much little, more/less, all,* etc.

 e.g. *You'll enjoy the singing.*
  Any cheating will be severely punished.
  I'm doing less driving now.

When used with an article, an *-ing* noun doesn't normally take a direct object.

Instead of:	* *The signing the treaty*
we say:	*The signing **of** the treaty*
Instead of:	* *The opening the motorway*
we say:	*The opening **of** the motorway*

* An asterisk indicates an incorrect utterance.

2   Verb + *-ing* form

Certain verbs are followed only by *-ing* forms (or nouns).

 e.g. *You know how he detests going to parties.*
  Let me know when you've finished working.

Note: *need* + *-ing* form has a passive meaning.

 e.g. *Your house needs painting.*

There is a list of verbs which are followed only by *-ing* forms on page 154. A few verbs can take both *-ing* forms and infinitives with little difference in meaning, while there are others which can take both forms but with a difference in meaning (see lists on page 154).

3   Other expressions + *-ing* form

Other expressions which take *-ing* forms, such as *can't stand* and *no use,* are listed on page 154.

4   Prepositions/conjunctions + *-ing* form

4.1   *-ing* forms can be used after **any** preposition.

- verb + preposition + *-ing* form
 *I finally succeeded **in** starting the car.*

- noun + preposition + *-ing* form
 *Doing yoga is a good way **of** relaxing.*

- adjective + preposition + *-ing* form
 *He's good **at** coming up with solutions.*

Other verbs, nouns and adjectives followed by prepositions are listed on page 154.

4.2   *-ing* forms are used after the following time conjunctions: *before, after, when, while, on, since.*

 e.g. *After checking the door was securely locked, she left.*

For more detailed information about participle clauses, see Grammar File, pages 144–145.

5   Possessive + *-ing* form

An *-ing* form after a verb, preposition or other expression may be interrupted by a possessive pronoun (e.g. *her*) or noun + *'s* to show a change of subject.

 e.g. *We appreciated **Helen's** offering to help.*
  *We appreciated **her** offering to help.*
  *I hope you won't mind **my** interrupting you.*
  *I look forward to **your** joining us.*
  *It's no use **her** trying to get out of it.*

In informal speech, a noun or personal pronoun may be used instead.

Modal verbs

1 Introduction

Modal verbs are a special kind of auxiliary verb. Like other auxiliary verbs, they are always used with a main verb but modal verbs express an *attitude* to what we say. They can express how certain or uncertain we are about an event, or how willing or unwilling we are to do something, for example.

There are three so-called semi-modals: *dare*, *need* and *used to*. These have some special characteristics which are described later.

The modal verbs in English are:

can   might   shall   would
could   must   should
may   ought to will

2 Special characteristics

2.1 Modal verbs are followed by the base form of the verb or by the base form of *be* (present) or *have* (past) + participle.

> e.g. *I might go.*   *You could rent a car.*
> *Would you like to sit down?*
> *They might be having dinner.*
> *He could have left the country.*

2.2 Modal verbs do not inflect, i.e. they do not take an *-s* in the third person or *-ing* or *-ed*.

2.3 Modal verbs do not take the auxiliary *do*. The negative is formed by adding *not*.

> e.g. *You can't go in there.*
> *It mightn't rain after all.*

2.4 Questions are formed by inverting the subject and the modal. Modal verbs are also used in question tags.

> e.g. *Must you make that noise?*
> *May I come in?*
> *You'd join, wouldn't you?*

2.5 Modal verbs have no infinitive. Other expressions must be used instead.

> e.g. *(can) Will you **be able** to help me?*
> *(must) I'm going to **have to** leave.*

2.6 Modal verbs have no past form, and other expressions must be used instead. (For special uses of *could* and *would*, see notes below.)

> e.g. *(must) **I had to** change the tyre.*

> *(can) **Were** you **able to** find a bank?*
> ***Did** you **manage** to find a bank?*

3 Detailed information

3.1 Ability: *can, could, able to*

3.1.1 *Can* is used to talk about present ability and awareness.

> e.g. *Holidays can damage your health.*
> *Can you hear me?*

It can also be used to talk about future ability (but not awareness), often with the idea of personal willingness.

> e.g. *Can we meet tonight?*
> *I can give you a lift tomorrow, if you like.*

3.1.2 As *can* has no infinitive, *be able to* is used with *will*, *going to*, *used to*, etc.

> e.g. *We'll be able to give you an answer soon.*
> *Will you be able to see the stage?*
> *I used to be able to swim 20 lengths without stopping.*

3.1.3 *Could* is only used to talk about general ability in the past. To talk about a specific example of ability, we use *was able to*. *Couldn't* refers to both general and specific ability.

> e.g. *I could drive when I was 15.*
> *Luckily I was able to find a taxi.*
> *I couldn't drive till I was 25.*
> *I'm afraid I couldn't find a taxi.*

3.1.4 *Could* + perfect infinitive is used to talk about how things might have been different. It can also suggest criticism.

> e.g. *He could have been an actor. (But he didn't become one.)*
> *You could have telephoned me to say you'd be late. (But you didn't phone.)*

3.2 Degrees of likelihood, assumptions and deductions: *must, can't, could, may, might*

3.2.1 *Could*, *may* and *might* are used to talk about the possibility of something. Strong possibility is indicated by adding *well*; weak possibility is indicated by adding *possibly*.

> e.g. *Don't eat it! It could/may/might be poisonous.*
> *Prices might well rise.*
> *I might possibly be wrong.*

3.2.2 Negative possibility is indicated by *may/might +
not*. *Couldn't* indicates impossibility.

> e.g. *He might not have our phone number.*
> *The news couldn't be better.*

3.2.3 *Must* is used to say that you are certain that
something is true or is going to happen, while *can't* is
used to say that you are certain that something is not
true or is not going to happen (unavoidable assumptions
and deductions based on what you know).

> e.g. *It must be 6 o'clock. There's the time signal.*
> *It can't be her at the door. She's away on holiday.*

3.2.4 Assumptions and deductions about the past are
expressed by using a perfect infinitive.

> e.g. *He could have been held up by traffic.* (possibility)
> *You must have been terrified.* (certainty)
> *She can't/couldn't have taken it.* (impossibility)

3.3 Obligation: *must, need, ought to, should*

3.3.1. *Must* and *mustn't* are used to say that it is very
important to do, or not to do, something. This can be a
personal recommendation, a strong suggestion or an
obligation (see also 3.3.2 below).

> e.g. *You must try the ice cream. It's delicious.*
> *We mustn't forget to write and thank them for their
> hospitality.*
> *You must try to be more punctual.*

3.3.2 Obligation in the past is expressed by *had to*.
Obligation in the future can be expressed by *must* when
the obligation already exists now. If it will only exist in
the future, *will have to* is used.

> e.g. *He told me that I had to try harder.*
> *You must telephone first before you arrive next time.*
> *If I'm late, I'll have to take a taxi.*

3.3.3 *Must* v. *have to*: *must* usually expresses an
obligation which comes from the speaker while *have to*
generally expresses a more impersonal obligation.

> e.g. *You must send me a postcard.* (friend speaking)
> *You have to have a visa to enter the country.* (travel
> agent speaking)

3.3.4 *mustn't* v. *don't have to/don't need to*: *mustn't*
expresses negative obligation while the other forms
express absence of obligation.

> e.g. *You mustn't make too much noise or you'll wake the
> baby!*
> *You don't have to/don't need to make an
> appointment to see him.*

3.3.5 *Should* and *ought to* express strong advice or
obligation. They are very close in meaning, but note the
difference in word order in the examples below. The past
is formed with a perfect infinitive.

> e.g. *I should really tidy the house up.*
> *You really ought to tidy the house up.*
> *They should/ought to have been more careful.*

3.3.6 *Need* exists both as an ordinary verb and as a
modal auxiliary. It is used as a modal auxiliary mainly in
questions and negative statements in the present tense,
to express lack of necessity, and in the expression *needn't
have done* (see 3.3.7 below).

> e.g. *Need you ask?*
> *You needn't shout, I'm not deaf!*

3.3.7 *Didn't need to* v. *needn't have done*: *didn't need to* is
used when something wasn't necessary so wasn't done,
while *needn't have* is used when something was done
even though it turned out to be unnecessary.

> e.g. *He didn't need to go to court because the case was
> dismissed.*
> *I needn't have dressed smartly. When I got there,
> everyone was in jeans.*

3.4 Permission: *can, may could*

3.4.1 Talking about permission

Can and *may* are used to talk about what is and isn't
permitted in the present. *May not* is more formal than
cannot.

> e.g. *You can leave school when you are 16 but you
> cannot vote.*
> *Under the law you may make one photocopy for your
> personal use, but you may not make multiple copies.*

Could and *was/were allowed to* are used to talk about
activities which were generally permitted in the past.
Only *was/were allowed to* can be used to refer to
permission given on a particular occasion.

> e.g. *At school, we could wear any clothes we wanted,
> apart from jeans.*
> *When the World Cup was on TV, I was allowed to
> stay up late and watch.*

Will be able to/will be allowed to are used to talk about
future permission.

3.4.2 Asking for and giving permission

When asking for permission to do something, *can* is the least formal, while *could* and *may* are more polite. The addition of *possibly* or the use of the form *I wonder if I ...* makes the request more polite. *Might* is very formal.

> e.g. *Can I borrow your pen for a minute?*
> *Could I (possibly) use your telephone?*
> *May I use your name as a referee?*
> *I wonder if I could interrupt you for a moment?*
> *Might I make a suggestion?*

When replying to a request for permission, only *can* and *may* are used.

> e.g. *Yes, (of course) you can/may.*
> *No, (I'm afraid) you can't (cannot)/may not.*

4 Semi-modals: *need, dare, used to*

These verbs exist both as ordinary verbs and as modal auxiliary verbs. As modals, they have certain special characteristics and the main points of these are described below.

4.1 *dare* and *need*

These verbs are mainly used as modal auxiliaries in questions and negative sentences in the present tense.

The meaning is the same as when they are used as ordinary verbs.

> e.g. *I daren't walk through the park at night.*
> *How dare you speak to me like that?*
> *We needn't hurry. The film doesn't start till 8.*

4.2 *dare*

In the present simple, *dare* sometimes takes an *-s* in the third person singular, while the past simple is usually formed with *-d*. *Dare* can also be used with the auxiliary *do* and *didn't*, and with the modals *will*, *would* and *should*.

> e.g. *She's the only one who dares challenge him.*
> *Don't you dare do that again.*
> *Nobody dared leave before the end.*
> *We didn't dare tell him what really happened.*
> *Would you dare go there alone?*

4.3 *Used to*

Used to only refers to the past. In general, its use as a modal auxiliary (*Used you to ...? He used not to ...*) is more formal and less common than its use as an ordinary verb with *did*. In the negative, *never used to* is often used instead of *didn't use to*.

> e.g. *Didn't you use to play in the school orchestra?*
> *He never used (didn't use) to be so mean.*

Participle clauses

Introduction

Participle clauses are common in written English because they enable the writer to convey information in a concise, economical way, avoiding unnecessary words. There are two types of participle clause, which are described below.

1 Adjectival participle clauses (reduced relative clauses)

Adjectival participle clauses have the same function as relative clauses, which is to give further information about a preceding noun. They can be expanded into a full relative clause, and may be either defining or non-defining.

1.1 Present participle clauses generally have an active meaning. They are used to refer to actions that happen at the same time as the main verb.

> e.g. *The author's latest book, featuring the famous*

detective in another murder mystery, is her best yet. (= *which features*: non-defining)
> *Many of the people waiting outside the palace had been there for hours.* (= *who were waiting*: defining)

1.2 Adjectival clauses formed with a past participle have a passive meaning. The past participle shows how the noun has been affected by an action.

> e.g. *Trees blown over by the storm were blocking the road.* (= *which had been blown over*: defining)
> *We stayed at the hotel recommended by the travel agent.* (= *which had been recommended*: defining)
> *Many people, worried about their health, have switched to a healthier diet.* (= *who are worried*: non-defining)

2 Adverbial participle clauses

2.1 Participle clauses can indicate the sequence of events.

The present participle is used when the action in the

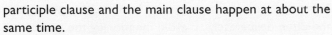

participle clause and the main clause happen at about the same time.

> e.g. *Turning the corner, I saw the old house.* (= *When I turned the corner, I saw ... / I turned the corner and I saw ...*)
> *He stormed out of the room, slamming the door behind him.* (= *... and ...*)

The perfect participle is used when there is a time difference between two actions.

> e.g. *Having finished the report, she went out for a walk.*

2.2 Participle clauses can replace adverbial clauses of reason, result and condition.

> e.g. *Not being an expert on the subject, I can't answer that question.* (reason)
> *Having lived in the country a long time, I know a lot about its customs and culture.* (reason/result)
> *Serviced regularly, the engine should last for many*

years. (condition: *If you service it regularly, ...*)

Participle clauses usually have the same subject as the main clause.

> e.g. *Knocked to the floor, the vase smashed into pieces.*

Not: * *Knocked to the floor, I smashed the vase into pieces.*

3 Participle clauses after prepositions and certain conjunctions

Participle clauses can be used after the following prepositions and conjunctions: *despite, on, as, before, after, when, whenever, while, since, until.*

> e.g. *I failed my driving test, despite having taken 25 lessons.*
> *In some jobs, you have to retire on reaching 60.*
> *He's perceived as being a hard man.*

Passive

1 Form

1.1 The passive puts emphasis on the person or thing affected by an action rather than on the agent (whoever does the action). To change a sentence from active to passive, the object must become the subject of the new sentence and be followed by a passive form.

> e.g. **Active:** *Someone has scratched my car.*
> **Passive:** *My car has been scratched.*

1.2 The passive is formed with the appropriate tense of the verb *to be* + past participle.

Present simple	*am/is/are* + p. participle *He is called 'Lofty'.*
Present continuous	*am/is/are being* + p. participle *I'm being followed.*
Present perfect	*has/have been* + p. participle *The door has been locked.*
Past simple	*was/were* + p. participle *It was made of silver.*
Past continuous	*was/were being* + p. participle *The cat was being chased.*
Past perfect	*had been* + p. participle *The cup had been broken.*
Future simple	*will be* + p. participle *They'll be criticised.*

going to	*going to be* + p. participle *You're going to be tested.*
Modals (present)	*modal + be* + p. participle *The car might be stolen.*
Modals (past)	*modal + have been* + p. participle *He could have been hurt.*
Infinitive	*to + be* + past participle *He's hoping to be invited.*

1.3 Get + past participle

Get + past participle can be used as an alternative to the *be* + past participle form in informal contexts. It usually suggests that the action described was accidental rather than intentional.

> e.g. *The trees got blown down in the storm.*
> *I'm afraid your file got lost in the move.*

1.4 An impersonal construction can be used after verbs of mental processes, such as *agree, allege, believe, feel, judge, know, rumour, say, think.*

a *It + passive + that* clause

> e.g. *It was agreed that membership fees should be raised.*
> *It is hoped that the summit meeting will be successful.*

b Subject + passive + *to* infinitive/perfect infinitive

> e.g. *She is believed to have a good chance of winning.*
> *He is rumoured to have had secret dealings with the enemy.*

2 Use

The passive is used:

2.1 when the agent is not known or not important, or when the agent is obvious from the context.

e.g. *The roof's been repaired at last.*
I'm hoping to be promoted next year.

2.2 when the agent is people in general (to avoid using *you* or *one*)

e.g. *Tickets can be reserved by calling the Box Office.*
The centre of town should be avoided during rush hour.

2.3 when the action or event is more important than the agent, as in describing processes or scientific experiments.

e.g. *The birds are first cleaned with mild detergent to remove the oil ...*
Water is then added to the mixture in the test tube

2.4 to make a statement more formal and impersonal, and often deliberately to avoid mentioning the agent.

e.g. *Your licence has been revoked.*
It was felt that he was at fault.
This is believed to be the only example in the country.

3 Special points

3.1 *make, hear, see* are followed by an infinitive without *to* in the active, but by the infinitive with *to* in the passive.

e.g. *They made me leave. I was made to leave.*
I heard them shout. They were heard to shout.
I saw him go into the building. He was seen to go into the building.

3.2 *let* has no passive form. Instead, the verb *allow* is used in the passive.

e.g. *They didn't let me pay for the damage. I wasn't allowed to pay for the damage.*

Relative clauses

1 Defining relative clauses

A defining relative clause makes it clear who or what we're talking about and is essential to the meaning of the sentence.

e.g. *I'm afraid I've lost the book that you lent me.*

Special points

a *That* often replaces *who* or *which*.

b The relative pronoun can be omitted when it is the object of the clause.

e.g. *The typewriter that you sold me has gone wrong.*
OR The typewriter you sold me has gone wrong.

c Commas are not used before the relative pronoun.

	subject	**object**	**possessive**
People	who/that	who/whom/that	
Things	which/that	which/that	whose
Place		where	
Time		when	
Reason		why	

Notes

a *Whom* is very formal and mainly used in written English.

e.g. *The man whom I met yesterday.*

Less formally, we would say:

The man (who) I met yesterday.

b *Whose* can refer to both people and things.

e.g. *The woman whose dog ran away; A house whose roof collapsed.*

c *That* normally follows superlatives and words like *something/anything/nothing/all/none/many* and *few*.

2 Non-defining relative clauses

A non-defining relative clause gives extra information about a person or thing and is not essential to the meaning of the sentence.

e.g. *We went on an excursion to a wild life park, which was interesting.*

Special points

a *Who* and *which* cannot be replaced by *that*.

b The relative pronoun cannot be omitted.

c A comma is normally used before the relative pronoun.

3   Relative clauses with prepositions

If a defining or non-defining relative clause contains a verb with a dependent preposition, this preposition is usually placed at the end of the clause:

> e.g. *There's the house (that) we used to live **in**.*
> *The President, who I spoke **to** yesterday, is very concerned.*

In more formal English, the preposition can be placed at the beginning of the clause. In this case the relative pronoun *which* or *whom* must be used.

> e.g. *There's the house **in which** we used to live.*
> *The President, **to whom** I spoke yesterday, is very concerned.*

See Study Box, page 188 for more examples of relative clauses with prepositions.

Reported speech

1   Reporting statements

To report what someone said, we use a reporting verb followed by a *that* clause. In informal speech and writing, *that* may be omitted.

> e.g. *She said she had been to an interview.*
> *I told you I'd be late.*

There is a list of reporting verbs which can be used with *that* clauses on page 155.

2   Reporting questions

Note: Reported questions use normal word order and do not have question marks.

2.1   *Yes/no* questions

To report a *yes/no* question, we normally use *ask* followed by an *if* clause or a *whether* clause. *Yes/no* questions with *or* are usually reported with *whether* clauses.

> e.g. *They asked if we had any children.*
> *I asked whether you wanted tea or coffee.*

There is a list of other verbs which can be used with *if* and *whether* clauses on page 155.

2.2   *wh* questions

To report a *wh* question, we use the *wh* word followed by the reported clause.

> e.g. *She asked why she had to pay a deposit.*
> *He wanted to know where the bank was.*

There is a list of verbs which can be used in this structure on page 155.

3   Reporting advice, orders, requests, suggestions, etc.

3.1   To report an order, request, etc. which has been made to someone, we can use a *to* infinitive clause.

> e.g. *He told me to wait in the queue.*
> *I asked her to switch off the central heating.*
> *Her doctor advised her to stop smoking.*

Other reporting verbs which can be used with this structure include *invite*, *order* and *warn*. There is a fuller list of such verbs on page 155.

3.2   To report a suggestion, we can use a *that* clause. This clause often contains the verb *should* but may also contain an infinitive.

> e.g. *The Manager suggested that we should put our complaint in writing.*
> *The Manager suggested we put our complaint in writing.*

Other reporting verbs which can be used with this structure include *demand*, *insist* and *recommend*. There is a fuller list of such verbs on page 154.

3.3   To report suggestions, advice, recommendations, etc. we can also use certain reporting verbs + *-ing*.

> e.g. *He suggested breaking the journey in Chester.*
> *The doctor advised taking a holiday.*
> *Steve recommended trying the steak.*

There is a list of these verbs on page 155.

4   Reporting intentions and hopes

To report a stated intention or hope, we can use either a *that* clause or a *to* infinitive clause after certain verbs.

> e.g. *I promised to be back before midnight.*
> *I promised that I would be back before midnight.*

Note: A *that* clause must be used if there is a change of subject.

Other reporting verbs which can be used in this way include *hope*, *propose* and *threaten*. There is a fuller list of such verbs on page 154.

5 Time reference

When reporting speech, the tenses and time expressions are normally changed as follows:

Direct Speech	Reported Speech
Present simple	Past simple
Present continuous	Past continuous
Present perfect	Past perfect
Past simple	Past perfect
Past perfect	Past perfect
shall/will	should/would
can/may	could/might
must	must/had to
now	then
today	that day
tomorrow	the next/following day
yesterday	the day before/the previous day
this	that
here	there
ago	before

Notes

a It is not necessary to change the tense when the reporting verb is in the present tense or when the original words are still true.

> e.g. *He says his car has broken down and he's waiting for a mechanic.*
> *Professor Cooper explained that family tensions often erupt when the family is thrust together incessantly.*

b Certain modal verbs (*could, would, should, ought to, might*) don't change in reported speech.

> e.g. *I might be back late.*
> *I said I might be back late.*

Spelling

I Capital letters

Capital letters are used:

I at the *beginning of a sentence*.

2 in *headings* and *sub-headings* for reports, articles and so on. Also in the *titles of books, plays, films, particular works of art, scientific laws*, etc. In this case, the main words have capitals while the articles and smaller prepositions usually do not.

> e.g. *Introduction   Focus on Advanced English   Hamlet*
> *Back to the Future   Mona Lisa   Boyle's Law*

3 with *names of people* (also animals and other things which have individual names), *manufacturers, shops, hotels, government departments*, etc.

> e.g. *Mr Martin Hall   Ford   Quicksave*
> *The Rome Hilton   Department of Education*

4 with *names of countries, cities, towns, regions, areas, streets*, etc., and with *adjectives* and *nouns* describing *nationality* or *place of origin* but not with east, west, etc. on their own.

> e.g. *France   Athens   the Middle East   Soho*
> *Fifth Avenue   French   a Dutchman   Bavarian*

5 with *names of rivers, mountains* and other *geographical features*. Also with *planets* but not the sun, earth or moon.

> e.g. *The Nile   Mount Everest   The Sahara Desert*
> *Mars   The Black Forest*

6 with *days, months, festivals* and *historical periods* but not seasons.

> e.g. *Tuesday   March   Easter   the Middle Ages*
> (but *summer, winter*, etc.)

7 with the names of certain *professions* or *positions* when used as titles for particular people but not when used generally.

> e.g. *Let me introduce you to the Principal.* (but: *I'd like to become the principal of a college one day.*)

2 Forming participles

2.1 Doubling consonants

The final consonant is doubled in verbs:

I which have only one syllable and which have one vowel followed by one consonant.

> e.g. *stop – stopping*
> *run, trap, swim, fit, clap*

Exceptions: Final -*w*, -*x* and -*y* are never doubled.

2 which have more than one syllable but where the final syllable is stressed and has one vowel followed by one consonant.

> e.g. *regret – regretting*
> *begin, admit, refer, occur, forget*

Exceptions: There are a few verbs where the final

consonant is doubled even though the stress is on the first syllable:

> e.g. *worship, kidnap, handicap*

3 which end in *-l* after one vowel.

travel*, cancel*, control, signal*, fulfil

> e.g. *quarrel – quarrelling*

Note that in American English there are some verbs where the final *-l* is not doubled. Examples are shown with a *.

The final consonant is therefore not doubled in verbs:

a where there are two vowels followed by a consonant

> e.g. *sweep – sweeping* (Rule 2.1.1)

b where there are two final consonants

> e.g. *warn – warning* (Rule 2.1.1)

c where the stress is on the first of two syllables

> e.g. *limit – limiting* (Rule 2.1.2)

d where final *-l* follows two vowels

> e.g. *steal – stealing* (Rule 2.1.3)

2.2 Other points

I Verbs which end in a consonant + *-e* normally drop the e before the ending *-ing*.

> e.g. *sneeze – sneezing*

Main exceptions: *age – ageing, dye – dyeing*

2 Final *-y* after a consonant changes to *-i* before *-ed*.

> e.g. *try – tried*

3 Final *-y* after a vowel does not normally change in this way.

> e.g. *enjoy – enjoyed, play – played*

Exceptions: *pay – paid, lay – laid, say – said*

4 The ending *-ie* changes to *-y* before *-ing*.

> e.g. *lie – lying, die – dying*

5 Verbs which end with *-c* usually add *-k* before *-ed* or *-ing*.

> e.g. *panic – panicked, picnic – picnicking*

Tenses: present

I Present simple

Form

base form + (e)s	e.g. *She plays the violin.*

Negative: *doesn't /don't* + base form

Question: *do/does* + subject + base form?

Use

1.1 The present simple refers to situations which are long-term or permanent and to general truths such as scientific facts.

> e.g. *She works for the Foreign Office.*
> *I love classical music.*
> *Nine planets travel round the sun.*

1.2 It can also refer to regular or repeated actions.

> e.g. *He swims during his lunch break every day.*
> *I always spend Christmas with my family.*

1.3 It is used with certain verbs to express thoughts, feelings, impressions and immediate reactions.

> e.g. *This tea tastes strange.*
> *Do you want to try the jacket on?*

Note: With certain verbs e.g. *think, feel,* there is a difference in meaning between the present simple and present continuous. There is a list of these verbs on page 155.

> e.g. *I think you're wonderful.* (opinion)
> *I'm thinking about what you said earlier.* (mental process)

1.4 The present simple also has certain special uses in reviews, sports commentaries, dramatic narrative and when reporting what you have heard or been told (with *say/tell/hear*).

> e.g. *Dustin Hoffman, who plays the hero, gives a fine performance.*
> *Black passes the ball to White but he misses ...*
> *There I am, all alone in the house, and the doorbell rings!*
> *I hear you've decided to move.*

1.5 The present simple can be used to talk about future plans with reference to timetables and itineraries (see Grammar File, page 150), and is also used in time clauses introduced by *when, as soon as, after, if,* etc. (The present perfect can also be used in time clauses; see section on present perfect below.)

> e.g. *The train leaves at midday.*
> *I'll let you know if a fax arrives.*

2 Present continuous

Form

is/are + -ing	e.g. He's washing his hair.

Negative: am/is/are not + -ing
Question: is/are + subject + -ing?
Note: Certain verbs do not usually occur in continuous tenses (see page 155).

Use

2.1 The present continuous is used to talk about actions which are happening at the moment of speaking or which are changing or developing at the present time.

  e.g. Don't disturb him, he's working.
  My typing's improving.

2.2 It can also refer to actions or situations which are temporary.

  e.g. I'm helping out in the kitchen until they find a new chef.

2.3 The present continuous can be used with always or forever to describe a habit which the speaker finds annoying.

  e.g. Why are you forever criticising me?

2.4 The present continuous is also quite often used to express pre-arranged future actions (see Grammar File, page 150).

  e.g. Nigel's coming round to see us tonight.

Tenses: expressing the future

Summary of forms and uses

Form	Use
going to	
e.g. We're going to have a party. Are you going to invite John?	1 To express personal intention. The action has usually been considered in advance and some arrangements may have been made.
e.g. I think I'm going to faint.	2 To make a prediction based on what you know, feel or can see.
Future simple	
e.g. He'll be forty in June. Tomorrow will be cold and wet.	1 To express a future fact or prediction.
e.g. I know, I'll phone for a taxi.	2 To express a sudden decision.
e.g. Shall I give you a lift? Will you help me with this bag?	3 To express an offer or request.
e.g. I'll hit you if you do that again. Don't worry, I won't be late.	4 To express a threat or a promise.
e.g. I suppose you'll be pretty busy. Do you think he'll come?	5 To express an opinion about the future after verbs like think, suppose, expect, doubt if and also with probably.
e.g. There's a car pulling up outside. Oh, that'll be Jim.	6 To express strong probability.
Present continuous	
e.g. What are you doing this evening? The car's being serviced tomorrow.	To express a pre-arranged future action. Similar in meaning and use to going to but with less sense of personal intention.
Present simple	
e.g. What time do you arrive at Heathrow? We call at Venice and Athens.	To express the certain future, a fixed future event usually based on a timetable or programme.
Is to	
e.g You are to do exactly as I say.	1 To express an instruction or order.
e.g. The President is to visit Rome.	2 To talk about an action or event which has been arranged, often officially.

About to/due to

e.g. *The building is due to be completed soon.* *He's about to announce the result.*	To talk about actions or events which are expected to happen, usually fairly soon.

Future continuous

e.g. *It's awful to think I'll be working this time next week!*	1 To talk about an action which will be in progress at a point in the future.
e.g. *The big stores will be having their winter sales soon.*	2 To talk about an action or event which will happen as a matter of course.
e.g. *Will you be checking out today?*	3 To express a request for information rather than a request for action.
e.g. *Where's Nigel tonight?* *He'll be performing somewhere with his band, I expect.*	4 To express strong probability.

Future perfect

e.g. *They will have received our letter by Monday.*	To talk about a future event which will be complete by a time which is further in the future.

Future perfect continuous

e.g. *I'll have been working in this company for 10 years next April.*	To talk about the duration of an action, as seen from a point in the future.

Tenses: present perfect

1 Form

Simple: | *has/have* + past participle |
| e.g. *He's sold his car.* |

Negative: *has/have not* + past participle

Question: *has/have* + subject + past participle?

Continuous: | *has/have been* + present participle |
| e.g. *I've been playing tennis.* |

Negative: *has/have been* + *-ing*

Question: *has/have* + subject + *been -ing?*

Note: Certain verbs are not usually used in continuous tenses. See list on page 155.

2 General use

2.1 Both the present perfect simple and the present perfect continuous are used to refer to actions or states which began in the past and have continued up till now. *Since* is used to express the starting point, and *for* is used to express its duration.

The following time expressions are often used:

lately   recently   so far   up till now

e.g. *I've had a cold for a week.*

He hasn't been practising on the piano so much lately.

How long have you lived in this flat now?

I've been going to Scotland every summer since I was a child.

2.2 The present perfect simple is used to refer to an action or state which was completed in the past but where the time is unknown or unimportant. The present result is generally more important than when or how the action or event occurred.

The following expressions are often used:

just, already, before, ever, never, yet, still

e.g. *Your father's just come in.* (= He's here.)

I've seen that film already. (= I don't want to see it again.)

The TV's been repaired. (= It is now working.)

Have you ever been to Nepal? (= Can you tell me about it?)

2.3 The present perfect can be used in time clauses introduced by *when, as soon as, after* to describe an action which will be completed before the action in the main clause.

e.g. *We'll make the announcement once everyone has arrived.*

You can buy a car after you've passed the driving test.

3 Simple v. continuous

3.1 In some cases there is little difference between the two forms.

> e.g. *I've lived here all my life.*
> *I've been living here all my life.*

3.2 The present perfect continuous tends to emphasise how long an action has continued.

> e.g. *It's been raining all day.*
> *I've been waiting for hours.*

3.3 The present perfect continuous may suggest that an action is temporary rather than long-term or permanent.

> e.g. *He's been staying with his sister till he finds somewhere to live.*

3.4 The present perfect simple suggests that an action is complete while the present perfect continuous suggests that it is still incomplete.

> e.g. *I've painted the kitchen.* (The job is finished.)
> *I've been painting the kitchen.* (The job is probably unfinished.)

3.5 The present perfect continuous can be used for a series of repeated actions but the present perfect simple must be used when the actual quantity of actions or finished products is mentioned.

> e.g. *I've been knocking on the door for ages.*
> *I've knocked on the door ten times.*

Tenses: past

1 Past simple
Form
Regular verbs:

base form + -(e)d	e.g. *They walked towards us.*

Negative: *didn't* + base form
Question: *did* + subject + base form?

Use

1.1 The past simple is used to refer to completed actions or events which took place at a particular time or over a period of time in the past.

> e.g. *We met last summer. Do you remember?*
> *I stayed with my uncle until I found a flat of my own.*

1.2 The past simple can also refer to repeated actions in the past.

> e.g. *He went for a walk every day before lunch.*

Note: It is also possible to use *used to* or *would* + base form with this meaning.

> e.g. *He used to go for a walk ...*
> *He would go for a walk ...*

1.3 When two actions happen quickly, one after the other, we usually use the past simple in each case.

> e.g. *When the oil warning light came on, I switched off the engine.*

1.4 When we report two actions which happened at the same time, and it is the result that is important, we can also use the past simple in each case.

> e.g. *As it grew darker, we found it more difficult to follow the path.*

2 Past continuous
Form

was/were + -ing	e.g. *It was raining.*

Negative: *wasn't/weren't* + -ing
Question: *was/were* + subject + base form?
Note: Some verbs do not usually occur in continuous tenses. See the list on page 155.

Use

2.1 The past continuous refers to actions or situations which were unfinished at a particular time in the past. It also emphasises how long an action continued.

> e.g. *You were living in Brighton then, weren't you?*
> *I was getting colder and colder all the time.*

2.2 It is often used to refer to an action which was going on when a second shorter action interrupted it.

> e.g. *I was driving home when I heard the news on the car radio.*

2.3 The past continuous is often used to describe the background to events in a story.

> e.g. *It was a beautiful day. The sun was shining and the birds were singing.*

2.4 The past continuous can be used to describe two actions which happened at the same time when we are more interested in the fact that they happened together than in the result.

e.g. *While I was waiting for him to ring, he was out having a good time.*

2.5 The past continuous can be used with *always* or *forever* to emphasise the frequency of an action. In this case, the speaker is often expressing criticism or annoyance.

e.g. *They were always having loud parties which went on till the early hours.*

2.6 The past continuous is used in the expressions *I was wondering if/whether* and *I was hoping (that) ...* as a way of making an invitation, a request, etc. more polite. These expressions refer to the present/future, not the past.

e.g. *I was wondering if you would like to join us?*

3 Past perfect
Form

Simple:

had + past participle
e.g. *He had already left.*

Negative: *hadn't* + past participle
Question: *had* + subject + past participle?

Continuous:

had been + -ing
e.g. *I'd been waiting for an hour.*

Negative: *hadn't been* + -ing
Question: *had* + subject + been + -ing?
Note: Some verbs do not usually occur in continuous tenses. See list on page 155.

Use

3.1 The past perfect refers to actions which happened, or situations which existed, before another action at a particular time in the past.

e.g. *The shop had closed by the time I got there.*
When I reached the front door, I realised I had lost my key.

3.2 The past perfect is used to make the order of events clear. It's not necessary to use it when the two actions happen quickly, one after the other, or when the order of events is clear anyway.

e.g. *I recognised him as soon as I saw him.*
After he left the office he went to collect his car from the garage.

3.3 The past perfect continuous is used when the first action continued for some time or was unfinished.

e.g. *The fire had been burning for some time before the fire brigade arrived.*
I'd been hoping to meet her for ages when I bumped into her by chance.

4 Past tenses used to talk about hypothetical situations

4.1 Past tenses can be used after the following expressions to talk about situations which do not exist or events which did not happen but which we are able to imagine.

I wish	would rather	suppose/supposing	if
if only	as if/as though		

The past simple is used for present or future reference.

e.g. *I wish I had a car.* (I haven't.)
I'd rather you didn't smoke. (You are smoking or may do in future.)
He behaves as if he owned the place. (He doesn't.)
Suppose you didn't get the job, what would you do?

Note: *I wish + would* is used to express a wish for something to change in the future. It cannot be used to refer to oneself.

e.g. *I wish the weather would improve.*
I wish you would stop going on about it.

The past perfect is used for past reference.

e.g. *If only he had telephoned before he came.* (He didn't.)
I'd rather you hadn't told me. (You did tell me.)
He speaks as if he had done all the work himself. (He didn't.)
Supposing you had had an accident! (You didn't.)

4.2 The past simple is also used after the expression *It's (high/about) time.*

e.g. *It's high time we left.* (It's late and we haven't left yet.)

153

Reference Lists

-ing forms and infinitive

1 Verbs followed by -ing forms

admit	detest	involve	resent
adore	dislike	keep	resist
appreciate	dread	lie	risk
avoid	endure	loathe	sit
celebrate	enjoy	mention	stand
commence	face	mind	suggest
consider	fancy	miss	
contemplate	finish	postpone	
delay	go	practise	
deny	imagine	report	

2 Verbs followed by a preposition + -ing form

admit to	benefit from	get on with	resort to
agree with	care for	insist on	succeed in
aim at	confess to	object to	think of
apologise for	count on	pay for	vote for
approve of	depend on	put up with	
believe in	feel like	rely on	

3 Nouns followed by a preposition + -ing form

hope of	idea of	way of
difficulty in	thought of	method of

4 Adjectives followed by a preposition + -ing form

bad at	capable of	guilty of
good at	excited about	tired of
good for	fed up with	keen on
bored with	fond of	nervous of

5 Other expressions followed by -ing forms

can't bear	go (e.g. camping)	no good
can't help	spend time/money (on)	no use
can't stand	not worth	

6 Verbs followed by a to infinitive

afford	decide	learn	swear
agree	demand	long	tend
aim	deserve	manage	threaten
appear	expect	mean	undertake
arrange	fail	neglect	volunteer
ask	fight	offer	vow
attempt	guarantee	pause	wait
beg	happen	plan	want
care	help	prepare	refuse
choose	hesitate	pretend	seem
consent	hope	promise	wish
dare	intend	prove	yearn

7 Verbs which take an object followed by a to infinitive

advise	forbid	leave	tell
allow	force	order	urge
ask	get	persuade	want
encourage	help	prefer	warn
expect	intend	recommend	
beg	invite	remind	

8 Verbs followed by -ing forms or a to infinitive

a With little difference in meaning

attempt	cease	fear	love
begin	continue	hate	prefer
bother	deserve	like	start

b With a difference in meaning

come + -ing	move in a particular way
come + to inf	gradually start doing something
dread + -ing	be fearful about a future action
dread + to inf	(used only with think)
regret + -ing	be sorry about an action in the past
regret + to inf	(with say, tell, inform and announce) be sorry about a present action
remember /forget + -ing	refers to an action **before** the moment of remembering or forgetting
remember/ forget + to inf	refers to an action **after** the moment of remembering or forgetting
stop + -ing	finish an action
stop + to inf	interrupt an action in order to do something else
try + -ing	make an experiment
try + to inf	make an effort to do something difficult

Reporting verbs

1 Verbs followed by *that* clauses

add	decide*	mention	state
admit	deny	observe	suggest
agree	doubt	persuade	suppose
announce	estimate	promise*	swear*
answer	expect*	propose	tell
argue	explain	remark	think
boast	fear	remember	threaten*
claim	feel	repeat	understand
comment	find	reply	warn
complain	guarantee*	report	
confirm	hope*	reveal	
consider	insist	say	

*These verbs can also be followed by *to* infinitive clauses.

2 Verbs followed by *if* and *whether* clauses

ask	remember	see
know	say	

3 Verbs followed by clauses beginning with *wh* words

decide	guess	reveal	think
describe	imagine	say	understand
discover	know	see	wonder
discuss	learn	suggest	
explain	realise	teach	
forget	remember	tell	

4 Verbs followed by object + *to* infinitive clause

advise	forbid	remind	warn
ask	instruct	teach	
beg	invite	tell	
command	recommend	urge	

5 Verbs followed by a *that* clause containing *should*

advise	insist	recommend
beg	prefer	request
demand	propose	suggest

6 Verbs + *-ing* form

admit	deny	mention	propose
recommend	regret	report	suggest

Verbs not usually used in continuous tenses

admire	detest	impress	mean	seem
adore	dislike	include	owe	sound
astonish	doubt	involve	own	stop
be	envy	keep	please	suppose
believe	exist	know	possess	surprise
belong	fit	lack	prefer	survive
concern	forget	last	reach	suspect
consist	hate	like	realise	understand
contain	hear	love	remember	want
deserve	imagine	matter	satisfy	wish

Verbs with a different meaning in simple and continuous tenses

Verb	Simple tenses	Continuous tenses
appear	= look/seem	= take part in (a trial/play/film)
expect	= feel confident that	= waiting for sth/to be pregnant
feel	= have an opinion	= physical sensation
have	= possess	= organising/actions (e.g. a bath)
hold	= have a certain capacity	= physical contact with hands
look	= have an appearance	= action of seeing
measure	= have a certain length	= action of taking a measurement
see	= use your eyes	= meeting
smell	= have a certain smell	= action of smelling something
think	= have an opinion	= mental process
taste	= have a certain taste	= action of tasting something
weigh	= have a certain weight	= action of weighing something

In some cases the meanings listed under 'Continuous tenses' can be used in simple tenses, e.g. *she's having a bath*, *she has a bath every morning*, but the meanings listed under simple tenses cannot be used in continuous tenses.

Writing File

A Informal Letters

A1 Layout

Write your address in the top right-hand corner.

Your address
The date

Write the date directly below.

Write the first line next to the left-hand margin.

Begin the next line under the name.

Dear ====,

====================================
====================================
====================================
=================

====================================
====================================
====================================
=================

Ending
Your name

A2 Example

22 York Street
Bridewell
BR8 4SO

24th Nov. 19—

Never put your name before your address.

Write the house number first, followed by the street, town (and postcode, if you know it).

Never begin with *Dear Friend*. Always use a name.

Begin the first sentence with a capital.

Dear Ken,
    Many thanks for your letter and for the photographs — they brought back very happy memories of our holiday.
    I'm glad to hear that your new job is going so well. It must be

    Do let me know when you're coming to England. It would be lovely to see you and you're most welcome to stay here — there's plenty of room!
    Hope to hear from you soon.
    Best wishes
    Sue

With closer friends, you could just put *Write soon*.

Best wishes, and *Yours* are useful general endings. For close friends, you can end with *Love*.

A3 Types of Letters

A3.1   Beginnings

In an informal letter to a friend, it may be appropriate to begin by mentioning a letter which you have recently received or by making general friendly comments.

Useful language:
Many thanks for your letter ...
It was lovely/very nice to hear from you recently ...
I was glad to hear that you had a good holiday
I hope you and the family are well.

A3.2   Invitation

Say what the event is and explain the details of date, time and place clearly. You may need to add other details such as who else is coming, what you would like your friend to bring (if anything), whether they can bring a partner or friend, when you need a reply by, and how to get there. Use separate paragraphs for each main piece of information.

Useful language:
I'm having a birthday party on Saturday the 22nd **and I hope you'll be able to come.**
I was wondering if you'd like to come to see 'Wild Lives' at the Theatre Royal with me?
Would you like to/Why don't you come and stay for the weekend?
Could you (possibly) let me know if you can come by ...

A3.3   Request

Describe the situation or problem and explain exactly what needs to be done. Make it clear how grateful you would be for the help you ask for and give an opportunity for the recipient to agree or refuse, if appropriate.

Useful language:
I'm writing to ask you a favour.
I wonder
I was wondering } **if I could ask you a favour?**
I'd be terribly grateful if ...
Please don't hesitate to say no if you can't manage it ...

A3.4   Apology

Explain why you are apologising, give reasons for your behaviour, express regret for any damage, inconvenience, offence which was caused, and offer to put things right if possible.

Useful language:
I'm writing to apologise
                        – about ...
                        – for the fact that (+ clause)
                        – for (not) (+ –ing)
I'm terribly sorry that ...
I do hope that ...
Please let me know where you bought it/how much it cost **and I'll gladly** replace it/pay for it.

A3.5   Information/News

Useful language:
I thought you'd like to know/hear about ...
This is just to let you know that ...

A3.6 Giving Advice

Useful language:
You asked me for advice on ...
Have you thought about ... ?
It might be a good idea to ...
One thing I would suggest is ...

A3.7   Thank you/Congratulations/Good Luck

Useful language:
I'm writing to thank you/Thank you so much for (+ noun/-ing)
It was very kind of you to ... (+ verb)
I'm writing to congratulate you/Congratulations on (+ noun)
I'm writing to wish you (the very best of) luck in/with (+ noun)

A3.8 Endings

It is usual to end letters which expect a reply with a sentence on a separate line. This could be:
Looking forward to hearing from you/seeing you.
Hope to hear from you soon/see you soon.
Write soon/See you soon.

Although it's important to know how to set out the address for real-life letter writing, you do not need to include addresses in exam tasks.

B Formal Letters

B1 Layout

Write the recipient's name and address on the left-hand side below the date.

Only use *Dear Sir* or *Dear Madam* if you don't know the person's name.

Your address

The date

Other person's name and address

Dear Sir/Madam, / Dear Mr Brandon/Mrs White,

===================================
===================================

Write your address in the top right-hand corner.

Write the date directly below.

===================================
===================================

Yours faithfully, / Yours sincerely,

Your signature

Your name – printed

If you begin *Dear Sir* or *Dear Madam*, end with *Yours faithfully*. If you begin with a name, end with *Yours sincerely*.

B2 Example

Write the name and/or title of the person you're writing to. Do not indent their address.

Write the first line next to the left-hand margin.

Begin the next line under the name.

Write *Yours* with a capital 'Y' and *faithfully* or *sincerely* with a small 'f' or 's'. These endings are followed by a comma.

22 York Street
Bridewell
BR8 4SO

24th Nov. 19—

The Principal
Clifton College
Clifton
CL5 2RE
Dear Sir,
   I am interested in applying for a place on a computer course at your college and I would be grateful if you could send me full details of the courses you offer and the fees, together with an application form.

I look forward to hearing from you.

Yours faithfully,

S. M. Gilchrist

S. M. GILCHRIST (MISS)

Never put your name before your address.

Write the house number first, followed by the street town (and postcode, if you know it).

Give your reason for writing at the beginning. If you are replying to an advert, say where you saw it and when. If you are replying to a letter, give the date of the letter.

Print your name clearly after your signature.

159

B3 Types of Letters

B3.1 Enquiry

Explain clearly what information you would like and why you need it. If there are different points you need to explain or to ask about, use a different paragraph for each.

Useful language:
I am writing to enquire about ...
I was interested in your advertisement in 'The Daily Times' and I would like to have further information about ...
I should be grateful if you would send me (full) details of ...

B3.2 Job Application

Explain clearly which post/job you are applying for and, if you are responding to an advertisement, say where you saw it and when. Give all the necessary information about yourself, including age, qualifications, past employment, relevant experience and any special hobbies or interests, and explain why you are particularly interested in this post. Use a new paragraph for each main topic. It's also helpful to say when you would be available to attend an interview.

Useful language:
I am interested in applying for the post of ... which was advertised in 'The Globe' on 22nd September.
My reason for applying is that I would like to broaden my experience and also ...
I would be able to attend an interview at any time which is convenient to you.

B3.3 Other Application

Explain clearly what you are applying for, where you heard about it and, if appropriate, who you represent. Give all the necessary information about your application, explaining how you intend to use the opportunity/money, what you hope to achieve, and why this is important or worthwhile.

Useful Language:
I am interested in applying for the grant/scholarship which ...
   – was advertised/mentioned in an article in last week's 'Globe on Sunday.'
   – I learnt about from my tutor/the college notice board.
The reason for my/our application is that this grant/scholarship would
   – enable me/us to gain valuable practical experience ...
   – make a real difference to my/our work/project.

Although it's important to know how to set out the address for real-life letter writing, you do not need to include addresses in exam tasks.

B3.4 Apology

Explain why you are apologising, give reasons for your behaviour, express regret for the damage/inconvenience/offence which has been caused and promise not to let it happen again or to make up for what you've done, as appropriate:

Useful language:
I am writing to apologise/I sincerely apologise
   – for (not) (+ -ing)
   – for the fact that (+ clause)
I'm so/really sorry (not) to have (+ p. part.)
I (do) hope you will forgive me for (not) (+ -ing)
I assure you that it/this will never happen again.

B3.5 Complaint

In the **first paragraph**, explain the reason for writing and in the **next**, explain exactly what the problem is. Give all the necessary details about where and when it happened and who was involved. Give other relevant information in **further paragraphs** if necessary. In the **final paragraph**, explain what action you want to be taken.

Useful language:
I am writing
   – to complain about ...
   – to express my concern about the fact that ...
   – to express my annoyance at ...
I must insist that you ...
I must urge you to ...

B3.6 Opinion

If you're replying or reacting to something such as a letter or an article, give the necessary details. Explain your opinion and the reasons for it clearly, using separate paragraphs for each main point. Sum up your argument in the final paragraph.

Useful language:
In reply to your letter of 12th September, I would like to say ...
I would like to respond to the article entitled '...', which appeared in Monday's edition of your newspaper.
In my opinion, ...
It seems (clear) to me that ...
I would suggest that ...

B3.7 Endings

It is usual to end letters which expect a reply with a sentence on a separate line. The most common ending is:
I look forward to hearing from you.

C Personal Notes and Messages; Memos

C1 Notes and Messages

Notes and messages are even more informal than informal letters and are written to friends and people you know well. They usually contain a brief message about one or two main subjects so they are generally shorter than a page. They may or may not be placed in envelopes and are often delivered by hand rather than posted. There are no fixed rules about their layout.

C2 Memos

Memos are a form of note or message between colleagues in a business context. They are usually written on official forms which have the heading 'Memo' and a place to write the name of the sender and the recipient, the date and sometimes the subject. There is no need to begin 'Dear ...'. The language is generally more formal than in a note to a friend but the degree of formality depends on the relationship between the writer and the recipient, and the subject matter.

C3 Examples

C3.1 Notes and Messages

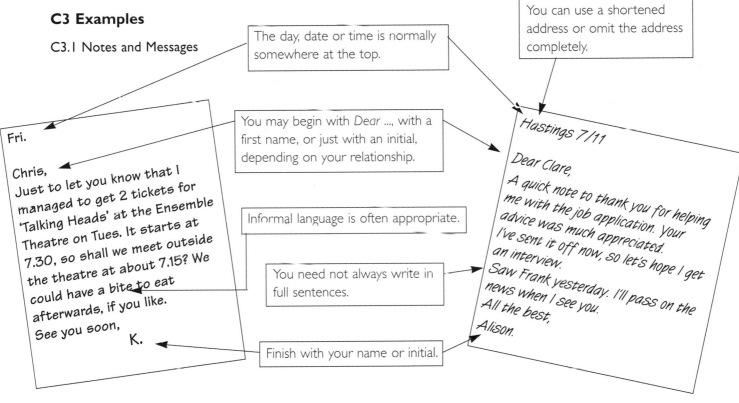

The day, date or time is normally somewhere at the top.

You can use a shortened address or omit the address completely.

Fri.

Chris,
Just to let you know that I managed to get 2 tickets for 'Talking Heads' at the Ensemble Theatre on Tues. It starts at 7.30, so shall we meet outside the theatre at about 7.15? We could have a bite to eat afterwards, if you like.
See you soon,
K.

You may begin with *Dear* ..., with a first name, or just with an initial, depending on your relationship.

Informal language is often appropriate.

You need not always write in full sentences.

Finish with your name or initial.

Hastings 7/11

Dear Clare,
A quick note to thank you for helping me with the job application. Your advice was much appreciated.
I've sent it off now, so let's hope I get an interview.
Saw Frank yesterday. I'll pass on the news when I see you.
All the best,
Alison.

C3.2 Memos

The heading includes names (or initials) and the date.

It's usual to put the subject, underlined, at the top.

```
                        MEMO
To:       HB
From:     SO
Date:     10/4


Subject:  Sales Conference 2 May

In order to compile the annual departmental report for
the above event, I need up-to-date sales figures for your
section. Could you have these on my desk by 22 April
at the latest, but sooner if possible?

I'd also like to take this opportunity of thanking you for
all your hard work over the past year. Enjoy your Easter
break.
```

There's no need to begin 'Dear ...'.

A memo can be unsigned or can have a name or initial at the end

C4 Types of Notes, Messages and Memos

In general, the language in a memo is more formal than in a note or message, but the degree of formality in all three types of writing depends on the relationship between the writer and the recipient, and also on the subject matter. A note to an acquaintance would be more formal than a note to a friend. A memo to a close colleague about servicing the coffee machine would be less formal than a memo to the boss apologising for a mistake you'd made.

C4.1 Query

Useful language:

Could you let me know

    – what happened about ...

    – what you('ve) decided about ...

Can you tell me

    – what you think about ...

    – if you're interested in ...

    – if you'd like to ...

Would you (please) *clarify the situation regarding ...*

C4.2 Information/News

Useful language:

Just to let you know *(that) ...*

(I) Thought you might like to know *(that) ...*

For (your) information, *the next meeting will be held ...*

C4.3 Request

Useful language:

Could you/Would you (please)

    – let me have ...

    – send me ...

    – look into ...

    – find out about ...

C4.4 Apology

Useful language:

(I'm) Sorry I *couldn't/wasn't able to/didn't/forgot to ...*

I (would like to) apologise for *missing the meeting.*

C4.5 Thank you/Congratulations/Good Luck

Useful language:

Many thanks for ... *(+ noun/-ing)*

Just to thank you for ... *(+ noun/-ing)*

I'd like to take this opportunity of thanking you/ to thank you ...

May I take this opportunity of thanking you/ to thank you ... ?

Congratulations on ... *(+ noun)*

Best of luck in/with ... *(+ noun)*

C5 Notes and Messages: Beginnings and Endings

C5.1 Beginnings

Useful language:

No special introductory phrases are necessary but notes often begin with expressions like:

Just (a note) to   *let you know/tell you/check (that) ...*

A quick note to   *ask/see if ...*

    thank you for/apologise (for/about) ...

C5.2 Endings

Useful language:

No special final phrases are needed but notes and messages may end with expressions like:

See you soon

Speak to you soon

All the best

D Information Sheets, Leaflets and Brochures

D1 Notes

Information sheets, leaflets and brochures are intended to **inform**, **advise**, **persuade** or **warn**. The two main aims are therefore to catch the reader's attention and to present the message as clearly as possible. To do this, layout and organisation need to be as effective as possible. Short paragraphs with clear headings are much easier to read and absorb than long blocks of text, for example. The best approach is to imagine yourself as the reader and to ask what you would want to know, and in what order you would find it easiest to absorb the information. Consider these points:

Main heading:

- Is this as direct and eye-catching as possible?
- Does it give the reader a clear idea of what the subject is?
- Does it make the reader want to read on?

Sub-headings:

- Are these short and clear? Asking a question in your heading may be more interesting than stating a fact. (See Example D2.2.)

D2 Examples

D2.1 Information Sheet

Text:

- Is the information broken up into short easy-to-read sections?
- Is the order logical?

Visual help:

Can you help the reader, for example:

- by indenting small sub-sections so that they stand out as small blocks which are clearly separate from the main text? or
- by putting important points on separate lines? or
6. by numbering your points? or
- by putting 'bullets' in front of main points? or

by using different **STYLES** and sizes of writing? or

by underlining, or

putting boxes round important words

You won't be marked on your design skills, of course, but you may make a good impression on the examiner!

BRISTOL HALF MARATHON

May 10th   11 a.m. start

The Event

On the 10th May this year Bristol will be staging its tenth Half Marathon. This is now the largest mass participation sporting event in the West Country.

The majority of entrants are not dedicated athletes but runners of all abilities, who like setting themselves a challenge and who enjoy the atmosphere of the day. Our course is exceptionally fast and flat, with leading finishing times regularly under 65 minutes.

Your Certificate

Each finisher will qualify for a certificate, which will be sent soon after the race.

The Closing Date

The last date to receive entries is 18th April. In recent years, entries have doubled, so PLEASE ENTER EARLY to avoid disappointment. You cannot enter the main event on race day.

The Charity

Children's Hospital Grand Appeal

The proceeds from individual runners' sponsorship will go directly towards the rebuilding of the Royal Hospital for Sick Children. We aim to raise £10,000 which will help provide a consulting room to be named after the event.

D2.2 Leaflets and Brochures

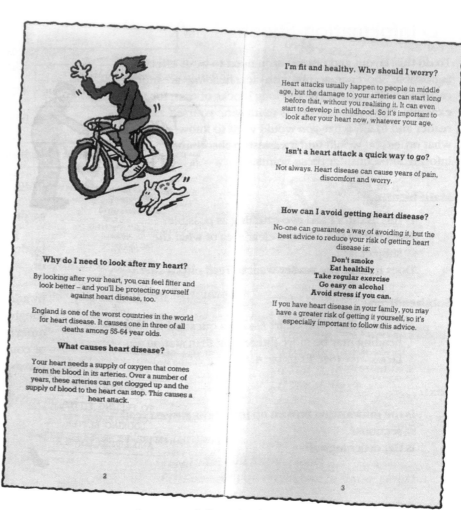

E Articles

E1 Notes

An article is a piece of writing on a particular subject which is written for publication in a newspaper, magazine or newsletter.

Approach:

A wide range of approaches is possible, depending on the subject matter. A light-hearted or humorous topic might be given a fairly personal treatment, for example, while a more serious topic would be treated in a more neutral, analytical way.

Headings:

Articles should have a heading which makes the subject matter clear but which also catches the reader's eye and makes him or her want to read. Newspapers and magazines often use dramatic statements or word play in headings for this reason, and sometimes add a sub-heading which gives more information. (See E3 for examples.)

Layout and Organisation:

As with any other kind of composition, it's important to have an interesting introduction and a suitable conclusion to 'round off' the piece, and to organise the information into paragraphs which help the reader to follow the argument or understand the different aspects of the subject. In addition, articles often include an outline of the story or the topic near the beginning so that the reader begins with a general picture and then reads on to find out more information.

E2 Example

HEADING

OPENING: Start in a way which catches the reader's attention, e.g. by asking direct questions.

Use separate PARAGRAPHS for different aspects of the subject.

ENDING: 'Round off' the article suitably, e.g. with an overview, a concluding remark, or a joke!

Screaming Tyres
By Tracy Cole

Have you ever wondered what it would be like to sit behind the wheel of a racing car? Are you looking for a really imaginative birthday present for a car-mad friend or relation? If the answer to either of these questions is 'yes', then you may be interested to hear about a course I took at Stoke Lodge Racing School recently.

My day as a racing driver was the first prize in a newspaper competition I had entered, and I must say that it was the most exciting prize I've ever won. The day began with theoretical instruction covering all aspects of safety. This was followed by practical tuition in a high performance saloon car. With no traffic to worry about, I was able to practise controlling the car on bends and prepare myself for the ultimate experience: the chance to drive a single seater racing car.

And finally, with crash helmet on and full harness seat belts secured, I was able to rev up the engine and edge my way out on to the circuit. Six breath-taking laps later, my dream had become reality.

For those not lucky enough to win a day at the racing school, the cost of the introductory course is £120, which includes all equipment and also an impressive certificate to hang on the wall. Anyone who can drive a car can enjoy the experience, regardless of age. The oldest participant so far has been 85, and I understand that he has booked a second course!

E3 Headings

Writers can use a variety of devices to make their headings eye-catching. Examples from texts in this book:

TODAY IS CANCELLED   (dramatic statement)

Your Mind: Do you make the best use of it? ⎫
You are caught in a fire – then what?   ⎬ (challenging question)

Must one be so polite that it hurts?   (interesting question)

Last chance to see ...   (unfinished statement – see what?)

US and Them   (word play: US = 1. United States; 2. personal pronoun)

For examples of different styles and approaches to writing articles, look through the texts in this book.

F Reports

F1 Notes

A **report** is a formal document prepared by one person or a group of people who have been studying a particular subject (e.g. *The committee published its final report, recommending legislation against racism.*). Both **articles** and **reports** may deal with similar subject matter but the treatment is different. While an **article** is designed to make a topic interesting for the general reader, a **report** is usually written for a more informed reader who already knows something about the subject. **Reports** are generally longer and more detailed than **articles**.

Approach:

There are two basic kinds of report:

- The first simply provides information on a topic and gives a brief conclusion or summary at the end. Example: a report on the educational system in a particular country, written to help someone research the subject.
- The second sets out to identify strengths and weaknesses in a particular situation and make recommendations for improvement. Example: a report on the library facilities in a college written at the request of the principal.

Language and Register

Reports are the most impersonal kind of writing and it is usually best to avoid expressing personal opinions or feelings, except, perhaps, in the conclusion. Instead of *I think that ...* or *I found that ...,* for example, you can use the impersonal '*It*' construction and a passive, e.g. *It seems that ... It was found that ...* (see F3).

It's also advisable to avoid making very definite statements unless you're absolutely sure they're true. Instead of saying *It is*, for example, you can use a modal verbs, e.g. It *could/might/may be* or a more tentative expression such as It *seems to be ...* or It *tends to be*.

Layout and Organisation:

Reports should have a clear, factual **heading** and may also have **subheadings** which divide the writing into shorter sections. The information should be organised and presented as clearly and logically as possible, with a short **introduction**, explaining the aim of the report and how the information was obtained and a suitable **conclusion**, summing up the information and making recommendations if necessary.

F2 Example

Clear, factual heading.

The introduction says what the aim of the report is and how the information was obtained.

Subheadings divide the information into logical sections.

The conclusion provides a brief summary of the information and may include recommendations for improvement.

LEISURE FACILITIES IN ANYTOWN

Introduction

The aim of this report is to describe and assess the leisure facilities available in Anytown. It is based on information made available by the Anytown Tourist Office, and on views expressed by local people who were interviewed.

Sport

Anytown has a wide range of sports facilities, both public and private. There is a large modern leisure centre in the High Street and facilities include a swimming pool, a sports hall for judo, fencing and other activities, and tennis courts. The centre runs courses in all these sports and these tend to be very popular. Membership costs £150 a year, which was felt to be rather expensive, but a special temporary membership is available to visitors. The public swimming pool on the outskirts of town at Downmarket is older, less attractive and often overcrowded, but entry is only £1.50.

Theatres

There are two theatres in town, the Kings Theatre in Bee Street, which offers mainly 'serious' drama and has a good reputation for its productions of Shakespeare plays, and the Little Theatre in Sea Street which specialises in lighter entertainment and the occasional pop concert. In general, it seems that the Kings Theatre is more popular with the older members of the community while the Little appeals more to people in their teens, twenties and early thirties.

Museums and Art Galleries

The City Museum has an extensive collection of maps, pottery and other articles connected with Anytown's history. The attendants are said to be very friendly and helpful, and there is also a small café with reasonably priced home-made snacks. Interestingly, few of the local Anytowners interviewed had ever been to the museum but it was recommended highly by several tourists.

Shopping

Conclusion

Anytown is well-provided with leisure facilities for a town of its size and these are well-used by the townspeople, on the whole. Sport seems to be the most popular leisure activity (after shopping) while cultural activities like visiting the museum or art gallery appeared to be the least popular amongst the Anytowners who were interviewed. Perhaps the City Council should consider launching a publicity campaign to show how much these facilities have to offer.

F3 Useful Language

Introduction:	*The aim of this report is to ...*	*It is based on ...*	
	This report is intended to ...	*It draws on ...*	
	This report looks at/describes ...	*It uses ...*	
Reporting an observation:	*It seems/appears that ...*	*It was found that ...*	
	... tend(s) to (do)	*It was felt that ...*	
	A/The majority/minority of ...	*... were in the majority/minority*	
Quoting:	*According to ...*	*As X said, ...*	*In the words of ...*
Speculating:	*It may/could/might (well) be that ...*		
	... may/could/might + (do/have done)		
Generalising:	*In general*	*On the whole*	*In the main*
Commenting:	*Interestingly*	*Curiously*	*Oddly*	*Strangely*	*Surprisingly*	*Predictably*
	As might be (have been) expected	*It is interesting that ... (etc.)*	
Making a recommendation:	*It is recommended that ...*		
	(Perhaps) It is/would be advisable for X to (do)		
	(Perhaps) X might/should consider + ing		
Summing up:	*To sum up/To summarise*	*On balance*	*In short*

G Reviews

G1 Notes

A **review** is an article in a newspaper or magazine in which someone gives their views on a book, play, film, TV programme, etc. The purpose of a review is firstly to give factual **information** about the subject, and secondly to give an **opinion** about it which will help the reader to decide where to buy the book, see the play or visit the exhibition.

Reviews normally contain the three main ingredients listed below. A review may not always fall in three neat sections, however. The writer may decide to describe an aspect of the subject and comment immediately on strengths and weaknesses, for example, before going on to describe another aspect of the subject.

G1.1 Overview – a description of the subject

Book – non-fiction:

What is it about? Who is it for? How technical is it? How is it organised? What topics are covered? What special features are there? How much does it cost? etc.

Book – fiction:

What kind of book is it (thriller/historical novel/science fiction, etc.)? Is it different in any way from other books of this type? What's the story? etc. (You can give an outline but don't give the ending away!)

Play/Film/Programme:

What is it about? Is there anything special/unusual about the production? **Play/film:** Where is it on? Are there any well-known actors? Who is the director? **TV Programme:** Which channel? Is it part of a series? Who is the producer?

G1.2 Pros and cons – detailed comments on the successful and unsuccessful features of the subject

Your comments will probably include both **objective** views (based on fact) – the photographs were poor quality or the costumes didn't fit the actors properly, for example – and **subjective** views (based on personal feelings) – the story wasn't interesting or the film was too violent. Make sure, however, that you give reasons for your comments.

You may have strong positive or negative feelings about the subject of the review and this is no bad thing. A strong opinion, clearly argued, is often more interesting to read than a carefully balanced assessment. Even so, try not to be completely one-sided.

G1.3 Verdict – summing-up and recommendation

The last paragraph should sum up your feelings and make it clear to the reader whether you recommend the subject without any reservations, recommend it with one or two reservations, or don't recommend it at all. In real life, readers often look at the last paragraph of a review first to see what the general verdict is. Make sure your review gives a clear verdict.

G2 Examples

G2.1 Book – non fiction

> **The Joy of Sandwiches – A Munch and Y Knott, The Take Away Press, Neasden, £35.**
>
> Despite its rather unpromising title, this is actually a fascinating and comprehensive study of a long neglected aspect of the cook's art.
>
> The first part of the book deals with the background to the subject. There is a detailed history of the sandwich from its invention by the Early of Sandwich in the 18th century to the latest creations of the present day. There are chapters on 'The Sandwich in Art' and 'The Sandwich in Literature', and this section ends with a survey of the place of the sandwich in the cultures of various countries around the world.
>
> The second part of the book is devoted to 'recipes', some traditional, some new, and each sandwich is beautifully illustrated with a full page colour photograph. The 'recipes' are clear enough even for a child to follow (although it must be said that a child might have difficulty lifting the book since it weighs nearly 2kg!). There are helpful line drawings showing some of the preparation techniques including the correct way to slice bread. All in all this is a superb book which should provide inspiration for all sandwich makers whether they are beginners or 'old hands'. Only the rather steep price of £35 may prevent it from becoming the best seller which it deserves to be.

G2.2 Book – fiction

> **Yes, Mr President – Ivan Oscar, Blockbuster Press, £12.50.**
>
> This is the unlikely story of a second-rate actor who becomes President of the United States. Young Donald Beagan seems set for a mediocre career in Hollywood in the 1940s until he ventures into politics and wins a nomination for Governor of California. Ten years and one marriage later, he runs for the White House and ends up the most powerful man in the world.
>
> Ivan Oscar, the author, is well-known for such best-selling thrillers as 'Live Now, Die Later' and this book is certainly packed with action and exotic settings but somehow the formula doesn't work. The hero, Beagan, never really comes to life and his wife, Mandy, (an ex-actress – what else?) is such a cardboard figure that it's hard to feel interested in their relationship. In the end, the story is just too improbable to hold the reader's attention. A very forgettable book.

G2.3 Film/Play

> **Crazy Plumber: Plaza Cinema**
>
> If you have seen the advance publicity, you might imagine that this was a funny film. Wrong. It's a film which tries very hard to be funny and fails consistently. The story concerns a plumber who isn't very good at his job. When his customers desert, and he can't pay the bills, he decides to turn to crime. He tries a little shoplifting (he's not very good at it, of course) but then he gets involved in bigger things.
>
> Wayne Gibson, who plays the hero, has one or two good lines but most of the time he's struggling with a terrible script. There are a few good moments – the car chase sequence is memorable – but the story line is very slight and the director seems to have run out of ideas very quickly. As the film progresses, the level of violence increases. Despite the publicity, this is not a film for young children.
>
> A great deal of money went into the making of Crazy Plumber but in the end, spectacular effects are no substitute for real humour.

G2.4 Radio/TV programme

> **The Secret Life of the Termite, 9.30 Tuesday, BBC 1.**
>
> This was the first in a new series of wild life documentary programmes presented by the well-known naturalist, David Buttonborough. Each programme will focus on one creature and looks at its habitat and life cycle in depth.
>
> This week's subject was the termite and we learnt, among other things, about the amazingly complex architecture of the termite hill. Termites are not particularly attractive looking creatures but the photography was so superb, and Mr Buttonborough's commentary so informative, that it was difficult not to become totally absorbed. I, for one, have certainly learnt a new respect for these industrious little insects. In the weeks to come, we can look forward to programmes on the earthworm and the sea slug. If they can maintain the standard set in this first programme, this will be a very successful series.

G3 Useful Language

G3.1 Overview

The	book film programme	concerns deals shows describes tells the story of contains includes

a	study survey history	of
a	chapter section	on

Each	chapter programme	focuses on is devoted to

The	book/script film/programme programme part costumes/set	is	written produced presented played designed	by

The story is based on

Books	Films	Plays	Programmes
chapter	plot/storyline	scene	episode
plot	script	act	series
characterisation	soundtrack	scenery	commentary
illustrations	set	costumes	photograph
design	special effects	cast	studio
contents	stunt	stage	broadcast

G3.2 Pros and cons

really absolutely	extraordinary fascinating amazing beautiful stunning superb brilliant original

quite fairly	interesting amusing entertaining exciting informative attractive successful unusual

really completely	boring unimaginative humourless hopeless awful amateurish over the top predictable

Despite/in spite of + noun	... while ...
Although + clause	... whereas ...
.... although/but + clause	... except that ...
On the one hand ..., on the other hand ...	... even if ...

G3.3 Verdict

All in all,	In the last analysis,	In conclusion
In the end	On balance,	To sum up,

Linking and Logical Devices

Addition	Cause and result
in addition to ... *as well as ... + N* *besides ...* *both ... and ... + N* *not only ... but also ... + N/clause* *Furthermore ...* *Moreover ... + clause* *... also ...* *... too/as well*	*Because ...* *as ... + clause* *since ...* *in case ...* *due to ...* *owing to ... + N* *as a result of ...* *so (that) ...* *so + ADJ/ADV + that ... + clause* *such + N + that ...* *therefore + clause* *consequently*

Concession	Contrast
although ... *though ...* *even though/even if ... + clause* *but ...* *yet ...* *despite ... + N* *in spite of ...* *however* *nevertheless*	*while ...* *whereas ... + clause* *but ...* *on the other hand, ...*

	Purpose
	in order that ... + clause *so that ...* *in order to/so as to ... + V* *to ...*

Similarity and comparison	Time
as ... *like ... + N* *as + ADJ/ADV + as ...* *as ...* *the same + N + as/that + clause* *as + ADJ/ADV + as ...* *not as/so + ADJ/ADV + as + N/clause* *not such + ADJ/ADV + as + N/clause* *as if/though ... + clause*	*before ...* *after + N/clause* *till/until* *as/as soon as/when/once/immediately + clause* *while + clause* *during + noun* *during that time* *then/next/after that/later/ subsequently/eventually/finally/ at last* *no sooner ... than ... + clause* *hardly ... when ...*

'Why can't a woman be more like a man?'
George Bernard Shaw, *Pygmalion*

Lead-in

Read through the cartoon and then discuss the questions below with another student.

1 How does she feel about him? How does he feel about her? What is the problem?

2 If you were an 'agony aunt' what advice would you give to her? Would you give him the same advice? If not, why not?

3 Do you think the man should always make the first move by asking a woman for a date? Or is it OK for a woman to ask a man out?

Text 1

SKIMMING

1 The article below is about some research into how men and women communicate, carried out by an American professor of linguistics. Read quickly through the main part of the text, ignoring the gaps, and answer these questions.

1 Do men and women 'speak a different language' in the opinion of this expert?

2 What evidence has she got for her view?

3 Why does she think the subject is so important?

GAPPED TEXT
► Paper 1, Part 2

2 For questions 1–7 you must choose which of the paragraphs A–H on the next page fit into the numbered gaps in the following text. There is one extra paragraph which does not fit in any of the gaps.

Remember to look for grammatical or logical links between paragraphs.

Different Wavelengths

Men: they cringe at the prospect of discussing anything personal, grumble they're being nagged when asked to take out the rubbish and, if they lose their way while driving, rage at the suggestion they ask for directions.
Women: they read things into the most innocuous comment, get upset when their man says 'I' rather than 'we' and demand impossibly detailed reports of every conversation they miss – who said what and how they looked when they said it.

And, says Deborah Tannen, it will all go on like this, each sex bristling at the other's peculiar ways, until we wake up to the simple truth – men and women don't speak the same language.

| 1 |

Since our lives are lived as a series of conversations, it's her belief that the sooner we start to appreciate and understand these differences – and the reasons behind them – the better.

| 2 |

For more than 20 years she has studied how people talk – what they mean by what they say and how it can be interpreted and often misunderstood. Eavesdropping in restaurants, collecting friends' anecdotes, watching hundreds of hours of taped conversations ... all in the name of research.

| 3 |

Men are concerned primarily with status, and prefer discussion of facts to dissection of feelings. Since feelings suggest vulnerability and thus inferiority, men see conversation as another way of scoring points.

| 4 |

So who's right? Neither, says Deborah Tannen. This sort of disagreement typifies the different approaches men and women have to asking for information. Since women are so used to asking for help, refusing to ask directions makes no sense to the wife. To her, asking for and receiving directions reinforces the bond between people.

| 5 |

This may sound a long-winded explanation but in the world of socio-linguistics, it is only scratching the surface of the male-female conversational anomalies in this particular situation. Mention any aspect of everyday chat and Deborah can give examples of the ways men and women's attitudes to it differ.

| 6 |

Apparently the main difference in the way we communicate is in the crucial matter of the metamessage – the unspoken attitudes, thoughts and intentions behind what is actually said. And while fact-oriented men tend to listen to the message, feeling-oriented women tend to listen for the subtler metamessage.
For instance:
She: Why didn't you ask me how my day was?
He: If you've got something to tell me, tell me. Why do you have to be invited?

| 7 |

Deborah maintains: 'Without understanding the gender differences in ways of speaking, we're doomed to blame other people, or ourselves, or the relationship. The biggest mistake is believing there is one right way to listen, talk and have a conversation.'

A The thrust of this study is that women use language to enhance intimacy, men to assert independence. Women, concerned primarily with making connections with people, regard conversation as a way to share feelings, create bonds and explore possible solutions to common problems.

B But in her husband's hierarchical world, driving round until he finds the way himself is a reasonable thing to do. Men are comfortable with giving help and information, but not with receiving it. So asking for directions would make the husband feel he was dropping in status by revealing his lack of knowledge.

C Their simplest exchange sparked off misunderstandings and irritation. Just before they separated, she attended a course in linguistics at the University of Michigan. Suddenly the light dawned. The problem wasn't what they'd been saying, but, of course, how. The divorce went through – but Deborah was hooked.

D It's not so much that the vocabulary and grammar we use are different, she explains. The differences lie in the way men and women talk.

E The lost-in-the-car scenario is an illustration of this. You know the scene – it's universal. Invited to a party, a couple have been driving round in circles for half an hour searching for the address which he is sure is nearby. She is fuming because he insists on trying to find the address himself instead of stopping to ask directions.

F She's fed up because she wants to hear evidence that he cares how her day went, regardless of what actually happened. And he, concerned principally with the fact-exchanging aspect of conversation, can't understand what she's complaining about.

G Take politeness. Men consider it subservient, women sensitive. Boasting. Men boast as a matter of course, battling to gain or maintain that all-important status. Women, who tend to gain acceptance with each other by appearing the same as, not better than, everyone else, take care never to boast.

H Tall, gentle, immediately likeable and mercifully spouting little of the jargon you'd expect of one of the world's leading lights in her field, Deborah Tannen is Professor of Linguistics at the University of Georgetown, Washington DC.

TASK ANALYSIS

3 a Compare your answers with another student.

b Draw a circle round the **reference links** which helped you to choose the **correct missing paragraphs.**
Remember that reference links can refer both backwards and forwards. For example, in the paragraph you chose for gap 1, there should be a word which refers to 'Deborah Tannen' in the previous paragraph **and** a parallel expression which links with 'conversations' in the following paragraph.

DISCUSSION POINTS

4 a **Work in pairs. Read through the remarks below and the replies. According to the information in Text 1, decide which of the replies is from a man (M), and which from a woman (W), and why.**

1 My boss gave me a week to write a report. The research alone would take a month if I did it right.

a *Don't you hate it when they do that?*

b *You should tell him if you do it in a week, it'll be a terrible job and it won't be your fault.*

2 What frustrates you about your partner?
a *X never gets to the point.*   b *X never tells me anything.*

3 What's a good way to impress someone you've just met?
a *Ask a personal question and listen to the answer.*
b *Have interesting information and witty things to say.*

4 You had a rotten day? I'm so sorry.
a *It's not your fault.*   b *Thanks for your concern.*

b **Change pairs and discuss what you think of Deborah Tannen's views.**

METAPHOR   5 **Each of the following excerpts from the text contains a metaphorical expression in which a noun is used as a verb. Read the dictionary definitions below and look at each expression in context. Then discuss with another student what the meaning is.**

1 ... each sex *bristling* at the other's peculiar ways ... (main text para. 3)
2 Their simplest exchange *sparked off* misunderstandings ... (para. C)
3 Suddenly *the light dawned.* (para. C)
4 Deborah was *hooked.* (para. C)
5 .... *spouting* little of the jargon you might expect ... (para. H)

bristle *n* a short stiff hair esp. on an animal
spark *n* a small bit of burning material thrown out by a fire
dawn *n* the time of day when light first appears
hook *n* a curved piece of metal used for hanging things on, catching fish, etc.
spout *n* an opening from which liquid comes out, such as a tube or pipe

Focus on Listening *Why men don't think like women*   ▶ Paper 4, Part 1

You will hear an extract from a radio programme about anatomical differences between the male and female brain. For questions 1–9, complete each of the statements. You will hear the recording twice.

The language-associated areas in women's brains are ☐ **1** than men's.	
Tests have shown that women have better ☐ **2** than men.	
Research has shown that when reading, men and women ☐ **3** differently.	
MRI, a brain imaging system, allowed researchers to monitor ☐ **4** in the body.	
The results showed that most women use ☐ **5** of the brain when they read.	
The left side of the brain is responsible for verbal abilities and ☐ **6**	
Researchers at Pennsylvania University asked men and women to lie in a dark room and ☐ **7**	
The women's brains were more active in the zones which deal with ☐ and **8**	
In the research at Yale University ☐ **9** of women's brains worked in the same way as men's.	

Focus on Grammar 1 *Review of -ing Forms and Infinitives*

1 All the quotations below deal with the subject of love. Choose one or two which you like and discuss your choice with another student.

A *'Love is like war: easy to begin with but very hard to stop.'*
H. L. Mencken (20th C)

B *'Parting is such sweet sorrow ....'*
Romeo and Juliet, Shakespeare (16th C)

C *'Love means never having to say you're sorry.'*
Eric Segal (20th C)

D *'It's love that makes the world go round.'*
Traditional

E *"Tis better to have loved and lost than never to have loved at all.'*
Alfred Lord Tennyson, poet (19th C)

F *'Life has taught us that love does not consist in gazing at each other but in looking outward in the same direction.'*
Antoine de Saint-Exupery, French writer (20th C)

G *'To get the full value of joy you must have someone to divide it with.'*
Mark Twain, American writer (1835–1910)

2 a Which quotations contain examples of *-ing* forms used:

1 after a **preposition** .... (Remember, *-ing* forms can be used after **all** prepositions.)
2 as a **noun** .... (These verbal nouns are also called 'gerunds'. See Grammar File, page 141.)
3 after a **verb** .... (See list in Grammar File.)

b Which quotations contain examples of an **infinitive without to** used:

1 after a modal verb ....
2 after *make* or *let* ....

c Which quotations contain examples of a **to infinitive** used:

1 after **adjectives** .... (also after ***too* + adj** and **adj + enough**, e.g. *too heavy to lift, not old enough to go alone.*)
    Note: We use the perfect infinitive (*to + have +* past participle) to refer to the past, e.g. *It's good to have had the experience of living abroad.*
2 to show **purpose** .... (You could also say *In order to ...*)

Remember, a few verbs can take either an *-ing* form or an infinitive verb with no difference in meaning. Some can take either form but with a difference in meaning. There are details of both kinds in the Grammar File, page 154.

For more information about the use of *-ing* forms and infinitives, see the Grammar File, page 154.

3 In the following letters, put the verbs in brackets into the correct form: ***-ing* form**, **to infinitive** or **infinitive without to**.

Date with disappointment

We met on the paradise island of Fiji. After (**1**) ...... (spend) several days together we had to continue our journeys but we arranged (**2**) ...... (meet) in Hawaii a month later. He managed (**3**) ...... (send) romantic messages to me along the route and he even telephoned me from LA (**4**) ...... (say) how much he was looking forward to (**5**) ...... (see) me. In spite of (**6**) ...... (send) a telegram with details of his arrival in Hawaii, he never arrived!

I often wonder just what made him (**7**) ...... (change) his mind. It's a hell of a long way to go (**8**) ...... (be) stood up.

LISA JONES
West Hampstead, London

While (**1**) ...... (stay) with friends in Ireland, I met a very pretty girl at a dance and she agreed (**2**) ...... (let) me (**3**) ...... (walk) her home. As we made our way along the cliff path, a full moon lit the harbour. It was so romantic and what a picture! I asked my companion if she'd mind (**4**) ...... (wait) a few minutes while I ran (**5**) ...... (fetch) my camera from my friends' house. When I returned, she'd gone.

I decided (**6**) ...... (take) a picture anyway. Was it worth (**7**) ...... (take)? Well it won first prize in a national photographic competition!

ROBERT TRUBSHAW
Weston-super-mare

Focus on Speaking *Family and Friends*

▶ Paper 5, Parts 1, 2 & 4

EXAM TIP Paper 5, Part 1

If you are paired with a student you know for the Speaking test, you may be asked to introduce each other. Before you go in, make sure you know the basic facts and also one or two interesting details about your partner.

1 Work in pairs. How much do you know about your partner? Could you answer questions about the following points? If not, check the details with your partner.
mother/father? – where they live, etc.
brothers/sisters? – ages/jobs, etc.
husband/wife/partner? – job, etc.
children/nieces/nephews? – names, ages, etc.
best friend? – how they met, etc.
favourite social activity?

Join another pair and work as a group of four.

Take it in turns to introduce your partners and talk briefly about their family, friends and social activities (about one minute each).

EXAM TIP Paper 5, Part 2

This task always has more than one part. In addition to describing the pictures, you may have to *compare, contrast, comment, identify* or *speculate.*
- You'll only have about one minute, so there isn't time for a detailed description of each picture. Keep this part fairly brief.
- Make sure you follow the instructions for the other part(s) of the task, and remember to express a personal reaction to what's shown in the pictures.

2 a Work in pairs and both look at the photographs on pages 236 and 239.

Student A: You should talk about the photographs on page 236. They each show a wedding, but were taken 50 years apart. You should

a) describe the similarities and differences between them, and

b) comment on the changes that have taken place since the first photo was taken. You have about one minute.

Student B: When Student A has finished, comment on what he/she has said. Say if you agree or disagree.

b Student B: You should talk about the photographs on page 239. They each show a family group. You should

a) compare and contrast them, and

b) comment on what life would be like for a child in each family.

Student A: When Student B has finished, comment on what he/she has said. Say if you agree or disagree.

DISCUSSION POINTS

3 Discuss these questions.
1 Do you think money spent on a big wedding celebration is well-spent?
2 What do you think are the advantages and disadvantages of
- living with your parents until you get married?
- having elderly parents living with you?
3 Is the trend in your country towards smaller families? Why/Why not?

Focus on Writing 1 *Informal Letter and Memo*

▶ Paper 2, Part 1

When you return from holiday, you find the following items of mail waiting for you: a wedding invitation dated three weeks ago, a more recent note from a friend and a letter from your boss.

WEDDING INVITATION

The pleasure of your company is requested
at the wedding of
Joanna Renshaw and Michael Woods
At St George's Church
On 14th February, 11 am
And afterwards at the reception to be held at
The Clifton Hotel

RSVP

Congrats/best wishes, etc. + profuse apologies

LETTER

As you may know, Marie N. was due to go to the international trade conference in New York from 12-15 February. However, in your absence she has been promoted to Regional Manager and her new responsibilities do not allow her to attend. For that reason, I would now like to ask you to represent the company at the conference.

This will be an exciting opportunity for you and I am confident that you will do an excellent job on our behalf.

Please let me know as soon as possible if you are able to attend, confirming at the same time that you hold a valid passport, so that the necessary travel arrangements can be made.

Yes!!!

NOTE

Help!

It's great news about Joanna and Mike, isn't it? I honestly thought they'd never get round to naming the day! Apparently they're having their honeymoon in Venice – so romantic! I've been worrying a bit about what to get as a wedding present. Have you seen the list? Some of the things on it are horrendously expensive but I think I've decided on a set of saucepans – not very glamorous but practical and within my budget.
Phone me and let me know what you're planning to buy them.

Love, Sheila

Ask J & M to send copy quickly! (maybe they could suggest something)

Read the three items above and then write:
a) a suitable **letter** to Joanna and Michael, explaining that you are unable to attend their wedding, and covering other relevant points (about 200 words);
b) a **memo** to your boss confirming your willingness to attend the conference (about 50 words).
You should use your own words as far as possible.

TASK CHECKLIST

Read the instructions and the three items very carefully, highlighting important points. For each piece of writing you need to consider:

- **Target reader and style:** Think about your relationship with each reader and about the circumstances. Make sure the style and tone are appropriate.

- **Purpose:** Be clear about the specific purpose of each piece of writing and take care to achieve this.

- **Layout and length:** Check the examples and notes in the Writing File and keep to the word limits. You must include all the key information but you can add extra details if necessary to increase realism.

Text 2

PREDICTION

1 Discuss in pairs. What changes do you think there might have been in the following aspects of marriage during the last 50 years?

- the age when people get married
- who does the housework
- the age when women have their first baby
- who pays the bills
- whether mothers go out to work

2 Text 2 is a magazine article about five women who married in different decades. Read the five sections quickly to see how far their experiences correspond with your ideas. Discuss any interesting points with a partner.

MULTIPLE MATCHING
▶ Paper 1, Part 4

3 For questions 1–18 answer by choosing from the list of women (A–E) on the right below. Some of the choices may be required more than once.

Note: When more than one answer is required, these may be given in any order.

According to the article, which woman ...		
thinks it's important to avoid arguments?	**1**	
feels her marriage has improved with time?	**2** **3**	
received a formal proposal of marriage from her fiancé?	**4** **5**	**A** Ivy Gould
is more extrovert than her husband?	**6**	
had a restricted social life at the start of married life?	**7**	**B** Sally Graham
let her parents influence arrangements for the wedding?	**8** **9**	**C** Lady Vincent
began married life with a large financial commitment?	**10**	
emphasises that she saw marriage as a lifetime commitment?	**11**	**D** Amanda Russell
had a wedding which departed from tradition in some way?	**12** **13**	**E** Stephanie Walter
has a husband who no longer does much housework?	**14**	
disapproves of lavish weddings?	**15**	
was able to economise on wedding expenses?	**16**	
says she had no illusions about marriage from the start?	**17**	
had arguments with her husband about housework?	**18**	

DISCUSSION POINTS

4 Discuss the following statements with another student. Decide if you agree or not and say why.

1 It's a good idea for newly-married couples to live with their in-laws until they have saved enough money for a home of their own.
2 A husband should be the breadwinner and his career should come first.
3 A wife should be able to keep her own name if she wants.
4 It's out of date for a woman to promise to obey her husband.
5 Marriage partners should have separate bank accounts.
6 A couple's career interests should determine when they have children.

State of the Union

A Ivy GOULD (The 40s)

Ivy married John Gould in 1947, when she was 23 and he was 26. He is now 73, and a retired engineer and she is 70, a former secretary. They have a daughter, Jayne, 41.

We lived in the same road, so we knew each other very well. Then when John came out of the airforce we met at a dance. John proposed at the same ballroom a few months later. He took me out on to the balcony and showed me a diamond ring. It was quite romantic.

I didn't want a big wedding, but my parents did, and in those days you did what they wanted. I'd done a tailoring apprenticeship, so I made my gown, all the bridesmaids' dresses and my going-away outfit. My parents had a big house, so we moved in with them and my grandmother. We had our own room but we shared the kitchen with Mum. It wasn't difficult. I stopped work when I got married; you did then. The man was supposed to be the breadwinner and it was his job that mattered. Because it was such a large house, I had plenty to do. John didn't do any housework, but he's changed since he retired.

When you first get married you think it's going to be brilliant. I'm not sure it lived up to all my expectations at first but it has since. I do think young couples who split up in the early years must regret it later. John and I have given each other a lot of security.

B Sally GRAHAM (The 50s)

Sally married Gordon Graham on February 19, 1955, when she was 26 and he was 30. He is a retired insurance worker, 71, and she is 67, a former secretary. They have two children and two grandchildren.

We helped out with the cost of the wedding. We didn't have grand weddings then, and it horrifies me how much people spend today. Then marriage was a step you took for better, for worse, for ever. I didn't know anyone who was divorced. We spent time getting to know each other and becoming friends before we married.

I was always busy. Babies didn't have disposable nappies, so I had washing every day. There were no women's rights, but we didn't moan or groan – we just got on with it. Of course, I gave up work; I didn't know anybody who worked when their children were small. My husband paid the bills – he was very much in charge – and gave me money each week to cover food and any make-up or stockings I wanted. We had friends in to play cards but we only went out on birthdays and anniversaries because there wasn't the money.

I think the 1950s were the best years to get married. It was before the explosion of everybody wanting to do their own thing. You can't do that without somebody suffering. We had to fit in and show consideration. And I think we did, by and large. Certainly in my circle, our homes and families were everything.

C Lady VINCENT (The 70s)

Christine married Sir William Vincent in 1976, when she was 24 and he was 25. He is now 44 and an investment consultant and Christine, 43, is a novelist. They have three sons, Eddie, 17, Charlie, 16, and John, 14.

The house we wanted to buy was way beyond our means, so we decided that when we were married we would put off having children for three years. In the event I got pregnant a bit sooner than we'd planned but I was absolutely thrilled. I meant to go back to work after Eddie was born, but I couldn't face it.

I had three children in three years, and luckily with each baby William seemed to get promotion. But I was careful not to become too obsessed with the babies. You have to take care your husband isn't an accessory instead of a companion. We both hate rows. I could row with a stranger but never with the family; you say such hurtful things that can't be unsaid. William is so diplomatic; he's just ace at quietly getting his own way and I don't even realise until a week later. The only thing we really disagree about is driving. I'm more aggressive than William, who is so well-mannered he gives way too often. We balance each other pretty well. I'm ebullient, William's reticent; he's a pessimist, I'm a dreamer.

D Amanda RUSSELL (the 80s)

Amanda Russell, a part-time designer, married Chris Gower, a market researcher, in 1982, when they were both 24. Now 37, they have two children, Imogen, 8, and Oscar, 5.

My parents wanted us to have a big party when we got married and I'm very glad we did. It was important to me, making the commitment with all our friends and family there. I kept my own name. I always wanted to get married and have children, but I didn't really see myself as an appendage. I don't want to be just Mrs Something. But the children have Chris's name; it just seemed to be the way to do it.

I wasn't particularly interested in housework, but fortunately Chris didn't expect an instant housewife. We shared most of the chores, though I do most of them now because I'm the one at home. I worked until Imogen was 18 months old, then gave up completely when I was expecting Oscar. We decided bringing up children was an important job in itself.

I don't suppose anybody else would read our marriage as perfect. But after 13 years we're still in love and we have a lot of mutual respect. I don't feel smug. I expected marriage to be quite hard work and it has been. It's almost like a job.

E Stephanie WALTER (The 90s)

Stephanie married Richard Walter in 1994, when she was 22 and he was 27. He is an insurance broker and she is a recruitment consultant.

I was the one who proposed to Richard, but when I said 'Let's get married', he told me to wait until I was asked. Six weeks later he proposed on one knee.

We dropped the promise in the marriage vows that I had to obey Richard; it's only a word but it's not a modern word and it's just not us. However, it never crossed my mind not to change my name; if you're not prepared to do that, why bother to get married?

We opened a joint account and now we each pay in half our wages, while the other half's our own, to do with as we wish. Housework was a novelty to start with, so I did everything – and Richard let me. It was my own fault but it really annoyed me in the end. We had a few barneys and now he does his fair share of most things.

They say it's the first year of marriage that is the hardest and I'd go along with that; it's difficult just learning to live together. But we argue a great deal less now; we've both mellowed. Eventually we'd like to have children, but not yet. Richard said he wanted them by the time he was 30, but now he's upped that to 35. It will depend on how my career is going. That's fairly important to me.

Focus on Grammar 2 *Cleft Sentences*

1 Type 1

The following sentence can be expressed in different ways to create special emphasis.

Jack lost his chequebook.

1 Jack was the person who lost his chequebook.
2 The thing (that) Jack lost was his chequebook.
3 What Jack lost was his chequebook.

Sentence 1 emphasises the subject, **who** lost the chequebook, while sentences 2 and 3 emphasise the object, **what** was lost.

Sentences like these are called **cleft sentences** (*cleft* means 'divided'). They are a common way of highlighting key information both in speech and in writing.

- This kind of cleft sentence often uses general terms like: *the person (who), the thing (that)/What, the one (that), the place (where), the reason (why), the time (when).*
  e.g. I was **the one** who proposed to Richard. (Text)
  Perhaps you think you are **the only person** who can solve the problem.

- Cleft sentences can also use more specific terms like: *the woman (who), the city (that/where), the film (that),* etc.
  e.g. Tokyo is a city (that) I've always wanted to visit.
  The composer whose music I like best of all is Handel.

2 Rewrite the following as cleft sentences to emphasise the part in italics.

Example:
  I meant to ask you for *your address.* (thing)
  The thing I meant to ask you for is your address.
1 *You* keep parking in my space. (person) *So you're ...*
2 I'm looking for *a beginner's guide to computing.* (What)
3 I borrowed your mobile phone *to call the hospital.* (reason)
4 She's only good at cooking *vegetable soup.* (thing)
5 I would never have thought of looking *there.* (place) *That's ...*

3 Complete the following cleft sentences with a suitable relative clause.

1 Alexander Fleming was the scientist ...... penicillin.
2 Burkino Faso is the country ...... Upper Volta.
3 Beethoven was ...... deaf in old age.

4 The FIFA World Cup is a ...... every four years.
5 1969 was the year ...... moon.
6 The reason ...... is that you haven't plugged it in.
7 The thing about English grammar ....
8 Of all my friends, the one ....

4 Type 2

The second sentence in each of the following pairs illustrates another type of cleft sentence, which can be used to emphasise almost any element of a sentence.

1 a They say that *the first year of marriage* is the hardest.
  b They say that *it's* **the first year of marriage** *that* is the hardest. (Text 2)
2 a Ivy Gould appreciates *the security of marriage.*
  b It's **the security of marriage** *that* Ivy Gould appreciates.
3 a Attitudes to marriage began to change *in the 1960s and 1970s.*
  b *It was* **in the 1960s and 1970s** *that* attitudes to marriage began to change.
4 a Ivy and John had a big wedding *to please their parents.*
  b *It was* **to please their parents** *that* Ivy and John had a big wedding.

Sentence 1b emphasises the subject, while sentence 2b emphasises the object. Sentence 3b emphasises the time adverbial, and in sentence 4b, it is the infinitive clause that is emphasised.

This type of cleft sentence often implies a contrast.
e.g. In the past it was the **man** who was supposed to be the breadwinner (**not the woman**).

5 Rewrite the following using a cleft structure beginning with *It + be* to emphasise the part in italics.

1 *Ivy's parents* wanted a big wedding, but Ivy didn't.
2 *Amanda* does most of the household chores now that she's at home with the baby.
3 Men seek *status rather than intimacy,* according to Deborah Tannen.
4 *His habit of keeping things to himself* frustrates me.
5 Women didn't get the vote in Britain *until 1918.*
6 *A woman, not a man,* discovered radium.
7 *What you say* isn't important; *how you say it* is.
8 I want *the opportunity to travel,* not a huge salary.

Focus on Vocabulary

COLLOCATION

1 **Choose the right verb to complete the following phrases. Most come from Texts 1 and 2.**

do   have   get   make

1 ...... a commitment
2 ...... your fair share of the work
3 ...... your own way
4 ...... no sense at all
5 ...... a row with someone
6 ...... an apprenticeship
7 ...... engaged to someone
8 ...... a good cry
9 ...... the ironing
10 ...... a big party
11 ...... your own back on someone
12 ...... a fuss about something

TOPIC VOCABULARY

2 **a** **There are mistakes in some of the following sentences. Make the necessary corrections.**

1 Haven't you heard? She got married with Tony last April.
2 I'm going to make a proposal to Linda tonight. Wish me luck!
3 They're honeymooning in Scotland until next weekend.
4 The stupid studio managed to ruin all our marriage photos.
5 We can't afford to have an extravagant wedding reception.
6 You'll need to keep your marriage certificate in a safe place.
7 I wonder why you have to fill in your marital status on this form.
8 She's going out with a 27-year-old divorced, who works in the same office.
9 They're upset because we didn't invite them to the marriage.
10 We got separated for a few months but we're back together again now.

b **Which of these expressions can be used for a man or a woman? What exactly do they mean? Check in a dictionary if necessary.**

*a confirmed bachelor   an old flame   u widower
a heartthrob   a spouse   a soul mate*

PHRASAL VERBS

3 **Fill in the gaps in the following sentences by completing the phrasal verbs with particles chosen from the list below.**

on   for   out   out   off   off   with   over   up   up   up

1 They used to be good friends but they fell .... over politics.
2 David's just split .... his girlfriend and he's feeling a bit low.
3 We arranged to meet outside the cinema but he stood me .... !
4 It was love at first sight. I fell .... you the minute I saw you!
5 She broke .... their engagement two days before the wedding.
6 If you like her so much, why don't you ask her .... ?
7 If I ever catch you cheating .... me with another man, we're finished!
8 We had a couple of dates but I went .... him when I realised how stingy he could be.
9 No matter how bad the row, they always kiss and make ..... in the end.
10 It's a year since his wife left him but I don't think he's got .... her yet.

Focus on Writing 2 *Information Sheet*

▶ Paper 2, Part 2

TASK

You have received the following memo from the President of the Students' Union at the college where you are studying English.

MEMO

From: M. S.
To: A. R.
Date: 13/4
Subject: Information for new students

If you remember, we agreed at our last meeting that one way of helping new international students to settle in would be to produce a series of information sheets for them, and I'm pleased to say that we've now been given the go-ahead to do this by the Principal.

I'm hoping you'll be willing to prepare the information sheet we decided to call 'Making New Friends'. The idea was to make some general suggestions about ways of meeting people (e.g. joining clubs, learning a new skill, maybe doing voluntary work), and also to mention some specific facilities which are on offer at the college or in town (including one or two forthcoming events?). I'm sure you'll have plenty of ideas!

Please include a friendly introduction and make the tone encouraging and fairly informal throughout (but remember to keep the English clear and simple).

Many thanks!

Write the **information sheet** as requested. Write approximately 250 words.

TASK CHECKLIST

- **Layout:** How should an 'information sheet' be laid out?
- **Target readers:** What are their likely ages?/interests?/needs?
- **Content:** How many formal and informal ways of meeting people can you think of? How should they be grouped? What sub-headings can you use?
- **Purpose:** What should your readers **know** and how should they feel?

GUIDANCE NOTES

1 An 'information sheet' is really a one-page leaflet. Check the notes in the Writing File (page 163) before you start.
2 The question leaves it up to you to decide where you are studying – in your own country or abroad. If you choose a town you know well (rather than an imaginary place), the task will be easier and also more realistic.

English in Use 1 *Word Formation*

▶ Paper 3, Part 4

For questions 1–15, read the two texts below. Use the words in the boxes to form **one** word that fits in the same numbered space in the text. The exercise begins with an example (**0**).

Some of the different ways of forming new words are listed in the introduction to this task type in Unit 1 (page 20).

LONELY HEARTS COLUMNS

A SUBJECT FOR RESEARCH

Researchers have recently studied lonely-hearts advertisements in 20 local and two (**0**) *national* newspapers and the (**1**) .... of the study could provide useful tips on how to get the most replies. (**2**) .... of the advertisements showed that men tended to offer wealth, professional status and property, and to seek attractive women with (**3**) .... and (**4**) .... . Women tended to emphasise their (**5**) .... but, above all, what they wanted in a man was (**6**) .... . Many men also claimed to be warm and caring – and did so more than the women. It is possible men are becoming 'new men' who are less (**7**) .... about advertising these (**8**) .... . Or it may be that they know this is what women want to hear.

(**0**) **NATION**
(**1**) FIND
(**2**) ANALYSE
(**3**) WARM
(**4**) SENSITIVE
(**5**) ATTRACTIVE
(**6**) SOLVENT
(**7**) HESITATE
(**8**) CHARACTER

A PERSONAL EXPERIENCE

I found it difficult to phrase the advertisement. How can you say you're good-looking without being accused of (**9**) .... ? In any case, it's all very (**10**) .... , and it's for someone else to judge. (**11**) .... isn't that important for me – I find (**12**) .... a more attractive quality in a person.

Of course, I had to put up with some (**13**) .... from my friends when they found out what I'd done, but I don't see the problem. When you work (**14**) .... long hours, as I do, the chances of meeting people are limited. This is just a way of helping the situation. I've had three (**15**) .... so far, and two of them look quite promising.

(**9**) VAIN
(**10**) SUBJECT
(**11**) APPEAR
(**12**) MODEST
(**13**) MOCK
(**14**) BELIEVE
(**15**) RESPOND

English in Use 2 *Structural Cloze*

For questions 1–15 complete the following extract from a newspaper article by writing each missing word in the space. **Use only one word for each space.** The exercise begins with an example (0).

WHAT IS THIS THING CALLED LOVE?

If you put a group of people who don't know (0) *each* other in a room together and ask them to pair up, they (1) .... naturally gravitate towards others of similar family background, social class and upbringing. We are all looking for something familiar, (2) .... we may not be aware of exactly (3) .... it is. Facial attractiveness is a big influence (4) .... our choice of partners, too. People tend to seek out and (5) .... long-lasting relationships with others of a similar level of attractiveness. Several studies have confirmed (6) .... . Researchers took a selection of wedding photos and cut them (7) .... to separate the bride and groom. They then asked people to rate how attractive each person's face was. When the researchers put the photos back into their original pairs, they found that most of the couples had (8) .... rated at similar levels. Not only (9) .... we rate others, but each of us carries a rough estimate in our heads of how facially attractive we (10) .... be. We realise subconsciously that if we approach someone who is significantly higher up the scale (11) .... we are, we run the risk of (12) .... rejected.

But (13) .... the explanation for how and why we fall in love, one thing is clear. Nature has made the whole process (14) .... blissful and addictive as possible (15) .... the purpose of bringing and keeping couples together.

Looking at the earth from afar, you realise it's too small for conflict and just big enough for cooperation.
Yuri Gagarin

Lead-in

1 a Work with another student to discuss the following questions and choose the most likely answer. One question has more than one correct answer.

GOOD NEWS/BAD NEWS

1 Four species of animals are becoming extinct every ...
a) hour   b) day   c) week

2 There were an estimated 250,000 blue whales in the Southern Ocean originally. Now about ...... are left.
a) 110,000   b) 55,000   c) 11,000

3 Destroying forests causes ...
a) flooding   b) drought   c) earthquakes

4 The nearly 2 billion Christmas cards posted in Britain every year use the equivalent of ...... trees to produce.
a) 200,000   b) 50,000   c) 1 million

5 A quarter of all cars in ...... run on fuel made from sugar cane.
a) Australia   b) Brazil   c) India

6 The number of vehicles on the planet is increasing at the rate of one new car for ...... babies born.
a) every two   b) every ten   c) every 100

7 1,000 times more usable energy than we need could be produced by ...
a) wind   b) water   c) the sun

8 In ...... 100% of electricity is produced by water power.
a) Canada   b) Norway   c) Switzerland

9 In many rural villages in India, simple 'biogas' plants make use of ...... to generate cheap electricity for people's homes.
a) crops   b) oil   c) rubbish

10 In some parts of China, ... are used to control harmful pests in the rice fields, instead of chemical pesticides.
a) ducks   b) rabbits   c) goldfish

b Check your answers on page 233. Which facts are good news? Why?

2 Look at the cartoons. What message are the cartoonists trying to convey?

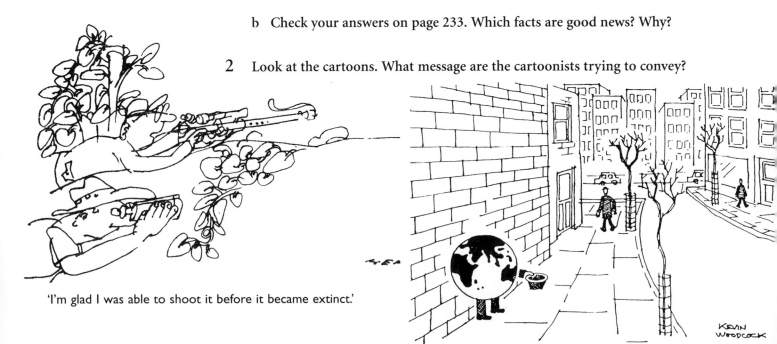

'I'm glad I was able to shoot it before it became extinct.'

Text

1 a Discuss these questions briefly with a partner.

1 Why are so many species are in danger of extinction?
2 How can animals be saved from extinction?
3 Which people are the most important in the success or failure of a conservation policy?

b Now read the text quickly in order to find answers the questions.

2 a Before you do the exam task, read the instructions and questions carefully.

b Check the words in italics in the questions and make sure you understand them.

c Look through the list of animals. You don't **need** to know what they are in order to do the task, but the text will be easier and more interesting to read if you have some idea. Which three are birds? What do A, B and C look like?

MULTIPLE MATCHING
▶ Paper 1, Part 1

Exam Tip Paper 1
These questions mainly test your ability to scan a text effectively. In the exam there isn't time to read the whole text.
Do
• read the questions first to see what kind of information you need.
Don't
• waste time trying to understand every word.
• spend time on parts of the text that aren't important.

3 For questions 1–15, answer by choosing from the animals listed A–G on the right below. Some of the choices may be required more than once.

Note: When more than one answer is required, these may be given in any order.

Which bird or animal ...

is endangered by the loss of its natural *habitat*?	**1** **2**	
has suffered from the effects of *pollution* on its food?	**3** **4**	**A** Florida panther
is the victim of illegal *poaching*?	**5**	**B** Polar bear
was once killed for sport by hunters?	**6** **7**	**C** Asian snow leopard
is unlikely to lose more of its habitat now?	**8**	
is now protected from harm by local people?	**9**	**D** Malaysian peacock pheasant
may be saved if it can be *reintroduced* to its native habitat?	**10**	**E** Arabian oryx
causes problems for local people?	**11**	**F** Bali mynah
has been successfully reintroduced to its native habitat?	**12**	**G** Bird of paradise
eats the same food as local people?	**13**	
is in danger because of its high value?	**14**	
cannot give birth to young	**15**	

The figures showing the rapid rate at which we are destroying the biodiversity around us are staggering. We are pushing a hundred species a day, four species an hour, into evolutionary oblivion. Some we know well – the elephant, the tiger, the rhino. Most are plants, insects, microbes and reptiles we haven't even figured out names for.

How are we doing it? Simply by demanding more and more space for ourselves. In our assault on the ecosystems around us we have used a number of tools, from the spear and the gun to the bulldozer and the chainsaw.

And as we destroy and reshape habitat locally and globally we will in the end be our own victims. Not only will we be creating a soulless place, devoid of birdsong with ever-expanding vistas of plastic and concrete, but the biodiversity we need to protect our bodies and sustain our spirits is the one thing we can never replace.

Endangerment is being caused not only in isolated habitats but almost everywhere, due to the effects of releasing agricultural and industrial chemicals into the eco-system. A small, isolated population of **Florida panthers** clings to existence at the edge of the Everglades. Many are in poor shape, unable to reproduce. Theo Colborn of the World Wildlife Fund in Washington, points to the chemical waste from Florida's massive agro-industry that ends up in the fish of the Glades, feasted on by the local racoon population. These racoons are the preferred dinner of the Florida panther.

The prevailing winds blow agro-chemicals and airborne industrial pollution to the furthest reaches of the globe. The fragile Arctic ecosystem is far from the sources of contamination, yet high levels of chemical residues are showing up in the fat of **polar bears** and other Arctic mammals. Colborn feels that their fish-based diets, shared by local Inuit people, account for increased reproductive abnormalities.

The New York Conservation Society not only runs all of New York's zoos, but is in the forefront of the struggle to preserve the beleaguered animals, birds and reptiles that are being crowded out of the world by human beings. Don Bruning, the Society's 'bird man', points to the plight of the **Malaysian peacock pheasant** as typical of many of the world's birds. 'Most of its natural habitat in lowland Malaysia

LAST CHANCE TO SEE ...

has been logged and converted to oil-palm and rubber plantations. We hope that we can reintroduce captive birds into some of the few wildlife refuges that remain.'

One of the birds that the Conservation Society has helped bring back from the brink is the **Bali mynah**. But now the poaching of these birds has dropped their wild population from 50 back to a perilous 35. Park rangers make $15 to $20 a month, while a Bali mynah sells for $500. Don Bruning says: 'The economics just aren't there. What we need to ensure is that enough Bali mynahs breed in captivity to swamp the market so it just isn't profitable to poach wild birds. This has already been done with a number of species, including the American alligator.

The Society participated with several other zoos in the reintroduction to Oman of the **Arabian oryx** – a small antelope whose habitat is some of the toughest terrain in the world. Jim Doherty, the Society's general curator, is quick to point out that only the support of local people keeps these antelopes out of the rifle sights of wealthy hunters who once slaughtered them.

The Society understands the mix of tactics needed to curb endangerment and also the complexities involved. Outside the **snow leopard**'s compound, a board gives the views of the different 'players' in the preservation of this shy and nomadic cat. A Western conservationist focuses on the uniqueness and beauty of the leopard. A local Himalayan herdsman stresses he can ill afford to lose 25 per cent of his sheep and goats. The wife of a local ranger talks about the difficulty of punishing those found with skins – they might be old and pre-date the anti-hunting law, they might come from a cat already dead. How was one to know?

The first task of any successful conservation policy is to get the local people on your side. Bruning is particularly enthusiastic about the Society's project to save the habitat of the **bird of paradise** in Papua New Guinea. 'We took 12 of the local leaders from a village in the centre of the bird's habitat and brought them down to the coast to visit two villages, one where logging rights had been sold and the area clearcut, the other where the forest had been protected. In the first village people told their visitors about the large amount of money they had received at the cost of their traditional forest livelihood. The money was now all gone. The other village never got the big payout but still had the forest, which they used to get a smaller but ongoing income from local eco-tourism. The group had never seen what clearcut forest looked like and they were devastated. These 12 people came back and discussed with all the local villages, and the first rule they came up with was that the area should never be logged. They are now looking at such things as local carving and handicrafts as well as butterfly farming. It gives them a stake in the forest and that's the key.'

STUDY BOX ▶ *Relative clauses with prepositions*

Look at these examples, which show the different positions for prepositions in defining and non-defining relative clauses. Two are from the text on page 187.

> The figures showing the rapid rate **at** which we are destroying the biodiversity around us are staggering.

> Most are plants, insects, microbes and reptiles we haven't even figured out names **for**.

> The New York Conservation Society, **to** which Don Bruning belongs, has helped rescue the Bali mynah from extinction.

In formal or written English, the preposition normally goes before the relative pronoun. In less formal and spoken English, it goes at the end of the clause.

Rewrite the second example so that it looks like the first. What extra word must be added?

Combine the information in these pairs of sentences in two different ways, one formal and one informal. Remember to use commas where necessary. (See the rule in Exercise 2, page 84.)

1 The giant tortoises are under threat. The Galapagos Islands are famous for them.

2 Many people depend on the forests for food. They are being destroyed quite unnecessarily. (The forests ...)

3 The destruction of the rainforest is a huge problem. We, as individuals, have very little control over it.

4 I am responsible for this area. It's too vast to police effectively against poachers. (The area ...)

5 David Young is a gifted scientist. We will be hearing a great deal about him in future.

Focus on Listening 1 *The Rainforest*

▶ Paper 4, Part 3

You will hear part of an interview with Dr Jeremy Knight, Director of an organisation called The Rainforest Foundation. For questions 1–9 complete each of the statements.

You will hear the recording twice.

Dr Knight says that an area of rainforest as big as a _____ **1** is disappearing every second.	
It upsets him that rainforest wood is used in products which _____ **2** from other materials.	
The people who live in the forests rely on them not only for food, but also for _____ **3**	
Staple food items which come from rainforests include tea, _____ **4**	
According to Dr Knight, rainforest plants are resistant to _____ **5** which affect cultivated crops.	
He thinks many of the plants which are being destroyed could be used to develop _____ **6**	
By absorbing rain water and then releasing it, rainforests help to _____ **7**	
Dr Knight makes it clear that he thinks destroying the rainforest is completely _____ **8**	
He says we can only stop the destruction of the rainforest if people change _____ **9**	

Focus on Grammar 1 *The Future 2*

1 a Underline the verb forms in sentences 1–5 below. Match them to the correct names a–e.

a present simple
b present continuous
c future continuous
d future perfect
e future perfect continuous

1 Panthers will probably have disappeared from Florida by the end of the century.
2 The New York Conservation Society is reintroducing the mynah bird to Bali next June.
3 The zoo reopens on January 1st.
4 They'll be opening the gates for the last time tomorrow morning.
5 By next month the villagers will have been waiting ten years for their share of the logging profits.

b Write the names of the correct forms in the explanations below.

- The ...... is used to talk about an action which will be in progress at a point in the future.

- The ...... is used to talk about a future event which will be complete by a time which is further in the future.

- The ...... is used to talk about the duration of an action, as seen from a point in the future.

- The ...... is used to express a pre-arranged future action. It is similar in meaning and use to *going to* but with less sense of personal intention.

- The ...... is used to express a fixed future event usually based on a timetable or programme.

2 Complete each sentence with a suitable verb form.

1 The doctor can't see anyone tomorrow because she ...... a conference in Cambridge.
2 It's our anniversary next week – we ...... together for a whole month!
3 Make sure you are at the station in plenty of time – the train ...... at ten on the dot.
4 I've booked a ticket for the concert next week and we ...... in the front row!
5 I'll be entitled to a pay rise next March because by then I ...... here for two years exactly.
6 He can't make it, he ...... for his boss this evening.
7 Hurry up, the show ...... in five minutes.
8 Unfortunately, they ...... the library in our village due to lack of funds.

3 a Read these 'visions of the future' and fill in the gaps using an appropriate form of the verbs in brackets.

Ecological Disaster

Professor Robert Tawnley, Institute of Ecological Research
'I'm not too optimistic about the future. My main worry is the greenhouse effect. The earth is heating up and at current rates the sea level (**1**) ...... (rise) by about 20 centimetres by the end of the 21st century. It might not seem like much but it (**2**) ...... (have) devastating effects. Large parts of the Indian sub-continent (**3**) ...... (be) under water during the monsoon season - an area that already suffers from famine. We have an observation centre in Antarctica and we (**4**) ...... (watch) the ice-caps carefully over the next decade. From what I have seen so far it's clear that the ice (**5**) ...... (continue) to melt at an accelerating rate in the future. And the destruction of the rain forests doesn't help. By 2035 over 95% of the rainforest in South East Asia (**6**) ...... (lose). I (**7**) ...... (fly) out to Brazil next month to chair a conference on this very subject and we (**8**) ...... (discuss) the loss of the natural habitat in the Amazon region. If we want the earth to survive we (**9**) ...... (have to do) something about it soon.'

Exploration and Ease

Caroline Brook, science-fiction author
'I'm excited about the future because I think, overall, things (**10**) ...... (get) better. Technology has already transformed out lives and I expect this (**11**) ...... (continue). If computers carry on improving at current rates, they (**12**) ...... (be capable) of near-human intelligence within the next half-century. It is quite likely that the average person in the year 2100 (**13**) ...... (lead) a life of leisure and (**14**) ...... (enjoy) themselves, while robots (**15**) ...... (carry out) all those boring day-to-day chores. And there are incredible possibilities in genetics and medical research. Scientists say most hereditary diseases (**16**) ...... (eradicate) by the end of the century. Space exploration is another area where I expect a lot of progress. The latest mission to Mars (**17**) ...... (land) on the red planet next July and two more probes (**18**) ...... (go) into orbit around Saturn in October. By the time our grandchildren grow up, a two-week holiday on Mars (**19**) ...... (probably become) as normal as a fortnight at the beach is for us!'

b Which do you agree with? What is **your** vision of the future?

189

Focus on Speaking I *Visual Prompts*

▶ Paper 5, Parts 2 & 4

1   Work in pairs.
Turn to the photographs on page 237.
Student A: You should talk about photographs A and B.
Student B: You should talk about photographs C and D.

You should:

- say what the scenes in your photographs have in common and how they are different.

- comment on the connection they have with wildlife conservation and say which you would prefer to do and why.

You each have about one minute.

When you have each finished, comment on what your partner has said. Say if you agree or disagree.

2   **Discuss these questions.**
1   Do you think tourism can help preserve endangered species? Why/Why not?
2   Do you believe zoos play a part in protecting wild animals, or do they violate animals' rights?

Focus on Writing I *Article and Note*

▶ Paper 2, Part I

TASK

You are part of a team which produces the college magazine. One of your responsibilities is the 'Green Issues' page, which features news and views on various environmental topics.

A friend has sent you an advertisement as a suggestion for a gift for a fellow student who's leaving college soon at the end of his course. You don't think it would be suitable for this purpose, but you feel it is a novel idea which could well be of interest to readers of the 'Green Issues' page.

Read the note below and the advert on page 191, to which you have added some comments. Then, **using the information carefully**, write:

a) an **article** about the Adopt a Whale scheme for the 'Green Issues' page of the college magazine (approximately 150 words);

b) a **note** to your friend, explaining why you don't think the gift would be suitable and making an alternative gift suggestion, and also saying how you plan to use the advertisement (approximately 100 words).

You should use your own words as far as possible.

I spotted this ad in one of the wildlife journals in the library and I was wondering if a whale adoption might make a suitable present for Peter when he leaves? I know he likes animals because he's always going on about his dog, and it would certainly be something different! We've got just about enough money in the kitty, so could you let me know what you think asap?

Jan

Adopt a Whale £17.50

AN ORIGINAL (GIFT) FOR YOUND AND OLD ALIKE

INCLUDES

✓ Free video
✓ Colour wall poster
✓ Colour brochure about natural history of whales

✓ Whale Adoption Certificate
✓ Black and white photo + biography of your whale
✓ 'I luv my whale' sticker

WHEN YOU adopt one whale you help all whales

Whales are extremely susceptible to the hazards of whaling and natural calamities. All whales are recognised by their tails. Choose the whale you would like to adopt from fully detailed Whale Adoption List sent with every FREE VIDEO kit.

BAT
Large female seen in Caribbean.
Photographed with first known calf in 1990.

COLT
One of best-known males in study group. Constantly approaches very close to whale watch and research boats.

OUR GUARANTEE: Your money will be spent directly on the protection and survival of whales.

Registered Charity

TASK CHECKLIST
ARTICLE

Format and approach: The main aim is to interest your readers (whether they are specially concerned about whales or not). Think about what makes the Adopt a Whale scheme unusual, what its key features are, and how best to present this information.

Your approach can be enthusiastic, humorous, or slightly sceptical, but your headline should reflect this approach, so it's worth spending a few minutes deciding on a suitable one. Check the other features of an article in the Writing File page 164.

Content and organisation: Once you've read the advert, jot down the key information in your own words. Decide on the best order to present this in.

Target reader: Would a reader be interested enough by the headline and opening sentence to read on? Would he or she find the key information?

NOTE

Content and organisation: The important thing here is **tact**. You need to include four elements: **thanking** your friend; **explaining why you don't agree with** his/her suggestion, **suggesting an alternative gift** and **saying how you intend to use** the advertisement. Decide the best order for these, and how to finish the note.

Target reader: When you've planned what to say, ask yourself how your friend will feel on receiving your note. Make sure there will be no cause for offence.

Focus on Grammar 2 *Quantifiers*

Each US citizen throws away the equivalent of three conifer trees *every year*.

1 The words in italics in the example above and in the sentences below are quantifiers, whose meaning and use are often confused. Identify the incorrect example in each group below, then answer the questions.

1 a Cars lined *each* side of the street.
  b Cars lined *every* side of the street.
  c *Each/every* street in the village was lined with cars.

Each refers to one of a group of ...... or more.
Every refers to one of a group of ...... or more.
Are *each* and *every* singular or plural?

2 a *None of* the students were Spanish.
  b *None of* the students was Spanish.
  c *Not all* the students were Spanish.

None of is always followed by a ....
Is *none of* singular or plural?
What is the difference between *none* and *not all*?

3 a *Neither of* the six animals was hurt.
  b *Neither of* the two animals was hurt.
  c *Neither* was hurt.
  d I don't know if *either* of the two animals was hurt.

Either and *neither* refer to one of ...... things.
Are *either* and *neither* singular or plural?
Either and *neither* can be used as ...... (in place of a noun).

4 a *All* animals have the right to survive.
  b *All of* the tigers in the zoo was healthy.
  c *All* the wildlife in the area was endangered.

When can *all/all of* be used with a singular verb?
What is the difference between *all* and *all of*?

5 a *Both* Sylvia and Marian aren't married.
  b *Neither* Sylvia *nor* Marian is married.
  c *Both* Sylvia and Marian are single.

Is *both* singular or plural?
The negative form of *both* is ...

6 a *A few* students have enrolled on the course.
  b *Few* students have enrolled on the course.
  c *Little* is known about the extinction of the dinosaurs.
  d Unfortunately, we had *a little* success with the conservation policy.

Is *few/a few* singular or plural?
Is *little/a little* singular or plural?
Few/a few is usually used with ...... nouns. *Little/a little* is usually used with ...... nouns.
A few and *a little* have a ...... meaning (more than expected/better than nothing) whereas *few* and *little* have a ...... meaning (not as much/many as we would like/expect).

2 Complete the following text with suitable quantifiers from Exercise 1. Use only one or two words for each space.

FACTFILE: **WHALES**

The whale is an aquatic mammal found in (1) ...... the oceans of the world. (2) ...... species of whale is different but scientists have divided them into two major groups: the toothed, including the sperm whale, the beluga whale and the narwhal; and the toothless, including the humpback and the blue whale. Whales in (3) ...... these groups share common characteristics such as a fishlike shape and nearly hairless skin. They have a dorsal fin and a flat tail which moves up and down to provide propulsion. There is a flipper on (4) ...... side of the head which is used for steering.

In common with (5) ...... mammals, whales produce living young. Unfortunately, (6) ...... is known about the reproductive behaviour of whales. However, there are (7) ...... exceptions, particularly the gray whale and the humpback. (8) ...... these two species produces more than a single calf per pregnancy. It is believed that the gestation period is (9) ...... ten or twelve months, depending on the species. Whales have a long lifespan; in the case of (10) ...... species such as the larger toothless whales this may be as long as 100 years.

(11) ...... the toothed (12) ...... the toothless whale poses a threat to humanity, yet we continue to hunt and kill them. Recent international treaties have attempted to ban whale-hunting. Unfortunately, not (13) ...... the whale-hunting nations have signed these treaties and (14) ...... of the most endangered species still face extinction.

Focus on Listening 2 *Helping the Environment*

▶ Paper 4, Part 4

You will hear five short extracts in which people talk about their attitudes to 'green issues'. For questions 1–10, choose the correct option A, B or C.

You will hear the recording twice.

1 What change has the first speaker made in her transport to work?
   A   She goes by public transport.
   B   She drives, using lead-free petrol.
   C   She uses her bicycle.

2 What action did her children recently take?
   A   They went on an organised cycle ride.
   B   They planted some trees.
   C   They joined a fitness club.

3 The second speaker says his company's environmental practices
   A   are decided by the Marketing Director.
   B   play a relatively minor part in the business.
   C   are advertised once a year.

4 The company's wood policies have been criticised by
   A   a business organisation.
   B   environmental groups.
   C   the national press.

5 Why doesn't the third speaker recycle her household waste?
   A   It would take up too much time.
   B   Not enough other people do it.
   C   She always forgets to do it.

6 What does she think is the best way to help the environment?
   A   going on demonstrations
   B   writing to politicians
   C   attending meetings

7 Which action does the fourth speaker think is the most important to stop?
   A   leaving windows open
   B   wasting paper
   C   using plastic cups

8 What system does he hope to introduce?
   A   new heating
   B   rewards for good ideas
   C   car-sharing

9 According to the fifth speaker, people tend to be most concerned about
   A   food packaging.
   B   air quality.
   C   water shortage.

10 Which of these areas of business has increased most?
   A   financial planning schemes
   B   environmentally-friendly building design
   C   organically grown food products

Focus on Speaking 2 *Interpreting and Discussing* ▶ Paper 5, Part 3

You have been asked to prepare a small leaflet called 'Four Ways to Save the Planet' for a student environment group you belong to. Look at the pictures, which all show suggested ways of helping the environment. Discuss what they each represent and how much difference you think they make to the environment. Then decide which four topics to include in your leaflet.

Focus on Writing 2 *Formal Letter* ▶ Paper 2, Part 2

WE CAN HELP YOU SAVE THE ENVIRONMENT!

Have you got an idea for a project to improve the environment in your area?

If so, write to us with the details and your project could receive a grant of £3,000 from the **Green Trust.** Send your letter to the Trust Director, explaining:

• what your project is, and why it is needed;

• who is involved, and how it will be organised;

• exactly how the grant money would be used;

• what you aim to achieve.

The grant will be awarded to the project which is considered the most worthwhile and practical in the view of the Trust.

You have seen this announcement in a newspaper. Write your **letter** to the charity using approximately 250 words.

Format: Check the layout for a formal letter (omitting addresses), and decide on the best way to begin and end.

Content and organisation: If you base your project on a real area you know well, it will be easier to think of ideas and your answer will sound more convincing. Before you begin, look at the pictures above again and think about the points that were raised in the Speaking activity. Discuss these and other possible issues with other students in order to stimulate ideas and activate relevant vocabulary.

Target reader: Remember that you need to convince the Trust that your project is really needed and will make a real difference, and that you have a realistic plan of action which will achieve results.

English in Use 1 *Lexical Cloze*

▶ Paper 3, Part 1

For questions 1–15, read the text below and then decide which word best fits each space. The exercise begins with an example (0).

GLADYS, THE AFRICAN VET

Last year Gladys Kalema became the Ugandan Wildlife Service's (0) .... (and only) vet after (1) .... from the Royal Veterinary College in London. She was the first person to fill the (2) .... for 30 years and, at the age of 26, easily the youngest.

If Gladys did nothing else, caring for the world's (3) .... population of 650 mountain gorillas would (4) .... justify her wages. Since the 1970s gorillas have (5) .... severely from war and poaching. Now for $150 each, tourists can be led through the forest and (6) .... within five metres of a gorilla - no closer, for (7) .... of transmitting diseases such as measles and flu.

The gorillas here make a small but viable population. (8) .... in the national parks the usual animals, elephants, rhinos, giraffes, are either not there or present in (9) .... numbers which are dangerously out of (10) .... with the creatures around them. If Uganda stays calm, wildlife may, in (11) .... , return by itself. But Gladys believes the country cannot wait. Animals must be brought in to (12) .... tourism and provide (13) .... to expand her work.

Despite her difficulties, Gladys feels more useful and fulfilled than she would be anywhere else. 'At this moment, my friends from vet school are reading the best way to (14) .... a cat or dog, and here am I planning to translocate elephants. In my small (15) .... I am part of the reconstruction and rehabilitation of my country.'

0	A top	B main	C first	(D) chief
1	A leaving	B qualifying	C graduating	D passing
2	A post	B occupation	C appointment	D career
3	A living	B surviving	C continuing	D lasting
4	A only	B alone	C just	D merely
5	A endured	B harmed	C suffered	D died
6	A come	B reach	C progress	D meet
7	A risk	B danger	C fright	D fear
8	A Somewhere	B Anywhere	C Nowhere	D Elsewhere
9	A slight	B little	C insignificant	D minor
10	A balance	B relation	C comparison	D equality
11	A term	B time	C ages	D years
12	A raise	B swell	C boost	D multiply
13	A figures	B savings	C accounts	D funds
14	A prescribe	B treat	C heal	D operate
15	A way	B manner	C method	D means

English in Use 2 *Discourse Cloze*

For questions 1–6 read through the following text and then choose from the list A–J the best phrase given below it to fit each of the spaces. Write one letter (A–J) in the spaces. **Some of the suggested answers do not fit at all.** The exercise begins with an example (**0**).

Looking After our Heritage

Would you care if the Parthenon in Athens vanished forever? Or if someone decided to tear down Rome's Colosseum? The questions seem too absurd (**0**) ..J... Of course, you'd care. Most people have no wish to see the remains of past civilisations destroyed or mutilated. Yet this is precisely what has already happened to numerous ancient buildings all over the world. The future of many more is, (**1**) .... , uncertain. The threat comes from many quarters – rain and floods, frosts and stone diseases, earthquakes, war and thoughtless destruction by bulldozers and other instruments of what we like to call progress.

It's easy (**2**) .... , who so often regarded classical sites as convenient piles of ready-made building blocks. But we have contributed our share. The Parthenon, for example, has suffered from aerial assault of rock-eating fumes emitted by chimneys and cars. Sadly, some governments seem (**3**) .... . Tourists have insisted on carving the dates of their visits on statues and columns and have broken off 'bits of old stone' (**4**) .... .

Happily there are some splendid examples of conservation. A large and dedicated army of archeologists and other enthusiasts is actively engaged in the task of protecting and restoring the masterpieces of earlier civilisations. More, much more, needs to be done. Tourism, now one of the largest industries in the world, plays an important role in this. It is fashionable these days (**5**) .... and, of course, some of the criticism is justified. But there is another side of the story. Our interest in antiquities has helped (**6**) .... . It has made politicians and local inhabitants aware that their ruins have economic value. The entrance money paid by tourists to enter archeological sites, or to visit museums has contributed to their preservation and upkeep.

A to be totally indifferent to their heritage
B to portray it as a negative force
C to do damage to them
D to enter archeological sites or visit museums
E to conserve much of what might otherwise have been lost
F to say the least
G to respect the heritage and culture of the country
H to blame past generations
I to take home as souvenirs

J to merit consideration

12 Living Dangerously

'Courage is the fear of being thought a coward.'
Horace Smith (1779–1849)

Lead-in

1 a Which of the following adjectives describe people who act without thinking about any dangerous consequences, or the actions they perform?

*reckless   hard-hearted   ruthless   foolhardy   daredevil   stingy
rash   chancy   dreary   conceited   hot-headed   troublesome*

b One of these words can also be used as a noun to describe a person who would act without thinking of the consequences. Which is it?

2 Choose nouns from the list below to complete the following sentences.

ice   fire   ground   hands   den   corner   depth   death

1 You'll be taking your life in your ...... if you try to cross the road here.
2 The course was pretty academic and I felt out of my ..... .
3 I've got to enter the lion's ...... this morning – the boss wants to see me.
4 Don't mention politics or you'll be treading on dangerous ....
5 I'd much rather take country roads than dice with ...... on the motorway.
6 You'll be playing with ..... if you try to outwit her.
7 He's skating on thin ..... by leaving his revision so late.
8 I've got myself in rather a tight ..... financially.

Focus on Listening 1 *Why do people take risks?*

▶ Paper 4, Part 1

You will hear part of a radio programme on why people take risks. For questions 1–9, fill in the missing information. You will hear the recording twice.

The number of British people taking part in adventure sports every year is	**1**
The bungee tower at Adrenalin Village is [**2**] in the world.	
According to statistics, bungee jumping is less dangerous than	**3**
The oldest bungee jumper at Adrenalin Village was	**4**
Simon Mayes says people like telling their friends how	**5**
The challenge for primitive man was to find food and somewhere	**6**
High sensation seekers like to experiment in [**7**], films and holidays.	
It's important to them that an activity makes them feel	**8**
In Professor Gunter's study, 'wallflowers' are people who are happy to watch others	**9**

Text 1

1 Newspaper readers recently sent in these examples of warning notices. Why do you think they sent them in?

a

For a compact camera:
Do not use this camera when it is emitting smoke or is unusually hot to touch. Use of the camera in any of these conditions may cause a fire.

b

On a pack of sleeping tablets:
May cause drowsiness.

c

At the bottom of the label on the back of a bottle of Californian wine:
Open Other End.

2 For questions **1–6** choose which of the paragraphs **A–G** on the next page fit into the numbered gaps in the following magazine article. There is one extra paragraph which does not fit in any of the gaps.

LIVING DANGEROUSLY

I spend a good deal of my time inventing or designing equipment and gadgets. I do so in a responsible way, paying due regard to safety, simply as a matter of common sense. But sooner or later I am invariably confronted with the problem of safety regulations.

1 ⬚

This problem arises, not because I want to make devices that are dangerous: it is because of the nature of the safety regulations – additional precautions designed to reduce risks that already appear insignificant to a point where they become negligible. Not surprisingly, I often find such regulations irksome and even unreasonable, and I have therefore been speculating on the curious and often contradictory attitude that we take, both as individuals and as a society, towards risk.

2 ⬚

But what about the effect that all these safety regulations have on our lives? Is it right that science teaching in schools is now so restricted by safety considerations that much of the practical science that stimulated my own interest in the subject can no longer be done? In my own field, the keen scientist who wants to get on with his research in the evening or at the weekend may actually be prevented from working alone with certain pieces of apparatus.

3 ⬚

The interesting thing, however, is that as this industry has grown, removing all sorts of risks from people's lives and adding substantial overheads to many industrial and everyday activities, so a parallel industry has developed which allows people to buy back those risks. It was not always so.

4 ⬚

Today, however, nearly everyone – possibly with a preponderance of men – spends money on buying back risk. We buy fast cars, and use them to exceed speed limits as a matter of course. We go on adventure holidays. We participate in increasing numbers in dangerous modern sports. We indulge ourselves in activities of proven danger such as smoking and over-eating, and yet we see no contradiction between this behaviour and increasing expenditure on industrial and institutional safety.

5 ⬚

For example, nearly every car advertisement these days offers safety as a major selling point. And yet those same advertisements almost invariably offer danger – in the form of lightning acceleration and three-figure top speeds – as a selling point too. How can this be explained?

6 ⬚

Among academics, the phenomenon is known as 'risk compensation'. Traffic experts express this in terms of 'accident migration'; making an accident blackspot safer merely means that motorists drive faster through the area in question, leading to more accidents somewhere else.

The simplest conclusion is that people never allow anti-risk measures to work. You can introduce laws requiring all cars to have better brakes, but the average driver will see such brakes as a justification for driving faster. Each potential safety benefit, in other words, will simply be consumed as a performance benefit.

A On the one hand, it seems to me, taking a risk is enjoyable. Why else do people queue for a go on the extraordinary machines of the modern fairground, except to be frightened? In other words, there does not seem to be any natural human drive to reduce risk absolutely. On the other hand, we live in an age of extreme safety consciousness. Every aspect of our lives, at home, at work and in between, is covered by rules designed to eliminate the risk of accidents and injury.

B The more one thinks about this phenomenon, the more absurd it begins to seem. Surely no sane society can simultaneously devote large amounts of time and money both to exposing itself to less risk and exposing itself to more risk? Yet the evidence suggests that this is exactly what we do.

C A further result of this development is that there is now a large safety industry with a vested interest in society continuing to perceive all risks as bad things which must be eliminated at all costs, with the cost not necessarily bearing any relation to the magnitude of the risk. There are large profits to be made from supplying new products to replace those that have been declared unsafe.

D Play, both in animals and among people, often involves a deliberate exposure to quite serious risks. Throwing yourself in front of the studded boots of a rugby player would certainly not get past many safety committees considering an industrial process in which similar behaviour was being considered.

E My personal belief is that we always arrange our lives in such a manner as to preserve a certain degree of risk, and even take on new risks whenever some existing avenue of risk-taking is closed, and this turns out to have a certain intellectual respectability.

F Almost as invariably, the requirements of safety regulations will compromise the design, add to the expense, make manufacture more difficult or even, occasionally, render the idea useless.

G In the 19th century, when everyday life really was full of danger, hardly anybody ever paid money in order to bring extra danger into their lives. (The exception were the rich, whose lives were safer anyway, who spent money on the thrillingly dangerous pursuit of hunting, and occasionally on expensive adventures such as exploration or ballooning.)

EXAM TIP   Paper 1, Part 2

In order to answer questions on the gapped text, you need to take a **broad perspective**, considering the development of ideas in the text as a whole, as well as a **close-up view**, looking at links between individual sections.

Do

- read through the gapped text first so that you have a general idea of its structure and meaning.
- see if there are reference links in the paragraphs before and after each gap to help you identify the missing sections. If not, look for a section which fits the logical development of the text.

GUESSING MEANING
FROM CONTEXT

3 **a** **Find the following expressions in the text and try to work out what they mean.**

irksome (para. 2)   a vested interest (para. C)
overheads (para. 4)   at all costs (para. C)
preponderance (para. 5)   render (para. F)
avenue (para. E)

b **Match the expressions with these meanings.**
*a personal advantage   greater number   means of doing something
annoying   cause to be   extra costs
as the most important consideration*

Focus on Listening 2 *Rescue at Sea*

▶ Paper 4, Part 3

1 In 1997, the British yachtsman Tony Bullimore was competing in a single-handed, non-stop, round-the-world yacht race called the Vendée Globe. In the Southern Ocean, 1,500 miles from the coast of Australia, his boat, Exide Challenger, capsized in a storm and Tony found himself beneath the upturned hull.

You will hear an interview in which Tony Bullimore talks about his terrifying experience and his dramatic rescue. For questions 1–10, fill in the missing information.

You will hear the recording twice.

One reason the Southern Ocean is called 'the Everest of Oceans' is that the waves can be as high as [_____ **1**] buildings.

One of the most frightening aspects of the storm was the [_____ **2**] which came from the sea.

The real emergency occurred when the keel [_____ **3**] and the boat turned upside down.

Tony knew that if his distress beacon [_____ **4**] he had no hope of rescue.

The only food he had was a few [_____ **5**]

He saw the biggest danger facing him as [_____ **6**]

The Australian defence forces sent a [_____ **7**] which eventually rescued him.

The first sign Tony had that somebody had found him was a noise [_____ **8**] the boat.

The injuries he had suffered included [_____ **9**]

Tony is determined to enter the next Vendée Globe race, which he sees as [_____ **10**] business.

DISCUSSION POINTS

2 Read this short text about a real-life emergency and discuss the questions.
You are in a very important round-the-world yacht race, with high prize money for the winner. You are in front and have a good chance of winning the race. Suddenly you hear an SOS signal. One of the other competitors is in serious trouble. Yours is the nearest boat to his. Would you:
a go back and help?
b radio the emergency services and carry on?
c do nothing and hope that the emergency services picked up the SOS signal?

Find out what actually happened by looking at page 234.

Focus on Writing 1 *Article*

▶ Paper 2, Part 2

TASK

You have seen this announcement in a magazine called *Out and About*, which is aimed at young people and focuses on travel, hobbies and outdoor activities.

COMPETITION   Win a BALLOON RIDE !!

Have you had an interesting adventure in your life? We'd like to hear about it!

It could have been your introduction to a daring sporting activity, your involvement in a challenge of some kind, or perhaps a journey where things didn't go quite to plan!

Tell us about your experience and about the effect it had on you in an article of approximately 250 words.

The best five entries will appear in the autumn issue of *Out and About*. The best overall entry, in the opinion of the judges, will win a balloon ride for two.

Closing date for entries: May 23rd

Write your **article**.

TASK CHECKLIST

Format and approach: What special features does an article have? Check the Writing File, page 164.
Content and organisation: What two elements must you include? Will this involve description? narrative? argument? How should you begin and end?
Style: What language features are needed for this content? (e.g. tenses? vocabulary?) What style is appropriate for this audience? How can you keep them reading? Should you include humour?
Target reader: Who are the magazine readers? (ages? interests? reasons for reading?)

KEY STRUCTURES

This is an opportunity to use some of the structures you have come across for adding emphasis and creating a dramatic effect.

a Rewrite these sentences using inversion. (See Study Box, page 127.)
1 I have never felt so frightened in my life. (Never ...)
2 The boat had just left the harbour when a storm blew up. (No sooner ... than)
3 We had lost our tent and the radio had been damaged as well. (Not only ...)

b Rewrite these sentences using a cleft structure to emphasise the part in italics. (See Focus on Grammar, page 180.)
1 I had always wanted to try *white-water rafting*. (a sport)
2 *I didn't know* that you had to have a visa to enter the country. (What ...)
3 The real emergency occurred *when the boat capsized*. (It ...)

Focus on Speaking 1 *Problem Solving*

▶ Paper 5, Parts 3 & 4

1 According to statistics for the whole of the United Kingdom, the main causes of fires in buildings are:

- faulty electrical appliances and wiring
- cooking accidents
- careless handling of smokers' materials
- heaters
- arson

1 One of these is by far the greatest cause of fire in people's homes. Which do you think it is?

2 A different factor causes most fires in offices, factories and hotels. Which do you think it is?

You can find out the answers on page 233.

2 a Work in pairs. Imagine you come back from school or work to find your home on fire. All the members of your family are safe, but the building cannot be saved. Then a fireman tells you he can go back in and save just one thing. Decide what you would like him to rescue. You can choose from the visual prompts.

b Briefly explain to the rest of the class the decisions you came to, and say how far you agreed or disagreed.

3 Now discuss these points.

1 What skills and qualities do fire fighters need to have?

2 Do you think fire fighters should be expected to go into burning buildings to rescue people? property? animals?

3 Which other rescue services can you think of? How many are voluntary?

4 What should happen to people who call out the rescue services unnecessarily?

> **EXAM TIP   Paper 5, Part 4**
> In the last part of the interview, you have to **explain** and **summarise** your conversation in Part 3, and also to develop the discussion further.
> **Do**
> - listen and respond to what your partner says.
> - allow your partner to comment on what you say.

Text 2

▶ Paper 1, Part 3

1 Before you read Text 2, see if you can guess whether these statements are true or false. Discuss your ideas with another student.

1 People are often too quick to imagine there's a fire in a building.

2 Men are less willing to leave a building in a fire than women are.

3 People frequently panic when there's a fire.

4 If there's a fire in a public building, most people look for a fire escape.

5 999 (emergency) calls often take longer than necessary.

2 Read Text 2 quickly in order to find out:
1 who devised the Survival Game, and why
2 which important aspect of a real fire the game misses out
3 if your answers in Exercise 1 are correct.

You are caught in a fire then what?

• •

You are asleep in your bedroom on the fifth floor of a hotel. Suddenly you are woken at 1.30 am by the sound of breaking glass. You get out 5 of bed to investigate, and look out into the corridor. There is nothing to be seen, but there is a smell of smoke. There seems to be a fire. What would your reactions be?

10 For many people they are never tested until it's too late – they are caught in a real fire. But visitors to the International Fire Safety and Security Exhibition in London this 15 week will have a chance to test their responses, and the consequences, in a specially devised game, The Survival Game.

The game was devised at Surrey 20 University where a team of scientists led by Dr David Canter is researching human behaviour in fires under contract to the Fire Research Station.

25 Their game cannot reproduce the stresses of a real fire, but it does bring out two very important points: the number of decisions that have to be taken on inadequate information, 30 and the importance of time. A correct decision at the beginning, for example, leads to a trouble-free escape, but there is no way of telling which is the safe route. It is a matter 35 of luck. And a delay closes even that route.

One of the most important discoveries the researchers have made from their hundreds of 40 interviews with people involved in fires is the problems of recognising that there is a fire at all. A fire is such an unusual experience that people will accept almost any other 45 explanation of the early signs of a fire first.

In one hotel fire, for example, 100 guests woken by the sound of breaking glass put it down to 50 someone smashing bottles outside – an event that had occurred on other occasions; in another incident, 105 residents in a block of flats, hearing cracking and popping noises, put it 55 down to vandals at work, made sure their doors were locked, and went back to the television.

Similarly, the research has shown that fire alarms are usually 60 interpreted as drills, tests or malfunctions – in the vast majority of cases quite correctly. The 115 assumption implicit in all fire regulations – that on hearing the 65 alarm the occupants of a building will evacuate – bears little relation to people's behaviour in practice. 120

In fact, faced with evidence of a possible fire nearly everyone seeks 70 further information. "There is a strong social stigma attached to getting it wrong," says David Canter. 125 So people are reluctant to make fools of themselves by rushing out into the 75 street or calling the fire brigade at what may be a false alarm.

Even when a fire is definitely 130 identified there is no immediate rush for the doors. Smoke is the thing 80 which most frequently persuades people to leave a building, but there are differences in the reaction of 135 various groups. Women are more ready to leave than men, the young 85 than the old, people at home than people at work, and people familiar with their surroundings than people who are not.

Under the stress of a fire many 90 people do things they afterwards see to have been inappropriate. There is a record of one man who twice carried a bucket of water right past a fire extinguisher.

95 Nevertheless, the Surrey team feel that people "panicking" in fires is something that often happens in press reports, but seldom in reality. Given the lack of information 100 normal in fires and the rapidly changing situation when a fire gets a hold, what appears to be senseless may be perfectly reasonable behaviour in the circumstances. In 105 the hotel fire of the game, for example, someone who dashed for the stairs by the lift, found them impassable, dashed to the other stairs to find them impassable too, 110 and then returned to his room would behaving perfectly rationally. But to somebody else he might appear to be dashing about at random.

The chief lesson to be learned 115 from this research, Canter thinks, is that more emphasis might be laid on the early detection of fires and training people to deal with them before they get out of hand.

120 Often the fire escape arrangements are not in normal use and are therefore forgotten when they are really needed. Or they may be cut off. Of 85 people involved in 125 fires where there was a fire escape available they were successfully used by only five. The vast majority did not even try to use them.

Even the simple 999 call could 130 be streamlined. Analysis of a large number of recordings has shown that it often takes several minutes for the caller to get over the location of a fire. A little training in 135 the best way to elicit the information for the people at the other end could save precious minutes.

MULTIPLE CHOICE QUESTIONS **3**
▶ Paper 1, Part 3

Now answer questions 1–6. Give only one answer to each question.

1 What can we learn from the game?
  A how to choose a safe escape route
  B which actions are most dangerous
  C when to leave the building
  D how to fight a fire successfully

2 Why did residents in the flats ignore the unusual sounds?
  A They guessed there was a party next door.
  B They wanted to watch the end of a television programme.
  C They thought it was only people mending the road.
  D They assumed young people were causing damage nearby.

3 What do people usually do when a fire alarm goes off?
  A telephone the fire brigade
  B pay no attention
  C leave the building
  D arrange to have the system tested

4 Why are people often slow to react when they think there's a fire?
  A they're afraid of making a mistake
  B they don't know the best way to leave the building
  C they can't think what to do
  D they don't want to leave their friends

5 If there was a fire in the Wonderpaint office building, who would probably be most unwilling to leave?
  A Miss White (30), the managing director's secretary
  B Mrs Brown (40), the office cleaner
  C Mr Green (60), the new managing director
  D Mr Grey (50), the resident caretaker

6 The research suggests that most people need training in
  A how to prevent fires from starting.
  B how to make 999 calls.
  C how to recognise the first signs of fire.
  D how to fight a major fire.

4 Try the Survival Game with a partner.

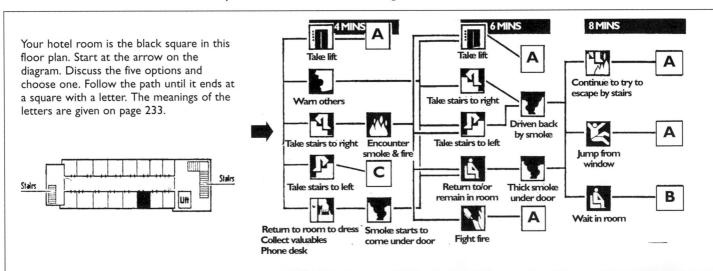

Your hotel room is the black square in this floor plan. Start at the arrow on the diagram. Discuss the five options and choose one. Follow the path until it ends at a square with a letter. The meanings of the letters are given on page 233.

LANGUAGE CHECK ▶ *Phrasal verbs*

Use a verb and a particle from the following lists to make phrasal verbs which can replace the italicised verbs in the sentences below. You may need to use a verb or particle more than once. You can find all the phrasal verbs in Text 2.

find	break	bring	put	get	cut

out	down	to	off	over

1 The Survival Game was designed to *discover* how people would react if a fire *started* in their hotel.

2 The game cannot reproduce the stresses of a real fire but it does *reveal* two very important points.

3 In one hotel fire, guests woken by the sound of breaking glass *interpreted* it *as* someone smashing bottles outside.

4 Often the fire escape arrangements are not in normal use. Or they may be *blocked* (by fire).

5 Analysis of a large number of recordings has shown that it often takes several minutes for the caller to *explain* the location of the fire.

6 Small fires have often been *extinguished* before the fire brigade arrives.

Focus on Grammar *Review of Tenses and Conditionals*

1 Past tenses

a Find six mistakes with tenses in these sentences, and correct them.

1 Paul is a firefighter since he left school.

2 The fire was burning for several hours by the time firefighters arrived.

3 I've been owning this watch for years and years.

4 When I was a child I was always getting into trouble.

5 'What's the matter?' ' I've been cutting my finger.'

6 During the last year I've been to the theatre twice.

7 I arrived last Saturday so I'm here for a week already.

8 Did you ever see this man before he attacked you?

b Put the verbs in the following passages into the correct past tense forms.

A

Until the invention of matches, lighting fires (1) ...... (be) not easy. Certain tribes in New Guinea (2) ...... (not know) how to light fires until recently and they (3) ...... (keep) their fires alight night and day. If they ever found that a fire (4) ...... (go out), they (5) ...... (go) and (6) ...... (borrow) glowing embers from a neighbouring tribe.

B

The first matches, invented by the Chinese in about 600 AD, (1) ...... (consist) simply of pieces of wood which (2) ...... (be/dip) in sulphur. These (3) ...... (burst) into flame when they (4) ...... (touch) smouldering wood. Modern safety matches (5) ...... (come) into use in Britain in the early 1900s when earlier friction matches, which people (6) ...... (use) for a hundred years, (7) ...... (become) illegal.

2 Conditionals

a Find five mistakes with conditionals in these sentences and correct them.

1 People are less likely to respect you if you are shabbily dressed.

2 If you wait there, I will let the MD know you are here.

3 Things will be a lot quieter if we had different neighbours.

4 If the company had installed sprinklers, the fire wouldn't have spread so fast.

5 We would be there by now if you wouldn't have spent so long on getting ready.

6 You would have enjoyed yourself if you were there.

7 If you had known about this, you should have told the police.

8 He could have been hurt if he weren't driving slowly.

b Answer these questions by writing suitable conditional sentences.

How would life be different if ...

1 matches hadn't been invented?

2 we didn't have electricity?

3 the telephone had never been invented?

4 there were no cars?

5 penicillin had never been discovered?

Focus on Speaking 2 *Spot the Difference*

▶ Paper 5, Part 2

Work in pairs. In this activity you will each have a picture to look at. The pictures are of the same scene but there are twelve differences between them.

a Student A should describe the left-hand side of the drawing in detail while Student B listens carefully and notes any differences (without interrupting). When A has finished, B should mention the differences he/she has noticed.

b Student B should then describe the right-hand side of the drawing in detail, while Student A studies his/her picture for differences.

c When you have finished both parts of the task, look at the two pictures together. You can compare your answers with the list on page 234.

Student A should turn to page 235. Student B should turn to page 238.

Focus on Writing 2 *Report/Memo*

▶ Paper 2, Part I

TASK

Recently there has been a spate of car and property thefts at your college. The college authorities haven't taken any specific action yet, and you decided to carry out a mini inspection of the college car park and classrooms to see whether anything could be done to prevent further crime. You reported your findings at the last Students Union meeting and you also jotted down some ideas for security measures which were suggested then. You have now been asked to prepare a report for the Principal, describing the main areas of poor security in the college, and outlining the measures you think need to be taken.

Read the notes you made during your inspection and the suggestions from the Students Union meeting. Then, **using the information carefully**, write a report and memo as instructed below.

NOTES ON INSPECTION OF COLLEGE PREMISES

NB My visit was between 12 and 2 on March 2nd

Car Park
Cars:
Two driver's doors unlocked (but didn't check all); 8 windows partly open and one sunroof completely open. One key even left in ignition! Very few steering wheel locks (or other security devices) in evidence.
Several car radios looked vulnerable; two briefcases, one holdall and a tennis racket left in full view on rear seats.

Bicycles:
Too many bikes for spaces available. Seven others chained to railings but three simply propped against the wall just asking to be stolen!

Classrooms
Equipment:
Obvious targets = TVs and videos (most rooms) – these not very securely fixed to stands; cassette players also left unattended in two rooms
Windows:
Hot day – several windows open. None of the ground floor windows had proper locks.
Doors:
Only computer rooms locked.
Personal property:
Several bags and/or jackets left in rooms during lunch hour.

SUGGESTIONS FROM STUDENTS UNION MEETING

- Car park lighting – improve, especially in far corner
- Bicycle parking – increase no. of designated spaces
- Signs reminding people to lock car doors and windows/remove valuables, etc.
- Leaflet giving advice on basic security, e.g. locking cars and bikes, taking care of wallets, handbags, mobile phones, etc.
- Local Crime Prevention Officer to give talk?
- Identity cards for registered students (and staff?) - this idea controversial!

Now write:

a) a **report** for the Principal (approximately 200 words);

b) an appropriate **memo** to the Principal to accompany the report (approximately 50 words).

You should use your own words as far as possible.

TASK CHECKLIST
REPORT

Form and Style: How should a report be laid out? What style is appropriate? Are there any special language features? See the notes on writing reports in the Writing File (page 165).

Content and Organisation: Have you included all the relevant information? Is it logically organised? Are the introduction and recommendations clear?

Purpose/Target reader: Will the Principal find the information clear and easy to read (or will he/she put the report back in the in-tray without reading it)? Are your recommendations reasonable and well-argued enough to persuade the Principal to take action?

MEMO

Form: A memo is a formal note. See the notes on writing memos in the Writing File (page 161).

Purpose: This is the first thing the Principal will read. What do you need to say, and how to do you say it, in order to explain why you are sending the report and to encourage the Principal to give it his/her attention?

LANGUAGE CHECK ▶ *recommend, suggest, advise, urge*

Not all these patterns are possible. Tick the ones you think are correct, then check your answers in the Grammar File, page 154.

I recommend	I suggest	I advise	I urge
a you to do this.	a you to do this.	a you to do this.	a you to do this.
b that you do this.	b that you (should) do this.	b that you do this.	b that you do this.
c doing this.	c doing this.	c doing this.	c doing this.

English in Use 1 *Structural Cloze*

▶ Paper 3, Part 2

For questions 1–15, complete the following article by writing each missing word in the correct space. **Use only one word for each space.** The exercise begins with an example (**0**).

SAVED

Tony Bullimore, Little, Brown

Geoffrey Moorhouse is thrilled by the tale of a yachtsman's heroic will to live

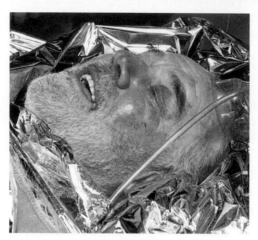

It is hard to think of a more terrifying thing than what happened to Tony Bullimore last January, (**0**) ..*or*.. of a more inspiring story than the epic of his rescue. (**1**) .... he was, trapped for four days in the darkness of his upturned yacht, deep in the Southern Ocean, where the waves are frequently four storeys (**2**) .... , and where (**3**) .... fall overboard without a survival suit usually means death (**4**) .... the hour. The (**5**) .... that Bullimore refused to give up hope is testimony enough to the old-fashioned guts of a very brave man.

For the airmen and sailors of the Australian Air Force and Navy, it was a race (**6**) .... time and the probability that (**7**) .... the end there would be total failure. The boat was much nearer the Antarctic than any other land, (**8**) .... meant that the rescue ship HMAS Adelaide had to sail (**9**) .... south than any Australian warship had ever gone before, (**10**) .... distant from port that a naval tanker was dispatched to refuel her in order that she (**11**) .... return home safely. The operation was that hazardous, that astonishing.

The story of all this (**12**) .... racily told, partly in narratives by Bullimore or his wife, who shared his ordeal back home in Bristol; partly in reportage logging the efforts of the rescuers. I sense that there has been a great deal of (**13**) .... the Americans call 'in-house editing'. (**14**) .... matter; it is a terrific story, and (**15**) .... without a discreditable figure anywhere.

English in Use 2 *Error Correction*

▶ Paper 3, Part 3

In **most** of the lines of the following text there is **one** unnecessary word. It is either grammatically incorrect or does not fit in with the sense of the text.

Read the text, put a line through each unnecessary word and then write the word in the space provided at the end of the line. Some lines are correct. Indicate these lines with a tick (✓) against the line number. The first two lines have been done as examples.

'... And we also fight fires'

Being a firefighter in today's Fire Service ~~that~~ is one of the most	**0** *that*
varied, satisfying and exciting of careers. Indeed, one of the main	**0** ✓
qualities required is in adaptability. Firefighters spend only a	**1** ......
small part of their time about fighting fires, in fact. As well as	**2** ......
having responsibility for the fire prevention, they deal with just	**3** ......
about every other kind major and minor disaster, such as road, rail	**4** ......
and air crashes, floods, chemical spills and rescuing people trapped in lifts.	**5** ......
Every year men and women join with the Fire Service from a	**6** ......
variety of different backgrounds. Entrants range from those with	**7** ......
only a few academic qualifications to those university graduates.	**8** ......
The important thing is that all recruits who receive the same	**9** ......
basic training and are encouraged to acquire any specialist	**10** ......
qualifications as they progress. A firefighter of exceptional ability	**11** ......
could not gain promotion to the rank of Station Officer after 5 years.	**12** ......
The Fire Service is a closely-knit organisation, based on teamwork	**13** ......
It offers plenty of opportunities to make up rewarding friendships.	**14** ......
In addition to the material benefits, and there are excellent sports	**15** ......
and social facilities. The Fire Service is also involved in a great deal of charity and community relations work.	**16** ......

A Career in the Fire Service

Crown Copyright

*"We feed the address into the computer and it shows us a map
of the area together with the exact location of the fire."*

13 ▷ Mind and Body

*'**Brain**: a two-room cottage occupied by an artist and an accountant engaged in a perpetual tug-of-war.'*
Rick Bayan, *The Cynic's Dictionary*

Lead-in

What kind of thinker are you? Work with another student. Discuss each of the statements below and fill in the answers **for your partner**. Tick 'yes' or 'no' according to whether your partner thinks the statement sounds like him or her or not.

		YES	NO
1	You like putting things in a sequence or order.		
2	You are spontaneous and sometimes jump to conclusions.		
3	You like puzzles and word games.		
4	You love to daydream, and your dreams at night are very real and alive.		
5	You have patience and stick to a problem, trying various approaches, until you get a solution.		
6	You like art, music, dance and creative expression.		
7	You can speak a few words in several languages.		
8	You cry easily and your feelings are easily hurt.		
9	You categorise things easily, and your files are in perfect order.		
10	You are visual; you get impressions of places in colour and form.		

Scoring
Count the number of 'yes' answers you gave to odd-numbered statements (1, 3, etc.). These indicate the use of the left brain, which is associated with logic and verbal ability.
Count the number of 'yes' answers you gave to even-numbered statements (2, 4, etc.). These indicate the use of the right brain, which is associated with visual and emotional matters.

Analysis
If one of your scores is much higher than the other, this indicates that you have a left- or right-brain preference. If, however, your scores are balanced, then you probably don't have a clear-cut preference for one mode of thinking or the other.

Text 1

SKIMMING
Paper 1, Part 3

1 Text 1 explains that there may be a connection between our facial features and our particular talents. Read the article quickly to find out about the theory of 'facedness'. Then answer questions 1–6 on page 212.

PHYSIOLOGY: Our features may reveal hidden talents, says Rebecca Fowler

  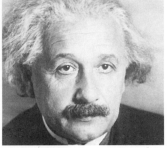 

Famous four: Beethoven and Prince Harry are left-faced, while Einstein and Burton fall in the right camp.

At first glance, you would be hard put to find any common ground between the angry features of Beethoven and the shy boyishness of Prince Harry.

Of course, if you were Karl Smith, emeritus professor of psychology at America's Wisconsin-Madison University, and had spent 15 years in research, you would know that both are left-faced.

'Facedness' is the new theory that proposes, just as most of us are either left-handed or right-handed, we have a more dominant facial side. It also claims to reveal the physiognomy of musical genius.

Left-facers, according to Smith's studies, are better able to tune into the right side of the brain, which is associated with musical performance, while right-facers tap into the left hemisphere, which is specialised for cognitive process – to the layman, thinking.

His surveys show that 85–90% of people are right-faced. 'With rare exceptions, all musically talented people are left-faced,' he says.

Wagner has one of the most marked left-faces that Smith has looked at, 'dominant to the point of deformity'. He is joined by Mozart, Beethoven, Brahms, Schubert, Tchaikovsky and Liszt. 'I have yet to come across a great musical talent who is not left-faced,' says Smith.

His work at New York's Metropolitan Opera shows that over 98% of opera singers of a 50-year period have been left-faced. Most contemporary musicians looked at also had a dominant left side, from jazz musicians to pop stars.

'The Beatles were all left-faced,' says Smith, whose work suggests that facedness ratios are the same in Europe as in the United States.

Prince Harry is the only member of the royal family who may have a career in music as a left-facer.

'Parents should not be wasting their money on right-faced children,' says Smith. It is not, contrary to popular belief, hands or ears that will suggest a Mozart in the making, but facial features.

The test for dominance is simple. Researchers measured signals from muscles and recorded resistance changes in jaw and lip movements.

But simply looking in a mirror will reveal a larger, more muscular side that is more flexible in speech and has a deeper dimple when you smile. The eyebrow will be higher and the skin smoother.

But right-facers should not despair. Dexterity in cognitive processes means that most great mathematicians and scientists have been dominant on the right. 'The marked right-facedness of Einstein is remarkable,' says Smith.

Right-facers also have the edge in speech. Most great orators and all British prime ministers have been right-side dominant, from Walpole to Thatcher. And we have yet to see a pope or monarch cloaking musical genius.

While left-facers have a better control of vowels, right–facers have the hold on consonants. Smith can recall no American newsreader who has been left-faced.

Actors should also be looking for a higher right brow, since most of the greats have been right-faced – such as Richard Burton.

Smith's theory also maintains that right-facers make better dancers and athletes. They depend on a highly articulate understanding of movement and cognition, born out in the elation between a dominant right face and left brain.

All athletes in the last Olympics were right-faced, he found, and a study of the Chicago and New York ballets showed 99% of dancers were right-faced. The one group of people who did not fall clearly into right or left were painters.

'The evidence has been astoundingly consistent right across the board,' says Smith. As a music lover, he is reconciling himself to his own right-facedness.

Unlike handedness, which develops at the age of three or four, facedness is determined before birth. For would-be composers and politicians there is no defying facedness, and parents should take note before signing up hopeful youngsters for music lessons – a glance in the mirror will tell if the expense will be worth it.

© The Sunday Times

1 What does the writer suggest about a first comparison between the faces of Beethoven and Prince Harry?
  A   They seem to have a lot of similar features.
  B   They look completely different.
  C   They're both left-faced.
  D   They're both right-faced.

2 Among left-facers, Wagner is said to be
  A   an extremely attractive example.
  B   a faulty example.
  C   an unusually clear example.
  D   a typical example.

3 What is different about the side of the face that is dominant?
  A   There are more wrinkles.
  B   It moves more easily.
  C   It is flatter.
  D   The eyebrow is thicker.

4 What advantage do right-faced people often have?
  A   They are optimistic.
  B   They are successful athletes.
  C   They pronounce different words more correctly.
  D   They are able to reason clearly.

5 What does Karl Smith's claim about the facedness theory?
  A   It is extremely convincing.
  B   It has been confirmed by the whole academic community?
  C   It is generally accepted by music lovers.
  D   It contains a number of interesting exceptions.

6 How is facedness different from handedness?
  A   It's of interest to politicians.
  B   It's easy to detect.
  C   You are born with it.
  D   You develop it as you grow up.

2   Discuss the ideas in the article with other students. See if you can tell what kind of face you each have.

EXPRESSIONS WITH 'FACE'

3   Choose idioms from the box to complete the sentences.
1   ...... , you're never going to be Einstein!
2   I saw her ...... him behind his back, so I guess things aren't quite as rosy between them as they were.
3   He'd been loyal to the company for years and when they promoted a younger man, it was a real ...... for him.
4   I don't know how you have the nerve to ...... round here after what you've done!
5   John's thought of a brilliant solution – he's not just a ...... , you know!
6   You're a married man now and you've just got to ...... your responsibilities!

slap in the face
pretty face
face up to
make/pull faces at
show one's face
Let's face it

Focus on Grammar *Past tenses to talk about hypothetical situations*

1 a One way to talk about a situation which does not exist but which we can imagine is to use *if* + a past tense. Look at this example from Text 1.

> If you were Karl Smith and *had spent* 15 years in research, you *would* know that both are left-faced.

There are a number of other expressions which can be used in a similar way. These include:

I wish   as though/as if   would rather + object
If only   suppose/supposing   it's (high/about) time

When they refer to the present or future, these expressions are followed by a past simple or continuous tense. When referring to the past, they are followed by a past perfect tense. (You can find further information in the Grammar File, page 153.)

b Read the examples below and circle the option, a, b or c, which best explains their meaning. Decide if the example refers to the present/future or the past.

1 If only you hadn't taken it.
   a You didn't take it.   b You took it.
   c You aren't going to take it.
2 I wish I was slimmer.
   a I used to be slim.   b I'm very slim
   c I'm overweight.
3 It's time we went home.
   a It's getting late.   b We went home on time.
   c It took a long time to get home.
4 I'd rather you didn't take the car out.
   a She took the car out.   b There's ice on the roads.
   c She didn't take the car out.
5 Supposing she had been seen by the police!
   a She was seen by the police.
   b She is about to do something illegal.
   c The police didn't see her.
6 He acts as if he owned it himself!
   a He owns it.   b He doesn't own it.
   c He used to own it.

c *Wish* + past tense versus *wish* + would

In these examples, there are four incorrect sentences. Which are they and why are they incorrect?

1 I wish I had my own car.
2 I wish she will be quiet.
3 I wish he hadn't shouted at me.

4 I wish John took the driving test again.
5 I wish you didn't have to go so soon.
6 I wish I would have a better-paid job.
7 I wish the government won't interfere in our lives.
8 I wish they would build a leisure centre in our town.

(See the Grammar File, page 153.)

2 Rewrite these sentences beginning with the words in brackets.

1 I hate having short hair. (I wish)
2 Your hair's too long. You need a haircut. (It's time)
3 I regret not going to the party. (If only)
4 Mary's always complaining. I want her to stop. (I wish)
5 Please don't go out tonight. (I'd rather)
6 He pretends to know all the answers. (He talks as if)
7 I left school at 16. It was a stupid thing to do. (If only)
8 I could go and confess to the police. (Suppose)

3 Complete the following sentences by adding one of the expressions listed in Exercise 1, and putting the verb in brackets into a suitable past tense.

1 ...... I ...... (can) help you but I'm afraid I can't.
2 I ...... you ...... (not tell) me how the book ends, if you don't mind.
3 ...... you ...... (not find) a spare key, how would you have got in?
4 Don't you think ...... the children ...... (go) to bed?
5 ...... I ...... (learn) to read music at school! I'd love to be able to join a choir.
6 The trouble with Jim is that he treats everything ...... it ...... (be) a joke.
7 You shouldn't have done it. ...... the security guard ...... (see) you!
8 ...... Stella ...... (speak) more clearly, she's so hard to understand.

4 Complete the following sentences in your own way.

1 You shouldn't keep lending him your car. It's time ...
2 We rely far too much on the car. Supposing ...
3 Please don't treat me as though I ...
4 It was quite a good course but I wish ...
5 You shouldn't have spent so much money on my present. I'd rather ...
6 You've got the wrong attitude towards your work. If only you ...
7 My boss sometimes acts as if ...

Focus on Listening 1 *Fears and Phobias*

Paper 4, Part 3

You will hear part of a radio programme about extreme fears, or phobias, their effects and treatment. As you listen, for each question 1–9, choose the answer which fits best. You will hear the recording twice.

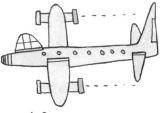

1 Paul's fear of flying means that he
   A   is going to give up professional football.
   B   is prepared to miss important matches.
   C   has only travelled by air once.
   D   will only fly for world cup matches.

2 On one occasion when he flew
   A   a bomb was reported in the papers.
   B   a reporter said there was a bomb.
   C   he imagined he saw a bomb.
   D   there was a bomb in the airport.

3 We are told that one in every four people
   A   actually enjoys flying.
   B   refuses to fly at all.
   C   is scared of flying.
   D   has never flown.

4 Denise started CAP because she felt
   A   people are scared of being attacked.
   B   she always wanted to be successful.
   C   people should understand their fears.
   D   her phobia was ruining her life.

5 What does Denise say about the 'rational' group of people?
   A   They tend to analyse their fear.
   B   They don't understand how planes work.
   C   They aren't really scared.
   D   They relate their flying to other things.

6 For Octavia, the worst part of her phobia about spiders was
   A   it caused inconvenience to others.
   B   she thought they would hurt her.
   C   it stopped her making phone calls.
   D   she couldn't go into some rooms.

7 Which part of the treatment did she find most unpleasant?
   A   having live spiders on her arm
   B   going to a shop to buy a toy spider
   C   discussing spiders with other people
   D   holding dead spiders in her hand

8 What is her attitude to spiders now?
   A   She still uses the treatment techniques.
   B   They are something she no longer thinks about.
   C   She suffers from frequent nightmares about them.
   D   They continue to affect other aspects of her life.

9 Which would make the most representative title for this programme?
   A Fear of flying
   B It's all in the mind
   C Accept your fears
   D Football terror

Focus on Speaking 1 *Visual Prompts*

Paper 5, Part 2

1 a Choose one of the pictures of businessmen and, without telling your partner which one, describe the man's expression and stance in as much detail as possible. (Don't use your hands to demonstrate!) Your partner should listen carefully and decide which picture is being described.

   b Discuss which details helped identify the right picture.

1

2

3

4

2 With a partner, discuss these questions about the businessmen.
   • Whose advice would you be most likely to take?
   • Who would you enjoy working with?
   • Who would you least like to meet?

3 Match the four pictures to these descriptions.
   A **The sergeant major:** Despite the strong message of physical self-assurance, there may be deeply-concealed anxiety.
   B **The gunslinger:** This stance may seem essentially masculine but women adopt it too, projecting a message of physical self-confidence.
   C **The village idiot:** Desperate to please an office audience, this unfortunate merely succeeds in looking rather insincere.
   D **The professor:** Although the body language reflects intellectual confidence, it sometimes hides emotional insecurity.

215

Text 2

GAPPED TEXT

Paper I, Part 2

For questions 1–6 below, you must choose which of the paragraphs A–G on page 217 fit into the numbered gaps in the following newspaper article. There is one extra paragraph which does not fit in any of the gaps.

Business of Body Language

What kind of signals do you send at work?

Are you a gunslinger or a sergeant major? A professor or an undertaker? Whatever job you do, you could be any of these, for this is just how you may look to other people. And that's what matters in business, according to Michael Howard of Talkshop, which offers training in personal communication and performance skills.

1

Michael offers his presentation skills to everyone from business consultants, lawyers and personnel managers to insurance salesmen and counter clerks. 'In fact anyone involved in face-to-face communication with the public could benefit,' he says. 'You cannot overstate how damaging bad presentation can be for business. A poor performer is embarrassing to watch and just makes people uncomfortable and bored.

2

He believes most people have a 'natural expressiveness' which can be unlocked by just a little training. His courses aim to turn you into 'an effective communicator, presenting yourself confidently in all situations'.

Michael, 40, set up Talkshop a year ago. He first trained as a quantity surveyor, then gave it up for drama school and an acting career that has taken in stage roles from Shakespeare to children's theatre. 'Talkshop was an ideal way to marry up my skills as a businessman and an actor.

3

Business 'performers' fall into several categories – examples are shown in the box below. If you can spot your 'type' it often helps to an awareness of the way you present yourself and how you might improve this.

4

'In fact, her sweeter tones should be seen as a positive asset rather than a problem. A warm, controlled voice conveys much more authority than a macho rant.

5

'For a woman in a top position there's no point in being a bully. Men will just be dismissive and resentful. Good use of eye contact is the best way of establishing high status.'

People from different cultures and professions also show marked differences in the way they talk and act, but it's important not to look at people as stereotypes.

6

But there is no one way to present, says Michael. 'It's horses for courses. While a salesperson may need to show that they are relaxed and chatty, a senior partner in a law firm may have to show more distance to create authority.'

The important thing is to get the right message across. 'It's all about releasing natural abilities,' says Michael. 'People coming away from my courses should not only be *able* to give a good public presentation, but should also positively *enjoy* it.

The gunslinger – legs apart, this type leans back and thrusts the pelvis forward showing physical confidence. But the head – intellectual confidence – is placed well back. This may sound like a masculine pose but women do the same. It shows you are sure of your physical attractions. But have you got anything to say?

The professor – legs together, the groin and chest are pulled right back while the head is pushed forward on the end of a long neck. This shows 'supreme confidence' in the intellect but also hides emotional insecurity.

The sergeant major – stands proudly with the chest out, appearing totally invulnerable. The stance says 'I'm afraid of no one.' But is he or she hiding some deep anxieties?

The village idiot – this type is 'open and full frontal'. With body swaying in the wind, he or she stands with a silly grin desperately 'eager to please' the audience. Unfortunately, they end up looking insincere.

The invisible man – rather than stand four-square in front of his or her audience, this type prefers to hide

behind a desk or lectern, looking down at sheaves of notes to avoid eye contact. He or she hopes to appear authoritative and learned, but instead appears shifty and insecure.

The undertaker – stiff as a board, these sombre characters just don't know how to relax. They speak in slow, serious tones, but the audience knows how racked they are with nerves and so feels edgy and uncomfortable.

A There are also important differences between the way men and women in business behave when dealing with people. 'A woman's higher, softer voice means she can be shouted down by more aggressive and domineering men,' says Michael. 'This often leads her to clam up in meetings.

B How can you convey to an audience that you are a confident, relaxed and authoritative speaker? Talkshop's Michael Howard offers the following tips to get you started: always look straight at your audience, make eye contact and keep it; project your personality by speaking loudly and clearly; don't fidget because too much movement will simply unsettle your audience

C The 'bluff businessman', for example, can turn to jelly when asked to speak to a small group for five minutes. In contrast, his 'shrinking violet' secretary may blossom when she is given the ear of an attentive audience.

D You may be offering the best financial advice around or selling the smartest computers, but if your body language is wrong your customers just won't want to know. And that could mean your business losing thousands of pounds. You may be trying to hide your nerves, your boredom or your aggression, but your body language will give you away.

E 'Drama training gives you a great knowledge of how body language works. You learn not only how your character works, but how the other characters react to that character. But if I hadn't been in the commercial world, I wouldn't have seen how that works in practice.'

F Women can learn to display confidence without being aggressive. Unfortunately, many women feel they should ape the male approach. This is a mistake. If anything, it should be the other way round.

G 'They will lose all trust in the person – and business. No one can afford that in today's competitive world.' Through his workshops Michael teaches relaxation and breathing techniques, how the voice works and – most importantly – body language.

LANGUAGE CHECK ▶ *Word formation*

Fill in the missing parts of speech. All the answers come from texts in this unit.

Adjective	Noun	Verb		Adjective
1 assured	......	9	dismiss	......
2 anxious	......	10	resent	......
3 bored	......	11	attend	......
4 aware	......	12	dominate	......
5 insecure	......	13	compete	......
6 sincere	......	14	flex	......
7 relaxed	......	15	chat	......
8 embarrassed	......	16	benefit	......

STUDY BOX ▶ *Concession*

If you concede something, you acknowledge, often unwillingly, that it is true, while at the same time countering it with another idea. The modal verb *may* can be used to express concession, often in a clause introduced by *while*.

> While a salesperson may need to show that they are relaxed and chatty, a senior partner in a law firm may have to show more authority. (Text 2)

Clauses of concession can be introduced by expressions including *although, but, despite/in spite of* (*the fact that*). (See Unit 1, page 17.)

Clauses that depend on a condition are introduced by *even if*
> e.g. Even if you double her salary, she won't stay.

Clauses that are true under all conditions can be introduced by:

> *no matter what/where/who*, etc. (See Unit 3, page 42.)

> *whatever, whoever, however*, etc. Whatever I do, I can't seem to please her.

> *hard as/much as* Hard as he tried, he couldn't solve the puzzle.

Rewrite these sentences using clauses of concession. Begin with the words in brackets.

1 It's true he is a good administrator, but he doesn't have very good interpersonal skills. (While)

2 I like her very much, but I wouldn't recommend her for this particular job. (Much as)

3 It doesn't matter how cold it gets, he never wears a coat. (However)

4 She has a degree from Oxford University, but she's still incredibly lacking in self confidence. (Despite)

5 I know it's received lots of awards, but I still think it's a terrible film. (No matter)

Focus on Listening 2 *Actions Speak Louder Than Words*   ▶ Paper 4, Part 2

TASK

1 You will hear part of a talk about Neurolinguistic Programming (NLP). This is a set of skills designed to improve communication and performance generally, which can be learnt through special training programmes. As you listen, complete the information for questions 1–8.

Listen very carefully as you will hear the recording once only.

NLP	
Content of a talk accounts for _____ **1** of effect on audience.	
NLP developed by student of psychology and _____ **2**	
NLP suggests that successful people should be studied and _____ **3**	
We can achieve rapport with someone by imitating their _____ **4**	
NLP stresses the importance of _____ **5**	
People benefiting from NLP training include: managers, salespeople, _____ **6**	
Salespeople with NLP training improved their success rate by _____ **7**	
European country where NLP is most widely used: _____ **8**	

Focus on Speaking 2 *Dress Codes*

▶ Paper 5, Parts 3 and 4

1 Work with another student. Decide which of the items in the pictures you think are appropriate to wear or take: a) to school, b) to the office.

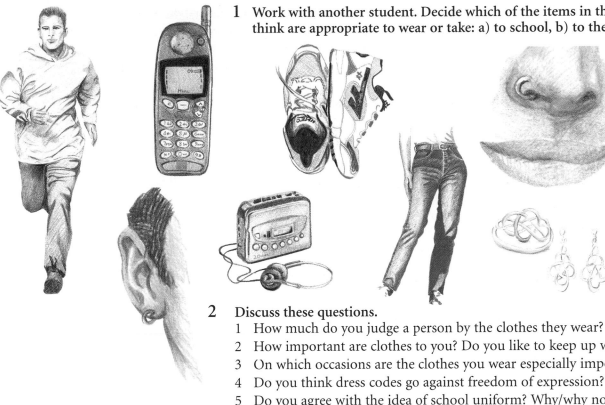
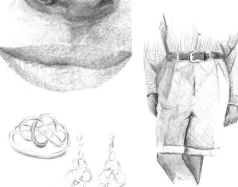

2 Discuss these questions.
1 How much do you judge a person by the clothes they wear?
2 How important are clothes to you? Do you like to keep up with the fashion?
3 On which occasions are the clothes you wear especially important? Why?
4 Do you think dress codes go against freedom of expression?
5 Do you agree with the idea of school uniform? Why/why not?
6 In a relationship, should you dress to please your partner? Why/why not?

Focus on Writing *Reference*

▶ Paper 2, Part 2

TASK

An American company is opening a new English language school in your town. Someone you have known for a long time has applied for the job of receptionist at the school, and has asked you to write a character reference. You should write a detailed **reference**, indicating how long and in what capacity you have known this person, and including relevant information about their abilities and personality, and why you would support their application. Write approximately 250 words.

TASK CHECKLIST

Content: Your answer doesn't have to be based on a real person, but it's usually easier to write about someone you know. Underline the main points the question asks you to include. Think about the role of a receptionist in a busy new language school, and the characteristics which would be appropriate.

Target reader: Put yourself in the shoes of the target reader. What information would it be helpful for an employer to know? If your reference contains nothing but unqualified praise, it may not ring true, so consider mentioning one or two minor weak points for balance, but make sure that the overall tone is positive.

Layout: Treat a reference like a formal letter, but without the usual beginning (*Dear ...*) and ending (*Yours sincerely*). Instead, write your friend's name at the top and underline it. Sign your name at the end, and add the date.

Focus on Vocabulary

COLLOCATION

1 a Match each word or expression (1–14) to its partner (a–n).

1	body	a	features	8	a knee-jerk	h	collision
2	eye	b	structure	9	fingertip	i	talk
3	facial	c	circulation	10	a thumbnail	j	story
4	hand	d	system	11	a hair-raising	k	noise
5	blood	e	contact	12	a heart-to-heart	l	sketch
6	bone	f	language	13	a head-on	m	reaction
7	digestive	g	signals	14	an ear-splitting	n	control

b Complete the following sentences using suitable collocations.

1 I'm sure your mother will understand if you have a ...... with her and explain why you're so upset.

2 When I learnt to drive you had to give ...... when you were turning left or right but now everyone uses their indicator.

3 Have you heard what happened when he disturbed a burglar in his flat? It's quite a ....

4 Look kids, I'm trying to work. Do you have to make that ...... while you play?

5 I don't need all the details yet but could you give me a ...... of the plan you're proposing?

6 The police asked me to describe her ...... in as much detail as possible so they could produce a photofit picture of her.

7 He sounded calm but his ...... suggested that he was nervous about something.

8 If I hadn't managed to swerve out of the way in time we would have had a ...... with that truck.

PHRASAL VERBS

2 The phrasal verbs in the list come from the previous reading and listening texts. Make the following sentences less formal by choosing phrasal verbs to replace the words or phrases in italics, and making any other changes necessary.

> *end up   marry up   take in   fall into   clam up   carry out*
> *give up for   shout down   set up   give somebody away*

1 The audience *expressed its disapproval by making his words completely inaudible.*

2 I know what I intend to say, but if he loses his temper I'm afraid *I'll be incapable of saying anything.*

3 What we have to do is *combine* Jeff's engineering expertise with your skills as a designer.

4 It was his extravagant spending that *revealed he was guilty.*

5 I was sympathetic at first but I *eventually began* to lose patience with her.

6 I'm sure she is capable of *performing* all the duties which the job entails.

7 Our tour *included* a number of places not normally on the tourist route.

8 He *established* his first company when he was just 18.

9 Visitors to the museum *can be divided into* several distinct categories.

10 He had a promising career as a journalist but he *abandoned* it for love.

English in Use 1 *Lexical Cloze*

For questions 1–15, read the following text and then decide which word below best fits each space. The exercise begins with an example (**0**).

A CHANGE OF MOOD

Most of us (**0**) .... our moods as being rather like the weather – it is something that colours the whole day, comes from somewhere else and over which we have little (**1**) .... . Not that there isn't a range of folk (**2**) .... for dealing with a bad one: 'Just snap out of it. Talk to a friend – a problem (**3**) .... is a problem halved. Pamper yourself.'

The problem is, as the latest American research (**4**) .... , all these favourite mood-swinging ploys are very ineffective. In his new book, Robert Thayer, professor of psychology at California State University, (**5**) .... forward a new theory about what to do to change our moods and why. There are a few surprises. For instance men, (**6**) .... to popular opinion, are actually better at dealing with their moods than women. Not only that, but the time-honoured female techniques of (**7**) .... it all out to a friend or (**8**) .... a good cry are often a waste of time.

His approach makes it possible to forecast moods and be much more precise about controlling them. For instance, we all have a daily energy rhythm – on (**9**) .... , we start low, build up to a (**10**) .... around midday, dip down, (**11**) .... up a bit in the later afternoon and then tail off towards the evening. So, because of the (**12**) .... between energy levels and mood, we can predict that an (**13**) .... in tension will produce a more gloomy (**14**) .... at those times of the day when our energy regularly takes a dip. Knowing that, you can take it into (**15**) .... .

0	**A**	regard	**B**	take	**C**	think	**D**	assume
1	**A**	selection	**B**	ability	**C**	decision	**D**	control
2	**A**	remedies	**B**	medicines	**C**	solutions	**D**	treatments
3	**A**	distributed	**B**	spread	**C**	divided	**D**	shared
4	**A**	informs	**B**	reveals	**C**	exposes	**D**	discovers
5	**A**	brings	**B**	gives	**C**	puts	**D**	calls
6	**A**	opposite	**B**	contrary	**C**	against	**D**	different
7	**A**	pouring	**B**	draining	**C**	dropping	**D**	spilling
8	**A**	giving	**B**	doing	**C**	having	**D**	making
9	**A**	general	**B**	ordinary	**C**	normal	**D**	average
10	**A**	point	**B**	height	**C**	peak	**D**	limit
11	**A**	pick	**B**	get	**C**	rise	**D**	lift
12	**A**	tie	**B**	link	**C**	line	**D**	combination
13	**A**	addition	**B**	improvement	**C**	enlargement	**D**	increase
14	**A**	vision	**B**	outlook	**C**	aspect	**D**	review
15	**A**	attention	**B**	mind	**C**	account	**D**	notice

English in Use 2 *Word Formation*

For questions 1–15, read the two texts below. Use the words in the boxes to form **one** word that fits in the same numbered space in the text. The exercise begins with an example (0).

Headaches and migraine

Headaches and migraine can vary in (0) *severity* from a dull thudding in the temples to a (1) .... intense pain. Most people suffer from headaches (2) .... but they can usually get (3) .... from the symptoms by taking a couple of pain-killers. Headaches usually create (4) .... in the shoulder and neck muscles and are most often caused by stress or (5) .... , though other triggers include eye strain and lack of sleep or food. Migraines are far more (6) .... than headaches, and attacks may last from four hours to three days. They are often confined to one side of the head and may be (7) .... by visual (8) .... , light intolerance, nausea and other symptoms.

(0) SEVERE
(1) FRIGHT
(2) PERIOD
(3) RELIEVE
(4) TENSE
(5) ANXIOUS
(6) ABLE
(7) COMPANY
(8) DISTURB

Self help for sufferers

There is a (9) .... of measures you can take to help prevent headache and migraine attacks. Keep a diary and note down the date and (10) .... of each attack, the symptoms and any possible trigger factors such as a (11) .... food or drink. Try to cut out these factors, one by one, and you should be able to identify the ones which trigger an attack. If you have a (12) .... drug from your doctor, it is important to take the (13) .... as soon as possible after the (14) .... of an attack. Finally, herbs such as feverfew have proved effective, but they should only be used under (15) ..... since they are still drugs.

(9) VARIOUS
(10) LONG
(11) SPECIFY
(12) PRESCRIBE
(13) TREAT
(14) SET
(15) GUIDE

14 ▶ Testing Times

'Examinations are formidable even to the best prepared, for the greatest fool may ask more than the wise man can answer.'
Charles Caleb Colton 1780–1823

Lead-in

Work with another student to discuss these questions.

INTERPRET AND DISCUSS

1 a Look at the cartoon below and discuss its connection with the title of this unit. What has the artist tried to illustrate?

b Briefly explain to the rest of the class how you interpreted the picture, saying how far you agreed or disagreed.

2 Tell your partner about the last exam you took.
- What was the subject?
- Where did you take it?
- What was the exam like?
- How did you feel about it?

3 How do you prepare for exams? Discuss the following points:
- revision
- health
- nerves

Text

TASK
MULTIPLE MATCHING

1 Answer questions 1–16 by referring to the magazine article on page 225 in which various writers are interviewed about their experience of examinations.

For questions 1–16, answer by choosing from the list of writers (A–D) on the right below. Some of the choices may be required more than once.

Note: When more than one answer is required, these may be given **in any order.**

Which writer or writers ...		
talks about school exams?	1 ...... 2	
describes an oral exam?	3 ..... 4 ..... 5	
found they minded more about an exam than they thought they would?	6	**A** Rose Tremain
often realised how little they knew?	7	**B** Tim Willocks
talks about how they prepared for an exam?	8 ...... 9	**C** A. S. Byatt
looks back on an exam with pleasure?	10	**D** Patrick Gale
mentions the value of exams?	11	
revised for the wrong questions?	12	
suggests that it's important to begin revising early?	13	
mentions a strong feeling of fellowship with other students?	14	
says that creative thought was discouraged at school?	15 ...... 16	

GUESSING MEANING
FROM CONTEXT

2 Find the following words and phrases in the first two sections of the text and think about the likely meaning. Then choose a suitable explanation from those on the right (a–f).

1	the knack	a	persuaded by praise
2	steal a march	b	so that it can be repeated without thinking
3	off-pat	c	secretly gain an advantage
4	taking the liberty	d	persuaded by fear
5	cajoled	e	trick/secret of success
6	bullied	f	doing something without asking permission

3 Now say what you think the following expressions from Section D mean.

1	in one fell swoop	3	scrawled
2	shrug it off	4	in the flesh

Discuss your ideas with another student and then check the words in a dictionary if necessary.

Testing Times

It's that season of the year again: Exam Time. Here, four authors reflect on their own experiences of a ritual that everyone fears and no one forgets.

A Rose Tremain

Exams come early. Always earlier than you'd expected. The knack is to see them from a long way off. At boarding school, I and a small group of friends tried to steal a march on them by giving up three hours of sleep each night, setting our alarm clocks and creeping down to our revision books at four in the morning, sustained by oranges saved from breakfast the day before.

It would be dark at first and awesomely quiet in the old school room, and we felt like burglars. Into our heads, as dawn came into the silent study, was crammed the information we needed. We learnt it all off-pat, by heart, because this was how we'd been taught it. In those days, at a girls' boarding school, nobody did much thinking. Information was given out, taken down, memorised and recycled.

But we all passed. We flew through Biology, History, Eng. Lit., Geography, French, Latin. What no one but us had witnessed was those early summer dawns where three hours of extra work had lain hidden. And all that remained of us, when the rest of the school began its day, was the astringent smell of oranges.

B Tim Willocks

In order to qualify as doctors, we had to take something over 50 examinations in six years, the failure in any one of which prevented us from progressing to the next. Exams walked at our side, day and night. Oral exams, multiple choice exams, essay exams, practicals, research projects and more.

Under these conditions there was an unspoken sense of an elite superiority, compared to other university students attending five lectures and one tutorial a week (less than we had each day). Or perhaps that was just me. I don't usually take it upon myself to speak for others, but in this case, the sense of shared struggle and discovery that I remember is so strong that I feel justified in taking the liberty. We all of us, I believe, were repeatedly humbled by our ignorance and by the scale of the endeavour before us.

But of all the exams I took, the type that provoked the greatest tension was the viva voce – the so-called 'orals'. One entered a large – usually dimly-lit – room in which anything from three to six bored, demi-gods sat in judgement behind a broad table and fired questions.

While I often hated the exams, I never resented them. I always acknowledged the fact that I would never have made the enormous effort necessary without being cajoled, threatened and bullied into the task by the seemingly endless series of trials that they set us.

C A. S. Byatt

Every year I dream that I am in an exam hall and cannot start to write until I have found the right size of paper from a heap like a mountain. Exams haunt our nightmares as sabre-toothed tigers haunted our ancestors.

But an exam is one of my best memories. I took the Cambridge Entrance exams in 1953, the only girl in my school, sitting in my headmistress's study. I was summoned to interview at Cambridge, and I was walking away when the secretary called me back – I was wanted for an oral examination for a scholarship. I remember lecturing the assembled dons, standing at a blackboard, and finding they were interested. Those exams were the first time I had really felt anyone was interested in what I was interested in, and in what I thought about. At school you had to hide what you were really thinking about, not speak of the music you were listening to or the poetry you were reading.

D Patrick Gale

I assumed the postcard from Oxford contained my degree result. A second would have been nice but I was quite prepared for a third. I didn't greatly care. Novelists had no need of degrees. Only it wasn't the result. It was a summons to present myself for a 'viva voce' examination the following week.

In one fell swoop my fragile adult life collapsed. Try as I might to shrug it off as a pointless ritual, I found myself caring deeply. I had kept my exam papers as a grim momento and now felt compelled to begin revising all over again. Assuming myself a borderline third, I concentrated on the questions I had answered poorly.

The exam was nightmarish, conducted with the solemnity of a job interview. Some six examiners faced me in a horseshoe formation. I was empty-handed. They had glasses of water and, I saw to my horror, photocopies of my scrawled exam papers. Thinking to put me at my ease, their leader explained that they had called me because several of my essays had been very good and if I could just expand on them sufficiently to raise them to excellence, I would win a first. They were giving no thought to the subjects over which I had just sweated a week's worth of blood. Oh no.

It was a disaster, of course. The subjects I had shone in were now dim in my memory, Where I was fluent on paper, I was a stammering dullard in the flesh, and the panel awarded me the second I would have been happy with all along.

METAPHOR

4 a Look at these examples from the text, and answer the questions.
1 We *flew* through Biology, History, Eng. Lit. (Section A)
Did they find the exams easy or difficult? What results did they get?
2 (The examiners) *fired* questions. (Section B)
How did they ask questions?
3 The papers I had *shone* in ... (Section D)
How did he do in those papers?

b Now choose words from the list below to complete the following sentences and say what the metaphor suggests.

staggering   blazing   saddled   spinning
blanketed   spoonfeeding   froze   snap

1 They gave me so much information that my head was ...... when I left.
2 There's no need to ...... at me – I only asked a perfectly civil question.
3 As a company, we seem to be ...... from crisis to crisis at the moment.
4 Half way up the stairs I .... I could hear footsteps on the landing!
5 Things finally came to a head and we had a ...... row last night.
6 His trouble is that he's ...... with that huge debt.
7 It's no use me ...... you the answers. You need to work them out yourself.
8 The whole city was ...... in smoke from the bush fires.

Focus on Speaking *Developing an Argument*

▶ Paper 5, Parts 3 & 4

Work with another student to discuss the following questions.

1 Consider the views on exams expressed in the following short text extracts. Which opinion do you agree with most/least?

A
'While I often hated exams, I never resented them. I always acknowledged the fact that I would never have made the enormous effort necessary without being cajoled, threatened and bullied into the task by the seemingly endless series of trials that they set us.'
Tim Willocks, author (Text Section B)

B
'[Exams] leave you brain-washed and stupid. I have learned many facts but not thought (no need).'
Diary entry written by 15-year-old Helen Simpson

C
'The thing about exams is that they do give you a clear goal to work towards. And there's a problem-solving element to some of the questions, which quite appeals to me too. It's a bit like doing crossword puzzles. The best thing is checking the answers and finding out how you've done.'
An exam candidate

D
'Exams are a necessary evil, I suppose. They can be nightmarish to prepare for and there's always going to be an element of luck on the day. All the same, I don't think anyone's come up with a really viable alternative yet.'
An examiner

E
'Exams encourage cheating. I think it's much fairer to have a system of continuous assessment, where you have to submit regular coursework.'
A teacher

2 What alternatives to traditional written exams can you think of? What are the advantages and disadvantages?

3 Are there certain subjects where a traditional written exam is the only way to test knowledge? Which ones?

Focus on Writing 1 *Article*

▶ Paper 2, Part 2

TASK

You see the following announcement in *English Across the World*, an international students' magazine.

Exams – should they be a thing of the past?

Readers – this is your chance to become a contributor to *English Across the World* by writing an article on the above subject. The treatment is entirely up to you – you can present a balanced argument, weighing all the pros and cons, or you can come out strongly on either side. What we do want is a well-written, well-argued piece, which our readers will enjoy, and which will make them think.

The best three articles will be included in a Special Examinations issue of the magazine. The winner will receive a year's subscription to *English Across the World*. With a prize like that, how can you resist the challenge? Get writing now and be sure to send in your article before the closing date of February 22nd.

Write your **article** in approximately 250 words.

Focus on Listening *How to Prepare for Exams*

▶ Paper 4, Part 3

You will hear a teacher giving some advice about exams. For questions 1–9, fill in the missing information.

You will hear the recording twice.

It's very important to prepare for [____] **1** of the exams.

Don't study too hard the night before an exam or you may be [____] **2** when you sit the exam.

In order to sleep well after studying you need to be able to [____] **3**

You have a limited amount of time in the exam and you don't get [____] **4**

If you try to take in new information shortly before an exam, there's a risk you might [____] **5**

Avoid discussions with [____] **6** just before the exam starts.

When tackling the exam paper, the key to success is [____] **7**

People who take exams divide into two categories: [____] and [____] **8**

After you've read through the questions on the paper, set yourself a [____] **9** and keep to it.

Focus on Writing 2 *Report*

TASK

> You are studying at an international college and you have just returned from a three-week Study Exchange scheme in Britain, which was arranged by an organisation called 'Open Frontiers'.
>
> Read the original advertisement, the questionnaire you completed at the end of your stay, and the postcard you sent to a friend. Using the information provided, write a **report** for your college giving your assessment of the scheme from your point of view, mentioning any problems you experienced, and making recommendations for improvements to arrangements in future.
>
> Write approximately 250 words. You should use your own words as far as possible.

◼ STUDY EXCHANGE SCHEME ◼

QUESTIONNAIRE

	Poor	Satisfactory	Good	Excellent
1 TRAVEL ARRANGEMENTS				
a) to destination		✓		
b) from destination		✓		

Comments:
Why such a late flight? Mine was delayed and got in at 2 am!! I then had to wait in the airport until I could get a bus into town, so I was exhausted for the first day.

	Poor	Satisfactory	Good	Excellent
2 ACCOMMODATION				
a) with family				✓
b) hotel				
c) flatshare				

Comments:
I was treated like a member of the family, and included on family outings, which was really nice.
NB: More advance info. re. accommodation would be helpful, e.g.
- distance from college (I was 45 minutes' walk away – OK for me but maybe not everyone)
- pets (my family had 3 cats)

	Poor	Satisfactory	Good	Excellent
3 COLLEGE				
General			✓	
Study programme			✓	
Teachers			✓	

Comments:
Small friendly college – it would have been harder to adjust to a very large institution. Programme was quite tough (6 hrs per day) but worthwhile. Maybe there could have been a <u>few</u> more English classes.

OPEN FRONTIERS
Live and Study in Britain

There are opportunities for students and young adults to undertake short study programmes in British colleges. Find out about the schemes and funding available by applying to the college's Student Services Officer. Requirements include: good knowledge of English and an ability to adapt to a different culture.

Dear N,

Having a great time here in the UK – now that I've recovered from the journey! I'm attending Business Studies lectures and also some English classes at the college I told you about. It took a couple of days to find my way around but I must say that the students and staff here have really bent over backwards to help me. Who said the British were stand-offish? Anyway, I'm getting a fascinating insight into British education and I feel my English is coming on by leaps and bounds! If you ever get the chance to do something similar, jump at it!

See you soon,

J

Focus on Grammar *Review*

The following exercises review the grammar you have done during this course. You can refer to the relevant sections in the Grammar File if necessary.

1 Tense forms and time

In the following sentences, the underlined verb form is incorrect. Rewrite the forms correctly.

1   I <u>have read</u> the latest thriller by John Grisham; I can't wait to get to the end.
2   We <u>will see</u> *Macbeth* at the National Theatre tomorrow night, Clare's just got the tickets.
3   He's looking at the house next week, so he'll tell us about it after he <u>will have seen</u> it.
4   I'm sorry I'm so dirty, I <u>cleaned out</u> the garage all morning.
5   I never stop working; if only my life <u>isn't</u> so busy!
6   By the time he retires in September Tom <u>is working</u> there for thirty years.
7   It's getting late, it's time we <u>had gone</u> home.
8   I <u>am living</u> here since last July.

2 Conditionals

Complete the sentences in an appropriate way.

1   If I'd known you were coming, ... extra food.
2   We'd be watching the match now if ...... the tickets.
3   I'll let you borrow the car provided you ......
4   If you knew him as well as I do, ... a job.
5   I wouldn't be an actor if my parents ...... when I was a child.
6   You go to prison if ......
7   Unless we hear from you in the next few days, ...
8   If the fire brigade hadn't arrived so quickly, ...

3 Structures after verbs

Fill the gaps using an appropriate verb in the correct form. In some cases you may need to add a preposition.

1   We missed the flight because Sarah forgot ...... the passports.
2   I'm tired ...... to your complaints.
3   Our teacher offered ...... us to the theatre one night.
4   I suggest ...... a different route to work today to avoid those road works.
5   My new boss has stopped employees ...... in the office.
6   The doctor advised me ...... on fatty foods and sugar for the sake of my health.
7   Those curtains really need ...... , they're filthy.
8   I'm interested ...... for the vacancy advertised in yesterday's paper.

4 Modals/Modal perfects

Fill the gaps using a modal verb and a suitable form of a main verb.

1   He ...... abroad yesterday. I saw him in the office this morning.

2   She drives a Mercedes so she ...... plenty of money!
3   You ...... the United States without a visa, they're compulsory.
4   We took a thousand dollars with us although we ...... so much because everything was so cheap.
5   The fax machine broke down yesterday but fortunately Jane ...... it.
6   He's got a wonderful voice. He ...... a professional singer if he'd wanted to.
7   We forgot to take our membership cards but luckily the man on the door recognised us, so we ...... them.
8   That cut looks nasty. You really ...... a doctor to look at it.

5   Passives

Change the following informal information into a more formal written style by removing all personal pronouns and using passive forms whenever appropriate. There should be at least eight passive forms in your answer.

This year we will hold the examination in the assembly hall on the third floor. We feel this is more convenient than the meeting room we used last year.
Summary of rules:
We don't allow candidates to bring calculators or dictionaries into the room.
Candidates should give proof of identity to the examination officer.
They must write all their answers in pen not pencil.
Students may not remove examination papers from the examination hall.
We will make students who arrive late wait until the following examination session.

6   Linkers: cause and result, contrast

Fill the gaps with an appropriate link word or phrase.

1   ...... I've done a lot of revision, I'm not expecting to do well in the exam.
2   Exam nerves can be ...... a number of different factors including lack of preparation.
3   Flights to Tenerife have been cancelled ...... adverse weather conditions.
4   Overeating can ...... obesity and serious health problems.
5   My brother can be very emotional, ... I've never seen him cry.
6   The introduction of computers is a major ...... of increased productivity.

7   New York has three international airports, ... London has five.
8   Hurricanes ...... the collision of areas of hot and cold air over the ocean.

7   Participle clauses

Rewrite these sentences using participle clauses (with -ed or -ing) to include the information in brackets.

1   Alan has access to a superb computer system. (he works at the London Business School)
2   I was able to apply for a much wider range of jobs than many people. (I studied languages at college)
3   He is finding it very difficult to get a job. (he hasn't got a degree)
4   I didn't recognise the woman. (she was in front of me in the queue)
5   The infection can be fatal to babies. (it is carried by mosquitoes)
6   I met my future wife in Italy. (I was teaching)
7   She has done several re-training courses. (she was made redundant)
8   My uncle paid for me to go to medical school. (he is known for his generosity)

8   Emphatic structures

a   Rewrite these sentences to make them more emphatic beginning with the word(s) in brackets.

1   I had hardly ever seen such an impressive performance. (Seldom)
2   She hadn't known a child to be so disobedient before. (Never)
3   The course is very long and extremely expensive. (Not only)
4   Just after the exam started, Sally fainted. (No sooner)

b   Rewrite the following as cleft sentences to emphasise the part in italics.

1   You should never *spend ages trying to work out a question* in an exam. (What)
2   I studied languages *so that I could get a job abroad*. (reason)
3   Our teachers didn't know that *we got up at four a.m. to revise* for the exams. (thing)
4   *Jane* went to university – my sister and I got jobs right after school. (It)

English in Use 1 *Error Correction: Spelling and punctuation* ▶ Paper 3, Part 3

In **most** lines of the following text, there is **either** a spelling or a punctuation error. For each numbered line 1–16, write the correctly spelled word or show the correct punctuation in the space on the right. Some lines are correct. Indicate these lines with a tick (✓) in the space. The exercise begins with three examples (**0**).

BANISH EXAM NERVES

If your heart starts <u>biting</u> rapidly, your mouth goes dry and	0	*beating*
you feel unable to cope don't panic. This thirty-second relaxation	0	*cope, don't*
exercise will get rid of anxiety and help keep exam nerves under	0	✓
control. First, calm the body. Sit or lie down in a quite place.	1	....
Remove your shoes and losen any tight clothing. Tense your	2	....
muscles like this clench your fists; try touching the front of	3	....
your rists to your shoulders; hunch your shoulders; frown hard;	4	....
clench your jaws; press the tip of your tounge to the roof of	5	....
your mouth; take a deep breath; flaten your stomach; stretch	6	....
your legs and paint your toes. Notice the tension and hold	7	....
the position as you count slowly to five. Now just let yourself	8	....
go. Flop out like a puppet who's strings have been cut. Feel	9	....
tension following freely away from your body. Next relax your	10	....
mind. With your eyes closed, breathe slowly and deeply.	11	....
Imagine being on a tropical island with a blue sky warm sun and	12	....
a golden, sandy beach. See yourself lying there very peacefuly.	13	....
Hold this image for 20 seconds – or longer if you like. Now open	14	....
your eyes and go calmly about your work. Do this relaxation	15	....
exercise last thing at night to ensure a good nights rest.	16	....

English in Use 2 *Register Cloze* ▶ Paper 3, Part 5

For questions 1–10, on page 232 read the notes on driving and the driving test in Britain, and use the information to complete the numbered gaps in the informal letter to a friend. Use **no more than two words** for each gap. The words you need **do not occur** in the notes. The exercise begins with an example (**0**).

NOTES

Legal Requirements

Before you learn to drive, you must
- be at least 17 years old
- be able to read in good daylight, with glasses or contact lenses if you wear them, a motor vehicle number plate 20.5 metres away
- be medically fit to drive
- hold a provisional licence
- be accompanied by a supervisor who is at least 21 years old and has held a full UK driving licence for at least 3 years
- ensure the vehicle being driven is legally roadworthy
- ensure the vehicle has a current test certificate, if it exceeds the prescribed age
- ensure the vehicle is properly taxed with the correct disc displayed
- ensure the vehicle is properly insured for its use
- display L plates that are visible from the front and the rear of the car

The Driving Test
- consists of a written Theory Test and a Practical Test of your driving
- you have to pass the Theory Test before you can apply for the Practical Test
- you must pass both parts in order to obtain a full driving licence.

INFORMAL LETTER

Dear Isabella

In your last letter you said you were wondering about the possibility of taking the driving test while you're in Britain, so I've done a bit of research, and these seem to be the main points. First, 17 is the (0) ..minimum. age you have to be to drive a car (so you're OK!) but there are a few other things which are required (1) .... . While you're learning, you'll need a provisional driving licence, and you can't go out on (2) .... - you have to have someone with you who's 21 (3) .... , and who's been (4) .... to drive for at least 3 years. How's your (5) .... ? With or without glasses you'll have to be able to read a number plate at 20 metres. Now the car: it must obviously be in a (6) .... to be driven safely, with an up-to-date tax disc and also a test certificate if it's (7) .... a certain age. You also have to make sure (8) .... covers you to learn to drive in it. Finally, you'll need to fix special L (Learner Driver) plates to the car so they can (9) .... from the front and back.

As for the test itself, there are two parts to get through - a Theory Test and a Practical Test - but you have to take them (10) .... times.

If you want to go ahead, let me know and I'll book some driving lessons for you.

All the best
Andy

Answer Key

Unit 5 Lead-in Travel Quiz (page 67)

1 a India b Japan c New Zealand d Brazil
2 a USA (Mardi Gras in New Orleans)
   b UK (Lord Mayor's Show in London) c Italy (Venice Carnival)
3 a Russia b Germany c India/Pakistan/Nepal
4 a Vatican City b Moscow c Alaska
5 a Sweden b Japan c Mexico
6 a Brazil b Australia c Hawaii
7 a Brazil b Belgium c Poland
8 a New York City b Chicago c Rome

Unit 5 Focus on Speaking 1 (page 71)

Scoring
Check your partner's results by following these instructions.
For question 1, note down the letter Z if your partner chose
answer a, W if they chose b, X if they chose c, Y if they chose d.
Treat the other questions in the same way.

2 a W	b Z	c Y	d X
3 a X	b Z	c Y	d W
4 a Z	b Y	c W	d X
5 a X	b Z	c W	d Y
6 a W	b Z	c Y	d X
7 a Y	b Z	c W	d X
8 a Y	b X	c Z	d W

Though we may display elements of more than one type of
behaviour, each of us has a particular tendency.
W – If you chose a large number of W options, it shows you are
a Good Holiday Person – flexible, adaptable and capable of
coping in awkward situations, everyone's ideal companion.
X – A large number of X options reveals a Blind Optimist. If
you're lucky, your blindness to reality may work for you, but you
tend to be a tiring holiday companion.
Y – A majority of Ys indicates a Selfish Pleasure Seeker –
determined to carry on with what you want to do, no matter
what's happening around you. While you are capable of having a
good time on even the most disastrous holiday, you do not
contribute to anyone else's enjoyment.
Z – if Z answers predominate, you are a Self-destructive
Grumbler – seeing trouble where none exists, and cutting off
your nose to spite your face.

Unit 5 English in Use 2 Exercise 2 (page 80)

1 Think about the kind/type/sort of word which is needed in each
space.
2 Make sure your answer is grammatically correct and makes
sense in the context.

Unit 6 Lead-in quiz (page 81)

Which language ...
1 Chinese (1,000 million speakers; English 350 million; Spanish
250 million) 2 English (official language population 1,400
million; Chinese 1,000 million; Hindi 700 million) 3 Hindi
4 Chinese 5 Eskimo 6 Esperanto 7 English 8 Eskimo

Unit 6 Text 1 Exercise 1 (page 82)

1 c 4,000
2 a more (around 10,000)

Unit 7 Focus on Speaking Exercise 1 (page 108)

The ideal ages suggested in a recent survey were:
racing driver 30 surgeon 50 gymnast 14
marathon runner 30 judge 65 airline pilot 45
footballer 25

Unit 9 Focus on Listening Exercise 4 (page 125)

1 Leave swiftly. One major disturbance is better than numerous
coughs.
2 Perfect politeness is to listen carefully and be as appreciative as
the first time. Next best is to remember it warmly, e.g. 'Yes, I
remember, that's a great story.'
3 Be careful: few people want the honesty they ask for. If the item
of clothing is awful, you can't really praise it – but good manners
prevent you from telling the truth. 'It's a nice shape, but I'm not
sure the colour really suits you' willl suggest it's bad news without
making the person feel a fool for buying it.
4 Sit in your car, or in the nearest café, until the correct time –
few social blunders are worse than arriving too soon.
5 Either introduce them, give them drinks and leave them to it or,
if it's an informal meal, invite them into the kitchen, or do some
preparation in the sitting room. Don't feel a failure. Guests who
normally are prepared can feel delightfully superior and those
who normally aren't can feel comforted.

Unit 11 Lead-in quiz (page 185)

1 a hour   2 c 11,000   3 a flooding and b drought
4 a 200,000   5 b Brazil   6 a every two   7 c the sun
8 b Norway   9 c rubbish   10 a ducks

Unit 12 Focus on Speaking 1 (page 202)

1 cooking accidents (40%); electrical appliances and wiring (15%);
arson (13%); smokers' materials (10%); heaters (7%)
2 arson (28%); electrical appliances and wiring (18%); smokers'
materials (9%); cooking accidents (8%)

Unit 12 Text 1 Survival Game (page 204)

A – You are probably severely injured or dead.
B – You may be slightly injured or suffering from shock.
C – Congratulations! The only course that leads to a trouble-free
escape.
In general, avoid lifts, don't waste time collecting valuables; if you
are trapped, wait by a window for the fire brigade rather than
jump, if you can possibly stay in the room for some time.

Unit 12 Focus on Speaking 2 (page 206)

Student A: left-hand side of picture
(Student B differences in brackets)
1 no glass on table (glass)
2 no lamp flex/wire running under mat to wall (flex running to wall)
3 no cigarette in ashtray (cigarette in ashtray)
4 rolled newspaper in woman's hand (electric fire in woman's hand)
5 girl wearing flowered skirt (girl wearing striped skirt)
6 train above fire (boat above fire)

Student B: right-hand side of picture
(Student A differences in brackets)
1 nothing above cooker (dishcloth above cooker)
2 cupboard door closed (cupboard door open)
3 1 pan on wall (4 kitchen tools on wall)
4 no child reaching for matches (child reaching for matches)
5 laundry basket empty (laundry basket full)
6 no electric fire by ironing board (electric fire)

Unit 12 Focus on Listening 2 (page 200)

In the 1996 Vendée Globe round-the-world yacht race, Pete Goss heard the distress signal of fellow competitor Raphael Dinelli. He turned back and rescued him, thereby giving up his chance of winning the race.

Visuals for Speaking

Unit 5 Focus on Speaking 2 (page 73)

Student A

Student B

Unit 3 Focus on Speaking 1 (page 42)

Student A

Unit 12 Focus on Speaking 2 (page 206)

Student A

Unit 6 Focus on Speaking 2 (page 90)

Student A

Unit 10 Focus on Speaking (page 176)

Student A

Unit 11 Focus on Speaking 1 (page 190)

Student A

A

B

Vets rescuing a sloth in a flooded rainforest

Visitors watching a panda at London Zoo

Student B

C

D

Watching lions in Kenya

Whale watching off the coast of Canada

237

Unit 3 Focus on Speaking 1 (page 42)

Student B

Unit 12 Focus on Speaking 2 (page 206)

Student B

Unit 6 Focus on Speaking 2 (page 90)

Student B

Unit 10 Focus on Speaking (page 176)

Student B

Addison Wesley Longman Limited
Edinburgh Gate
Harlow
Essex CM20 2JE

and Associated Companies
throughout the World.

ISBN 0 582 32569 2

Set in 11/13,5pt Minion
Printed in Spain by Graficas Estella
First published 1999
Twelfth impression 2005

Illustrations by Clinton Banbury, Ian Dicks, Martin
Fish, Spike Gerrell, Caroline Logan, Robert Loxston,
John Mac (Folio), Pat McCarthy, Nigel Paige,
Rosemary Woods

Designed by Cathy May (Endangered Species)

Project Managed by Helena Gomm

We are grateful to the following for permission to reproduce
copyright photographs:

Apple UK Ltd for 46 top left; AWL for 46 top right, 46 bottom
middle left and 46 far right; AWL/Trevor Clifford for 46 bottom left
and 215; AWL/Gareth Boden for 60 middle, 60 top, 60 bottom and
194 top middle right; BBC/Cunliffe & Franklyn Productions Ltd for
195; John Birdsall for 236 left and 239 bottom; Britannia Airways
for 119 left; Camera Press for 107 bottom, 225 top right (Mark
Gerson) and 237 top left (Richard Open); Jonathan Cape for 225
bottom left; Bruce Coleman for 198 top (Alain Compost), 186
bottom (Rod Williams), 186 far bottom (Steven Kaufman), 187
(John Cancalosi) and 237 bottom right (Johnny Johnson); Ecoscene
for 194 top left (Angela Hampton), 194 top right (Anthony
Cooper), 234 left and 237 bottom left (Sally Morgan); Greg Evans
International for 79 top; Mary Evans Picture Library for 211 far left
and 236 right; Helena Gomm for 235 ; Grayshott Hall for 64 top;
Robert Harding for 23 top right (G Williams), 67 left bottom (Ellen
Rooney), 71 top left (C Martin) and 239 top; Heather Jones for 194
bottom left; The Kobal Collection for 211 right; Frank Lane Picture
Agency for 186 far top (Gerard Lacz) and 191 left (J D
Watt/Earthviews); Panos Pictures/Jon Michell for 234 right;
Photofusion for 16 top; Pictor International for 16 bottom, 39
middle bottom, 71 bottom left, 97 (1, 2, 4, 5, 6, 7 and 8) and 238;
Popperfoto for 208; Powerstock Photo Library for 103; Rex Features
for 23 top left (Today), 23 bottom left (The Sun), 23 bottom right
(David Ademas/Sipa Press), 34, 82, 107 top (Brian Rasic), 119 right,
191 right (Catherine Leroy), 194 bottom middle (John Powell), 200,
211 middle left (Tim Rooke), 225 top left and 225 bottom right;
Science Photo Library for 35 (Hasler & Pierce/NASA and 211
middle right (US Library of Congress); Sony for 46 bottom middle
right; Sporting Pictures for 99; Still Pictures for 194 top middle left
(Martin Wright, 194 bottom right (Nigel Dickinson) and 237 top
right (Michel Gunther); The Stock Market for 79 bottom, 109, 196
and 201; Tony Stone Images for 39 middle top, 39 bottom (Chris
Baker), 39 top (Mark Dolphin), 67 top left (Randy Wells) and 67
right (Connie Coleman); Superstock for 64 bottom; Telegraph
Colour Library for 71 top right (Steve Bloom) and 97 (3) (FPG/A
Tilley), Universal Pictorial Press and Agency for 86 and John
Walmsley for 15.

We are grateful to the following for permission to reproduce
copyright illustrations:

Cartoon Gallery for 26; M H Jeeves for 69; The Observer
Magazine/Candy Guard for 171; The People/Gray Joliffe for 104;
Private Eye/Martin Honeysett for 125; Private Eye/Kevin Woodcock
for 185 right; The Random Century Group Ltd/Martin Honeysett
for 209; The Spectator/Heath for 185 left; Sunday Express /Peter Till
for 223; Sunday Times 9.3.97 for 74; Sunday Times/Michael Heath
for 122 and Times Newspapers for 204